Dfm.   162

Business Associations and the
New Political Economy of Thailand

Published in cooperation with
the East Asian Institute, Columbia University

The East Asian Institute is Columbia University's center for research, publication, and teaching on modern East Asia. The Studies of the East Asian Institute were inaugurated in 1962 to bring to a wider public the results of significant new research on modern and contemporary East Asia.

Business Associations and the New Political Economy of Thailand

From Bureaucratic Polity to Liberal Corporatism

Anek Laothamatas

Westview Press

BOULDER • SAN FRANCISCO • OXFORD

Institute of Southeast Asian Studies

SINGAPORE

Copyright © 1992 by Westview Press, Inc.

Published in 1992 in the United States of America by Westview Press, Inc., 5500 Central Avenue, Boulder, Colorado 80301-2847, and in the United Kingdom by Westview Press, 36 Lonsdale Road, Summertown, Oxford OX2 7EW

Published in 1992 in the Republic of Singapore by the Institute of Southeast Asian Studies, Heng Mui Keng Terrace, Pasir Panjang, Singapore 0511

Library of Congress Cataloging-in-Publication Data
Anek Laothamatas.
  Business associations and the new political economy of Thailand :
from bureaucratic polity to liberal corporatism / Anek Laothamatas.
    p.   cm.
  Includes bibliographical references and index.
  ISBN 0-8133-8285-8. — ISBN 0-8133-8528-8 (pbk.)
  1. Boards of trade—Thailand. 2. Thailand—Economic policy—
Decision making.   I. Title
HF331.T5A53   1992
338.9593—dc20   91-24169
                                                         CIP

Singapore Library Cataloging-in-Publication Data
ISBN 981-3016-05-1 (Hard cover. ISEAS, Singapore)
ISBN 981-3016-04-3 (Soft cover. ISEAS, Singapore)

Printed and bound in the United States of America

 The paper used in this publication meets the requirements
of the American National Standard for Permanence of Paper
for Printed Library Materials Z39.48-1984.

10   9   8   7   6   5   4   3   2   1

Contents

Tables and Chart

Tables

Chart

Note on Currency

Monetary values in this study are expressed in US dollar terms. To convert the bahts into dollars, the following rates are used:

-for the period 1949-1979, 20 bahts = 1 dollar,
-for the period 1980-1981, 22 bahts = 1 dollar,
-for the period 1982-1984, 23 bahts = 1 dollar,
-for the period 1985-1986, 27 bahts = 1 dollar,
-for the period 1987-1991, 25 bahts = 1 dollar.

Preface

The search for a bourgeois or business class capable of taking national leadership or imposing political control on the state has a noble origin in the works of both Marx and Weber. One major approach to this search is to look for a large number of political officers who have a business background. Another is to look for a business class which has gained a strong socio-economic foothold, and which, as a result, is able to force its demands on the state. I believe that the first approach does not necessarily establish the strength of business as a class or a collective entity; it may just tell us about individuals of this class. The second approach may tell us that the state is working "for" the capitalists, but it is not necessarily run "by" the capitalists, and this makes a big difference.

I have long been intrigued by business associations in Thailand which have been active in public policy-making since the early 1980s, for their story highlights well the two dimensions missed by the approaches mentioned above. They are thus indispensable if we are to detect the "political" rise of the bourgeois "class." I place the study of these associations in two theoretical contexts: the debate on the passage of the "bureaucratic polity" in Thailand, and, to a lesser extent, the discussion of the "East Asian statist" model of economic development.

To Marx and Weber, the political importance of the bourgeoisie lay in their challenge to a pre-established societal force, the feudal or agrarian aristocratic elite. However, I view recent Thai politics as being mainly the struggle between the military-bureaucratic elite and the extra-bureaucratic forces. My major thesis is that organized business, a major societal group, has become strong enough to break the monopoly of the military-bureaucratic elite with regard to the economic policy-making of the state. This being so, it is no longer correct to conceptualize politics in Thailand as being a "bureaucratic polity," as had been the case until the early 1970s. Please note that I use the term bureaucratic polity in the strict Riggsian sense, that is, the virtual monopoly of political power in the hands of a military-bureaucratic elite, not as a shorthand for the strong role of the military in politics.

xii

My point is that the bureaucratic polity model is no longer useful because business has a substantial share in political power, not because the military is no longer a significant factor in politics. In other words, Thailand has entered a significant phase beyond that of bureaucratic polity in that business and military-bureaucratic forces, instead of the latter alone, have come to dominate the political landscape.

Unhappy with most works on Thailand in the past which have tended to shy away from putting the country in comparative perspective, I have also set this study against the backdrop of the East Asian statist model of development. Briefly, the East Asian model presupposes that the government is both enlightened in setting economic goals and efficient in their implementation. Yet, it views societal actors (including business) as short-sighted, self-serving, and obstructive to the making of good policies. Their exclusion from public policy-making is thus held to be both necessary and justifiable. By contrast, the emerging Thai model of government-business relations neither idolizes the government nor belittles business in terms of policy-making. If the power equation between the government and organized business is in clear favor of the former in the East Asian model, it has a more balanced relationship in the Thai model.

In the course of writing this book, a labor of love, I have been assisted by several people and institutions. To begin with, James Morley and Philip Oldenburg effectively supervised the dissertation version of it at Columbia University. Funding for the field work which has informed the book was provided by the Pacific Basin Studies Program of that university and by the Asia Foundation. As the reader will realize, my work has greatly benefited from the scholarship of two eminent Thai scholars, Montri Chenvidyakarn and Chai-anan Samudavanija. Montri's dissertation on trade associations in the 1970s was the forerunner of, and source of inspiration for, this book. My accounts of modern Thai politics in the book have been built largely on the excellent scholarship of Chai-anan. Of equal importance, I am indebted to the following distinguished Western scholars of Thai and Southeast Asian studies for their helpful advice: James Guyot, Clark Neher, Ansil Ramsay, Jamie Mackie, John Girling, and Benedict Anderson.

I am grateful to all interviewees, but particularly to Snoh Unakul, Amorn Wongsurawat, Preecha Tanprasert, Chakramont Pasukwanij, Pratuan Ngam-kham, and Nikorn Wattanapanom. Without the help of the following friends and colleagues, my research and writing would have been much more time consuming: John Bresnan, Pitak Thawatchainant, Chaiwat Satha-Anand, Surachart Bamrungsuk, S. and S. Paleewong, Sanpet Guyot, Komkrit Sertnuansaeng, and Sri-Aporn Kerdtieng. The East Asian Institute of Columbia University and the Thai Khadi Research Institute of Thammasat University provided me with a stimulating and friendly working environment. Finally, my deepest love and gratitude go to my wife, Jiraporn, and my three little children, Katerut, Kemarut, and Indira, who were an unfailing source of comfort and encouragement throughout this long intellectual sojourn of mine.

Anek Laothamatas
Political Science, Thammasat University

Dedicated to my parents,

Uthai and Noi Laothamatas

1

Introduction

With careful diplomatic maneuvering, vigorous administrative and economic reform, and a certain degree of luck, Thailand remained independent throughout the era of Western colonialism. Thai modern political history began in 1932 when the ancient royal rule was toppled by a group of Western-educated, middle-ranking military and civil bureaucrats. While these officials staged a "revolution" which aimed to install a democratic constitutional monarchy,[a] in reality the post-1932 regime succumbed rapidly to the rule of military governments or civilian governments which had to rely heavily on the approval of the armed forces. During the four decades that followed the revolution, most premiers and cabinet ministers were serving or retired bureaucratic leaders—civilian or military—rather than professional party politicians.

In fact the bureaucracy was so dominant in politics and policy-making that Fred Riggs[b] identified the Thai political regime as a "bureaucratic polity." Such a polity, Riggs argued, was neither a traditional nor a modern system. Unlike a traditional system, it developed a wide range of differentiated

---

[a] It was not a "true" revolution in that it hardly mobilized the masses; however, its aim was revolutionary, for it sought to overthrow the absolute monarchy and establish a democratic form of government.

[b] Fred Riggs, *Thailand: The Modernization of a Bureaucratic Polity* (Honolulu: East-West Center Press, 1966). Before Riggs, some other American scholars, especially David Wilson and James Mosel had also viewed Thailand in a bureaucratic polity vein; however, Riggs was first in explicitly formulating the concept. See David Wilson, *Politics in Thailand* (Ithaca: Cornell University Press, 1962), and James N. Mosel, "Thai Administrative Behavior," in W.J. Siffin, ed., *Toward the Comparative Study of Public Administration* (Indiana University's Department of Government, 1957).

1

2

bureaucratic structures. Unlike a modern political system, it failed to create a nonbureaucratic mechanism to place accountability on the bureaucracy.[1] Neither a single official party along the lines of modern totalitarianism, nor competitive parties and interest groups along the lines of a modern polyarchy, arose to place effective control over the bureaucracy. Meanwhile, though Thailand has shared several features with authoritarian regimes commonly found in the Third World, not all kinds of modern authoritarianism are bureaucratic polities. There are several cases in which authoritarian regimes are led at the top by official mass-mobilizing parties or charismatic leaders, not a military-bureaucratic elite which has risen to power through successful coups or the support of the politicized army.

At the heart of the Thai bureaucratic polity was the weakness of extra-bureaucratic forces, be they governmental actors (such as the monarchy, the judiciary, and the legislature) or nongovernmental actors (such as social classes or groups). Of particular interest is the political passivity of the bourgeoisie or business class. If the society-centered model of Western industrialization and democratization may give any clue, one should expect that the business and middle classes would inevitably aspire to national leadership or at least try to force the government to become more responsible to their interests. This, however, was far from the case in the heyday of the bureaucratic polity. The explanation for the disjunction of wealth and power is to be found at least in part in the ethnic composition of the business community of Thailand.

Most of the local entrepreneurs in Thailand were ethnic Chinese. During the late 1940s and early 1950s, for example, ethnic Chinese accounted for 70 percent of "large" and "smaller" business owners or managers in Bangkok.[2] Their vulnerable foreign status aside, these businessmen came largely from a humble peasant background and had received little formal education. Worse yet, during the 1940s and 1950s they were confronted with nationalistic-minded governments. For all these reasons, ethnic Chinese businessmen chose to affect public policy in a covert and particularistic fashion, and their effect was felt chiefly in the implementation, rather than the formulation of government policies. To exert influence on government policy-making, businessmen typically gave bribes or nurtured "clientelistic" relationships with bureaucratic leaders by inviting these people to join their executive boards. As late as 1972 twelve of sixteen commercial banks in Thailand, for example, still had military or political leaders on their boards of directors.[3]

Contrary to the belief of several scholars and practitioners about the peculiarity of Thai politics, Riggs from the beginning held that bureaucratic polity was by no means unique to Thailand. Developing polities in general, he observed, were marked by "the lack of balance between political policy-making institutions and bureaucratic policy-implementing structures . . . and the weakness of their extra-bureaucratic political institutions in contrast with the burgeoning growth of their bureaucracies."[4]

Riggs' observation has been confirmed by the works of several other analysts. Writing a decade or so later, Karl Jackson and John Girling held that Indonesia could also be viewed as a bureaucratic polity.[5] Though not using the term "bureaucratic polity," Hamza Alavi, a prominent neo-Marxist author, asserted that unlike the historical Western bourgeois state, the post-colonial states of Pakistan and Bangladesh have been characterized by strong military-bureaucratic oligarchies which are relatively independent of the ruling classes—the international bourgeoisie, the local bourgeoisie and the landed class.[6] Finally, Peter Evans, a leading scholar of the "dependency" approach, noted that during the mid-1970s Brazilian politics was in fact an affair limited to the bureaucracy. Even the dominant factions of the bourgeoisie in that country, according to Evans, "were not in a position to shape state policies systematically or control the actions of the central bureaucracy."[7]

Certainly, the bureaucratic polity, according to all the above accounts, is not a phenomenon exclusive to Thailand. However, the country is a classic case par excellence. Whether electoral activities were allowed or not, the military-bureaucratic elite heavily dominated the Thai political scene. The best illustrations are that, of the 174 men who served in all cabinets of Premiers Praya Pahon and Plaek Phibunsongkram between 1933 and 1944, when electoral activities were allowed, only five were nonbureaucrats;[8] of the 85 men serving as cabinet ministers under Sarit Thanarat and Thanom Kittikachorn between 1959 and 1973, when electoral activities were largely banned, only five had a business background.[9] The political dominance of these bureaucrats was in part a result of the military coups which have taken place probably more frequently than in any other nation. Between 1932 and 1973 there were fourteen coup attempts; on the average, one coup was struck every three years.[c]

It must be quickly added, however, that the Thai bureaucratic polity was also founded on the distinctive political apathy of the populace. Historically there had been no foreign colonial rule in Thailand to provoke a nationalist movement, which in much of the Third World provided the ground for popular political participation after independence. Tellingly, the overthrow of the absolutist monarchy in Thailand, something comparable with the struggle for national independence in most of the developing world, was the

---

[c] What matters here is not only the frequency of the coup, but also the relatively legitimate status of it. Observing the political scene of the 1950s, Mosel noted that a striking feature of Thai politics was the "semi-officialization" of the coup as a device for gaining control of the state. See Mosel, "Thai Administrative Behavior," p. 299.

work of but a handful of military-bureaucratic leaders. As late as the 1950s when much of the Third World was thrown into the fire of mass-based nationalist, socialist, or democratic movements, a Western journal had this to say about Thailand:

> The contented Siamese, traditionally uninterested in politics and with an ingrained talent for obedience, have never shown the slightest desire for democracy—a phenomenon disconcerting to well-intentioned Western visitors. If they are now to enjoy the benefits of democracy, it is clear that these will have to be imposed from above.[10]

The Bureaucratic Polity Outgrown

Valuable as the bureaucratic polity model may have been for elucidating the political experience in the first four decades following the 1932 revolution, Thailand in the 1970s began to outgrow it. The dramatic economic development of the last three decades has spawned extra-bureaucratic forces that can no longer be denied. During the period of 1965-1980 Thailand enjoyed an average annual GDP growth of 7.2 percent.[11] Between 1965 and 1988 the Thai average GNP per capita grew 4 percent annually; of the 122 countries reported by the World Bank in 1990 only ten outranked Thailand in this respect.[12] Over the 1965-1988 period the share of agriculture in GDP declined from 32 percent to 17 percent, while that of manufacturing increased from 14 percent to 24 percent.[13] Even more prominent was the increase in the share of manufacturing in total exports which jumped from 5.5 percent in 1970 to 30.1 percent in 1980.[14]

Presently Thailand is classified by the World Bank as a lower middle income country. With a population of 54.5 million, its GDP of US$ 57.9 billion in 1988 was the twelfth largest of the 96 low-income and middle-income countries of the world.[15] In the whole of South and Southeast Asia only India (with a population of 815.6 million) and Indonesia (with a population of 174.8 million) had larger GDPs than Thailand.[16] On a per capita basis, the Thai GNP in 1988 was US$ 1,000, which was higher than that of Nigeria, Egypt, and the Philippines, but lower than that of Peru and Turkey.[17]

While agriculture still employs close to 70 percent of the country's work force, since fiscal year 1984-85 the share of manufacturing in the GDP has outstripped that of agriculture.[18] On the whole the Thai economy is now relatively balanced in terms of sectoral distribution as illustrated by the fact that rice, textiles and tourism have been the three largest foreign exchange earners of the country in recent years.

Since the middle of the nineteenth century, under pressure from Western powers at the beginning, Thailand has followed a capitalist path to development. Recently, the country has had one of the lowest government expenditures as a proportion of GDP among the developing economies of the world. In 1988 the Thai central government expenditure was about 16.4 percent of GNP, which was smaller than that of Malaysia, Indonesia, and Brazil.[19] Thailand's public investment during the 1980-1988 period was about 33 percent of total investment, about half that of Turkey (68 percent), Egypt (65 percent) and Argentina (58 percent).[20]

The predominance of the private sector in the Thai economy may be demonstrated also by the fact that in 1979 only nineteen of the 100 largest enterprises (in terms of assets) were government-owned, and these nineteen held only 36 percent of the total assets.[21] In comparison, in the early 1980s as many as 47 of India's top 100 enterprises (in terms of capital) were government-owned, and these organizations accounted for 76 percent of the total capital assets of the 100 largest enterprises.[22]

Thailand since the 1960s has actively encouraged foreign private investment. During the 1977-1981 period foreigners undertook about 30 percent of the gross fixed capital formation of the country.[23] Among the top 100 enterprises in Thailand, 29 firms were owned by multinational or foreign corporations. Japanese and Americans have been the two most important foreign direct investors. During the 1960-1977 period, for example, they held about half of the total foreign investment in Thailand.[24]

In this development milieu, some nonbureaucratic political forces have emerged. First were the college students. In 1973 they led a popular uprising that brought down a military regime which had been in power for sixteen years. This event was followed by years of political turmoil. The democratic regime which succeeded the deposed military regime was short-lived. Fearing the increased activism of left-leaning students, in 1976 the military seized power and ruthlessly suppressed the student movement. However, the repressive government that came into being as a result of the bloody coup could not return the country to authoritarianism for long. Within a year, amidst widespread resistance from the educated urbanites, it was deposed by yet another coup. The succeeding regimes thereafter recognized the need for power sharing with nonbureaucratic forces.

The most enduring post-1977 regime was that of Prime Minister Prem Tinsulanond, which lasted from 1980 to 1988. Prem's regime may be regarded as a "semi-democracy."[25] During this semi-democratic period, governments came to power by competitive elections. Three or more parties were usually needed to form a coalition government, and their leaders were unable to decide who among themselves would serve as prime minister. In addition, the support of the armed forces lingered on as an indispensable condition for stable rule. Consequently, the ruling parties opted to invite respected retired generals to serve as premier and ministers of key portfolios, such as Defense, the Interior, Finance, and Foreign Affairs.

Besides, the Prem administration necessarily took special heed of the monarchy, as the latter, while formally placed above politics, of late has effectively commanded the loyalty of both the ruling elite and the populace at large. The support of the much revered monarchy saved Premier Prem from coup attempts in 1981 and 1985.

In 1988 Premier Prem retired from politics and Chatichai Choonhavan, leader of the largest party, was chosen as the new prime minister. Virtually all members of successive Chatichai cabinets, including Chatichai himself, have been elected politicians. Consequently, in terms of democratic development, the Chatichai administration is a major improvement on the Prem administration. However, it is not yet a completely democratic regime as the military continues to exert strong influence on government affairs and poses a real threat to the stability and survival of the civilian rule. It remains to be seen just how long this kind of wholly elected government will survive.

The question to be posed is: How decisively have the post-1977 regimes moved away from the bureaucratic polity model? On the one hand, Chai-anan Samudavanija, Sukhumbhand Paribatra, and Suchit Bunbongkarn[26] have argued that Thailand is still essentially a bureaucratic polity, though one that is well adjusted to growing nonbureaucratic demands.[d] The nonbureaucratic groups, in their view, are divided and prone to official co-optation, and thus their share of power is minimal. Accordingly, the military, as these scholars have interpreted the situation, has regained its supremacy without the need to form an explicitly authoritarian regime. Viewed in this light, the prospects for democracy are rather bleak and there remains the possibility that direct military control may return in some form of a "corporatist state."[27]

On the other hand, Ansil Ramsay, Pisan Suriyamongkol, and James Guyot have claimed that Thailand has changed fundamentally.[28] Pisan and Guyot are keen on citing cases in which "the free run of the bureaucracy has been checked and held at bay by a variety of newly developed, as well as some older, extra-bureaucratic forces."[29] Ramsay, while admitting that as late as 1987 Thailand was still a "restricted democracy," holds that the country has moved "beyond the bureaucratic polity."[30] In an important sense, Ramsay argues, the regime of the 1980s was an incipient form of a "bourgeois polity,"

---

[d] It must be noted that I have not included in this camp J.L.S. Girling, *Thailand: Society and Politics* (Ithaca: Cornell University Press, 1981). Although Girling's work may be viewed as a modified version of bureaucratic polity which admirably takes into account nonbureaucratic forces, it covers only the period of Kriangsak and very early Prem. Thus, I have excluded Girling from the debate which is in itself a reflection of the political changes which have taken place after the period that he covers.

referring to a system in which business and the middle class have a major share in political power.[31]

Also in disagreement with Chai-anan, but looking at things from a different angle than Ramsay, is Patcharee Thanamai.[32] While Patcharee has not engaged directly in the debate, she suggests that the economic policy-making of the state that has taken place since the 1960s can best be explained by the "triple alliance" model.[33] In her view, the economic decision-making arena in Thailand is no longer occupied exclusively by the military-bureaucratic elite; rather, local and foreign capitalists have a substantial share of the power along with the state elites.[e]

Central to the dispute among these scholars is the nature of the relationship between the government and the nonbureaucratic groups. At issue are the questions: How influential are extra-bureaucratic groups in public policy-making? Are these groups independent of the government or, does the government effectively control the groups? If the nonbureaucratic groups are controlled by the state, how is this control exercised?

To try to resolve this issue, I single out for examination the political role of business associations, which have replaced student groups as the strongest of all the nonbureaucratic elements in Thailand. Since the late 1970s trade associations and chambers of commerce have proliferated and become very active. While the history of trade associations in Thailand goes back to the nineteenth century, in 1975 there were only 75 trade associations in Bangkok.[34] The number had risen to 124 by 1979,[35] and to 177 by 1987.[36] More striking was the proliferation of provincial chambers of commerce. In 1979 there was only one chamber in each of four provinces.[37] By 1987 chambers of commerce had spread to all 72 provinces, in addition to the Bangkok metropolis.[38]

Assertive demands from business associations are frequently reported in the press. Equally important has been the creation by the government, at national and provincial levels, of the Joint Public and Private Sector Consultative Committees (JPPCCs). These committees are highly regarded

Chai anan paper

---

[e] Kevin Hewison has made a very penetrating criticism of the bureaucratic polity model in his work, "The Development of Capital, Public Policy and the Role of the State in Thailand" (Ph.D. thesis, Murdoch University, 1983). However, he is not considered as part of this debate, since the debate has been among those who argue that the bureaucratic polity model was once, or is still, correct. Only the changes in the reality of the situation in the 1980s prompted these authors to reassess the model. Hewison, on the other hand, has never held that the model could be useful or valid for the analysis of modern Thai politics. In other words, he has been an "outsider" to this model throughout, whereas the authors engaged in the debate, including myself, were more or less advocates of the model, at least until the mid-1980s.

8

by both the government and the business community. At the national level the prime minister heads the committee, and representatives of the three most important central associations—the Thai Chamber of Commerce (TCC), the Thai Bankers Association (TBA), and the Federation of Thai Industries (FTI)—are among its members. At the provincial level the governor is the president of the committee (there is one for each province) and the provincial chamber of commerce, or the provincial branch of the FTI, or the provincial bankers club are represented in the membership.

If these business groups are merely a creation of the officials or have been co-opted by the officials and cannot exert any meaningful influence on the regime, then it is fair to say that bureaucratic polity, though an adjusted one, is still operative in Thailand. On the other hand, if business associations are independent of the government and are indeed effective in influencing public policy, then it may reasonably be concluded that the regime has entered a significant new phase beyond that of bureaucratic polity.

A Neglected Area

Business associations have long been a neglected area of inquiry among students of Third World politics. Parallel to what Philippe Schmitter and Wolfgang Streeck observed about political economic literature on advanced industrial countries,[39] to date there have been few studies of business associations in the Third World.[f] Political scientists with "pluralist" or "corporatist" bents seldom place a direct and exclusive focus on business groups.[40] Their focus is on interest groups as a whole and their question is limited to the politics of group activities or government-group interaction.

For that purpose, organized business is often studied by writers of both intellectual perspectives simply as one among the plethora of societal groups.[41] Writers with the pluralist bent are interested in "how people organize, what they organize for, how they attempt to influence policy, and what factors affect their attempt to influence policy."[42] In contrast, writers with the corporatist perspective are more interested in the ways Third World states have tried to control, restrain, or repress organized societal demands. Analysis of the economic effects of business associations by these scholars, to the extent that there has been any, has been on policy-derived benefits

---

[f] Richard Doner and Ernest Wilson III share my observation that the study of business associations in the developing world is a neglected area of inquiry. See their paper, "Business Interest Associations in Developing Countries," prepared for the annual meeting of the International Political Science Association, Washington, D.C., September 1988.

gained or lost by particular associations. The broader impact of organized business on the economy or on the role of the government in the economy has hardly been studied.[43]

Development economists are no better than political scientists when it comes to the study of the business and the economic activities of business associations and their overall role in economic development. This may be due to the fact that economists have a predilection for the role of individuals or firms on the one hand and the role of the government on the other, as key to the success of economic growth. The role of intermediate organizations, placed between individuals or firms and the state, such as business associations, has thus been overlooked. Usually, standard textbooks on economic development do not even have a section on business associations.[44] Bruce Herrick and Charles Kindleberger came close to giving due attention to them when they devoted a chapter to organizations needed for development. Unconventionally, the authors pointed out that,

> The institutional possibilities for organization of the development process are more varied and diffuse than were formerly realized. Early in the evolution of thought about economic development, governments and private, profit-seeking business firms were considered the only engines through which development might proceed. . . . A wider variety of possibilities is now seen.[45]

Herrick and Kindleberger then propose labor unions and producers' cooperatives as candidates for organizations with a substantial role in development, in addition to public agencies and private business firms. Surprisingly, they fail to mention business associations as one among such organizations.[46]

The role of Third World business associations is also overlooked by Marxist-inspired political economists. For scholars offering crude versions of the "neo-colonial" or the "dependency" approaches, the key to the dynamics of Third World development is the international (neo-imperialist) bourgeoisie and their states.[47] Local bourgeoisie in developing countries draw little of the attention of these writers, since such bourgeoisie are assumed to be neither effective nor independent political and economic actors, as compared to their international masters. Logically, there is no urgent need for scholars in this tradition to study any organizations, including the business associations, of the local bourgeois class.

Sophisticated variants of dependency theory, especially those put forth by the "triple alliance" school,[48] and the domestically oriented "class and state" school,[49] do have analytical room for the study of business associations in the Third World. Contrary to the crude versions of the dependency school, members of these schools entertain the possibility that participation in the world market may lead to the progress of Third World economies, rather than to their stagnation or destruction. More importantly, with the assistance of the relatively autonomous states, local capitalists may emerge as dynamic, significant and independent political and economic actors, despite the integration of these developing economies into world capitalism. Thus, Colin Leys has argued that, instead of being subservient to the needs and interests of the international capitalists, since independence the Kenyan capitalists have made successful inroads into economic activities previously dominated by Western investors. In addition, by 1966 the local capitalists had taken control of the state and was able to use this power to consolidate their position against the international bourgeoisie.[50] In Brazil, Peter Evans has contended, the indigenous bourgeoisie have formed with the state and the international bourgeoisie a triple alliance which has dominated the Brazilian economy since the 1960s.[51] In Thailand, as demonstrated by Kevin Hewison and Kraisak Choonhavan, the local Sino-Thai businessmen have become vibrant players in the political-economic arena.[52]

However, despite a high analytical priority assigned by these political economists to the indigenous capitalists in the Third World, they give inadequate attention to business associations. In the main they are content with showing that local firms have a substantial share in national investment, in total private assets, or in total domestic sales, especially in comparison with foreign firms or public enterprises.[53] From their class-focused perspective, these writers should have been theoretically concerned with the collective actions rather than the individual actions of the capitalists. In practice they have paid little attention to formal institutions, such as trade associations or chambers of commerce, which businessmen may use to organize their collective efforts to advance or defend their common interests. Accordingly, while the crucial political and economic roles of individual business persons or firms are generally substantiated, class solidarity and class action on the part of the Third World indigenous capitalists are in most cases simply postulated.

The "post imperialist" variant of Marxist scholarship on the Third World seems to be the only exception to the general trend described above. First propounded in Richard Sklar's seminal work,[54] the central tenet of the post imperialist school is that, unlike in Lenin's day, contemporary capitalism allows the harmonization of the global interests of the international bourgeoisie and the national aspirations of the various countries in which transnational subsidiaries operate. Accordingly, it is possible for there to emerge in the Third World local bourgeoisie, who, while participating as junior partners of the international bourgeoisie, do have an independent class interest of their own in national development. More importantly, scholars in this tradition have come to recognize the role of business associations in facilitating local capitalist collective political and economic action. For example, David Becker[55] examined the role of business associations in the process of the class formation of the Peruvian bourgeoisie.[56] Thus far, however, the focus of writers in this tradition has not gone beyond this process of class formation. The role of business associations in other aspects of development has not yet been analyzed by writers with the post imperialist perspective. Thus, it is fair to say that the story of business associations, especially the study of their role in the national development of Third World countries (apart from the formation of the local bourgeois class), has not been adequately studied by Marxist-inspired scholars.

Business associations have also been overlooked by the recent non-Marxist, state-focused literature on the political economy of the East Asian newly industrializing countries (NICs).[57] This new literature has attributed the success of the export-oriented market economies of Taiwan, South Korea and Singapore to the ability of the governments in these countries to devise appropriate economic strategies or policies. While acknowledging the importance of societal actors in the economy, especially entrepreneurs, writers in this emerging literature pay modest attention to the role of business in the formulation of public policy. It has been contended that these states have been able to shield their policy-making process from the influence of virtually all societal groups.[58]

There is, indeed, a profitable way to incorporate business associations into a study of the state-led development of the East Asian NICs. As theorized by Fred Deyo, a prime contributor to this new literature, the ability of the state to implement its economic strategies is enhanced by the existence of some representative organizations of the private sector. Through these organizations,

> state actors can effectively redirect the disposition and organization of capital, labor, and physical resources. Such organizations, which might include industry associations, oligopolized industries, and trade union federations, are "strategic levers" for policy implementation.[59]

Thus far, however, there has been no major study with a direct focus on business associations along these lines.

As almost everywhere else in the Third World, the role of business associations in Thai development has attracted few scholarly studies. It was not until the 1970s that the first such study appeared, that of Montri Chenvidyakarn.[60] Montri employed the concepts of "limited pluralism" and "state corporatism" to analyze government-business relations in the early 1970s and found that business associations had until then "been able to exert relatively little influence over government policy and actions."[61]

Also working during the first half of the 1970s, Narong Petchprasert found that trade associations, especially those dealing with the export of commodities were economically influential in some areas.[62] Generally, Narong saw business associations as a venue for businessmen to regulate prices and wages, often at the expense of farmers, workers and consumers. However, in terms of government-business relations, he seemed to agree with Montri that the government obviously dominated organized business. The success of business representation, in the view of both scholars, was largely due to the consent of the government, rather than to any pressure that the business associations were able to bear on the government.[63]

In the 1980s when business associations grew tremendously, only two works on relations between business associations and the government appeared. Suthy Prasartset's paper, "Some Aspects of Government-Business Relations in Thailand and Japan," attributed the recent proliferation of business associations to the rise of a strong "indigenous" capitalist class, due to the effective assimilation of the ethnic Chinese into Thai society, and the growth of large modern corporations.[64] Suthy also regarded the Joint Public and Private Sector Consultative Committees (JPPCCs) as a public measure to institutionalize business participation in national policy-making.[65] A major weakness of Suthy's work is that it was largely based on the account of Montri, whose data was limited to the earlier 1970s period.

Another study related to business associations in the 1980s was that of Sawaeng Rattanamongkolmas.[66] However, since it was an evaluation commissioned by the National Economic and Social Development Board of the Thai government, the study limits itself to the analysis of administrative and attitudinal problems in the operation of the JPPCCs.

Thailand as Liberal Corporatism

There are three major arguments in this study. The first of them is that in Thailand since the late 1970s business associations have become autonomous and effective extra-bureaucratic interest groups. To substantiate this argument, I will demonstrate that organized business has played an initiating role, leading to the creation of the JPPCC system which has come to be the centerpiece of government-business relations since the early 1980s. Then, several short cases will be constructed to illustrate the ability of organized business to initiate, transform, or block major policies or legislative measures put forward by the government in recent years. Finally, I will claim that the existence of corporatist features in the legal and institutional relations between the government and organized business has not seriously undermined the autonomous and effective role of business in the public policy process. This is due to the fact that the present system of business associations honors societal group autonomy in relation to the state as well as free competition among groups. If the current government-business relationship can be classified as a corporatist system, it is more likely to be a "liberal" rather than an "authoritarian" corporatism.

A pluralist model of government-group interaction is marked by a minimal role of the government in encouraging or restricting the formation of societal groups, or in structuring the relations within society, or between the government and groups.[8] Interest groups, usually organized into an unspecified number of voluntary, nonhierarchically ordered categories, compete for desired public policies or legislative measures as the government seldom recognizes or assists any particular groups. An extreme pluralism holds when public officials do not have their own interests or convictions but are pressured or controlled by competent and powerful societal groups to make policies that are compatible or consistent with the demands of those groups.

An alternative to pluralism is corporatism. While admitting the influence of interest groups on the policy and legislation of the government, corporatism conceives of the government as a largely autonomous actor with issues and ideas of its own. Moreover, the government may structure its formal relations with society as well as the intra-societal relations. Ideally, interest groups are organized hierarchically and then linked to the government. Group competition is thus expected to be limited since major conflicts will be solved by higher societal organizations or by public officials. Finally, groups in the corporatist model work not only as policy advocates; they are often in charge of some public duties and, accordingly, are delegated the necessary authority from public agencies.

While pluralism is closely associated with liberal democracy, corporatism is not necessarily connected with authoritarian regimes. Corporatist scholars, led by Philippe Schmitter, Leo Panitch and Gerhard Lehmbruch, have contended that there are two varieties of corporatism: "liberal (societal) corporatism" and "authoritarian (state) corporatism."[67] Although the functioning of both varieties requires a leading role of the government, they differ as to the degree to which groups are subordinate to, or dependent upon, the government.

Liberal corporatism is marked by a high degree of autonomy and spontaneity, and by the central role of private groups in the creation and

---

[8] My characterization of pluralist and corporatist models is based largely upon the following works: Philippe Schmitter, "Still the Century of Corporatism?" in Fredrick Pike and Thomas Stritch, eds., *The New Corporatism: Social-Political Structures in the Iberian World* (Notre Dame: University of Notre Dame Press, 1974), pp. 85-131; Alfred Stepan, *The State and Society: Peru in Comparative Perspective* (Princeton: Princeton University Press, 1978), pp. 7-17; 46-52; Alan Cawson, *Corporatism and Political Theory* (Oxford: Basil Blackwell, 1986), pp. 1-44.

14

operation of their representative associations, as well as systems of government-group interest mediation.[68] Authoritarian corporatism, on the other hand, is characterized by a high degree of dependence and subordination of groups in relation to the government. In such a system of state-society interaction public agencies usually subsidize, support, and control societal groups, which in turn work mostly as auxiliary organs of the government.[69] Liberal corporatism is claimed to exist in several Western countries, while authoritarian corporatism is viewed as a Third World phenomenon.[70] Although Thailand is a Third World fledgling democracy, this study contends that its current government-business corporatism is an emerging liberal corporatism.

All things considered, I suggest that Thailand has ceased to be a bureaucratic polity—in the realm of economic matters at least. This is so because organized business has formed politically effective extra-bureaucratic groups and the policy of the government is no longer determined solely by the bureaucratic elite.

Connected to this is the second major argument of the study: organized business has affected the Thai economy significantly. While some associations, as in the bureaucratic polity years, function mainly, if not exclusively, as a tool of the government in regulating prices, quality, or quantities of certain products or in implementing other public policies, a number of peak business associations, industry associations, tourist-industry associations, and provincial chambers of commerce have contributed to economic development in new and important ways. Through political and economic collective work (to be defined shortly), these organizations have urged and facilitated the shift of the national economic strategy to an export-oriented one. They have also pushed for an enhancement of the ability and efficiency of the government in supporting business operations. Last, but not least, provincial chambers of commerce have begun to exert their leadership in provincial development.

Political collective work means the efforts of business associations to initiate or shape government policies and legislative measures that are favorable to economic development in general or to the progress of particular economic sectors. Economic collective work, on the other hand, refers to activities that associations carry out to improve the economic and business conditions for the whole trade or industry they represent. These activities may include investment in necessary infrastructure, research and development in product quality, public relations campaigning, sales promotion efforts, and so on. Generally, these activities are too expensive or are administratively too difficult for individual members to undertake alone. At the same time, the government is not usually in a position to supply or subsidize these activities. Arguably, business associations in

15

Thailand have begun to step in to provide these necessary functions by pooling resources and the knowledge of member firms.

The final major argument is that the Thai liberal corporatism, compared to the government-business relations in the East Asian NICs, is less statist. I propose a view that Thailand now resembles South Korea, Taiwan and Singapore in that close and supportive relations between the government and organized business have emerged. However, while business associations in the East Asian NICs, especially in the 1960s and 1970s, have exerted only modest influence on economic policies, and even less influence on development strategies, Thai organized business has played a substantial role in initiating or shaping a new strategy and the associated policies to bring about economic development. Just as important, while the power equation between the government and business associations has been in clear favor of the former in the East Asian NICs, it has been more of a balanced relationship in Thailand.

Notes

1. Fred Riggs, *Thailand: The Modernization of a Bureaucratic Polity* (Honolulu: East-West Center Press, 1966), pp. 373-378.

2. Calculated from the data provided by G. William Skinner, *Chinese Society in Thailand: An Analytical History* (Ithaca: Cornell University Press, 1957), Table 21, p. 301.

3. Akira Suehiro, *Capital Accumulation and Industrial Development in Thailand* (Bangkok: Social Research Institute, Chulalongkorn University, 1985), p. 5.40.

4. Fred Riggs, "Bureaucrats and Political Development: A Paradoxical View," in Joseph LaPalombara, ed., *Bureaucracy and Political Development* (Princeton: Princeton University Press, 1967), pp. 120-121.

5. Karl Jackson, "Bureaucratic Polity: A Theoretical Framework for the Analysis of Power and Communications in Indonesia," in Karl Jackson and Lucian Pye, eds., *Political Power and Communications in Indonesia* (Berkeley: University of California Press, 1978); John Girling, *The Bureaucratic Polity in Modernizing Societies: Similarities, Differences and Prospects in the ASEAN Region* (Singapore: The Institute of Southeast Asian Studies, 1981).

6. Hamza Alavi,"The State in Post-Colonial Societies: Pakistan and Bangladesh" *New Left Review* 74 (July-August 1972): 59-81.

7. Peter Evans, "Reinventing the Bourgeoisie: State Entrepreneurs and Class Formation in Dependent Capitalist Development," in Michael Burawoy and Theda Skocpol, eds., *Marxist Inquiries: Studies of Labor, Class, and States,* supplement to *American Journal of Sociology,* 88 (1982): S.217.

16

8. Calculated from the data provided by Riggs, *Thailand,* Table 30, p. 316.

9. Calculated from the data provided by Krirkkiat Pipatseritham, *Karn Plianplang Tang Settakij Kab Panha Sitti Manusayachon Nai Pratet Tai* [Economic Change and Human Rights Issue in Thailand] (Bangkok: Thammasat University Press, 1985), Table 9-3, pp. 472-475.

10. The Economist, Vol CLXXVI, No.5845 (September 3, 1935), p. 779, as quoted in Rupert Emerson, *From Empire to Nation* (Boston: Beacon Press, 1960), p. 271.

11. World Bank, *World Development Report 1990* (Oxford: Oxford University Press, 1984), Table 2, pp. 180-181.

12. Ibid., Table 1, pp. 178-179.

13. Ibid., Table 3, pp. 182-183.

14. World Bank, *Thailand: Managing Public Resources for Structural Adjustment* (Washington, D.C.: World Bank Publication, 1984), Table 2.15, p. 32.

15. Ranked by the data provided by World Bank, *World Development Report 1990,* Table 3, pp. 182-183.

16. World Bank, *World Development Report 1990,* Tables 1 and 3, pp. 178-179 and pp. 182-183.

17. World Bank, *World Development Report 1990,* Table 1, pp. 178-179.

18. Government of Thailand, *Statistical Yearbook Thailand,* Vol. 34, 1985-1986 (Bangkok: National Statistical Office), Table 193, p. 448.

19. World Bank, *World Development Report 1990,* Table 11, pp. 198-199.

20. World Bank, *World Development Report 1988* (New York: Oxford University Press, 1988), Table 2.3, p. 47.

21. Suehiro, *Capital Accumulation,* Table VII-2, p. 7.10.

22. Calculated from the data provided by Lloyd Rudolph and Susanne Rudolph, *In Pursuit of Lakshmi: The Political Economy of the Indian State* (Chicago: University of Chicago Press, 1987), Appendix A, pp. 403-406.

23. Kraisak Choonhavan, "The Growth of Domestic Capital and Thai Industrialization" *Journal of Contemporary Asia* 14:(No.2, 1984): 136, Table 1.

24. Grit Permtanjit, "Political Economy of Dependent Development: Study of the Limits of the Capacity of the State to Rationalize in Thailand" (Ph.D. dissertation, University of Pennsylvania, 1982) Table 4.2, pp. 171-172.

25. The term "semi-democracy" is used by many authors, most importantly Chai-anan Samudavanija. See his article, "Democracy in Thailand: A Case Study of a Stable Semi-Democratic Regime," in Larry Diamond, Juan Linz and Seymour Martin Lipset, eds., *Democracy in Developing Countries: Asia* (Boulder, Colorado: Lynne Reinner, 1989).

26. Chai-anan Samudavanija,"Democracy in Thailand: A Case Study of a Stable Semi-Democratic Regime," paper presented at the Conference on the Comparative Study of Democracy in Developing Nations, Stanford University, 1985, later published in Larry Diamond, Juan Linz and Seymour Martin Lipset, eds., *Democracy in Developing Countries: Asia* (Boulder, Colorado: Lynne Reinner, 1989), pp. 305-346; Sukhumbhand Paribatra and Suchit Bunbongkarn," Thai Politics and Foreign Policy in the 1980s," paper presented at the Third US-ASEAN Conference, Chiangmai, Thailand later published in Karl Jackson, Sukhumbhand Paribatra and J. Soedjati Djiwandono, eds., *ASEAN in Regional and Global Context* (Berkeley: Institute of East Asian Studies, University of California, Berkeley: 1986), pp. 52-76.

27. Chai-anan Samudavanija,"The Military and Politics in Thailand," paper presented at the annual meeting of the American Association for Asian Studies, Philadelphia, 1985.

28. Ansil Ramsay, "Thai Domestic Politics and Foreign Policy," paper presented at the Third US-ASEAN Conference, Chiangmai, Thailand, later published in Karl Jackson, Sukhumbhand Paribatra and J. Soedjati Djiwandono, eds., *ASEAN*, pp. 30-51; Pisan Suriyamongkol and James Guyot, *The Bureaucratic Polity at Bay* (Bangkok: Graduate School of Public Administration, the National Institute of Development Administration, no date).

29. Pisan and Guyot, *The Bureaucratic Polity at Bay*, p. 75.

30. Ansil Ramsay, "Beyond Bureaucratic Polity," paper presented at the annual meeting of the American Association for Asian Studies, Boston, April, 1987, pp. 8, 12-13.

31. A concept derived from Samuel Huntington and Joan Nelson, *No Easy Choice: Political Participation in Developing Countries* (Cambridge: Harvard University Press, 1976), pp. 17-41.

32. Patcharee Thanamai, "Patterns of Industrial Policy-Making in Thailand: Japanese Multinationals and Domestic Actors in the Automobile and Electrical Appliances Industries" (Ph.D. dissertation, University of Wisconsin-Madison, 1985).

33. As propounded by Peter Evans, *Dependent Development: The Alliance of Multinational, State, and Local Capital in Brazil* (Princeton: Princeton University Press, 1979).

34. Narong Petchprasert, "Samakom Karnka Lae Ho Karnka Nai Pratet Tai" [Trade Associations and Chambers of Commerce in Thailand] (M.A. thesis, Thammasat University, Bangkok, 1975), pp. 170-176.

35. Montri Chenvidyakarn, "Political Control and Economic Influence: A Study of Trade Associations in Thailand" (Ph.D. dissertation, University of Chicago, 1979), pp. 514-517.

36. Data obtained from the Central Trade Associations and Chambers of Commerce Registrar's Office, Ministry of Commerce.

37. Montri, "Political Control," p. 519.

18

38. Data obtained from the Central Trade Associations and Chambers of Commerce Registrar's Office.

39. Philippe Schmitter and Wolfgang Streeck, "The Organization of Business Interests: A Research Design to Study the Associative Action of Business in the Advanced Industrial Societies of Western Europe" (October 1981 version), p. 1.

40. For a long time major exceptions had been two books by Stanley Kochanek: *Business and Politics in India* (Berkeley: University of California Press, 1974) and *Interest Groups and Development: Business and Politics in Pakistan* (Delhi: Oxford University Press, 1983). A more recent exception is Andrew MacIntyre, *Business and Politics in Indonesia* (Sydney: Allen and Unwin, 1991).

41. Examples of studies of this kind are Myron Weiner, *The Politics of Scarcity: Public Pressure and Political Response in India* (Chicago: University of Chicago, 1962); Philippe Schmitter, *Interest Conflict and Political Change in Brazil* (Stanford: Stanford University, 1971); Robert Bianchi, *Interest Groups and Political Development in Turkey* (Princeton: Princeton University Press, 1984).

42. Weiner, *The Politics of Scarcity,* p. xix.

43. Authors of Western corporatism, by contrast, have paid a greater attention to this issue. For example, Peter Katzenstein's two books: *Corporatism and Change* (Ithaca: Cornell University Press, 1984); *Small States in World Markets* (Ithaca: Cornell University Press, 1985) deal in detail with the ways in which corporatist orders have allowed the smaller European countries to weather economic difficulties generated by external factors.

44. For example, Everett Hagen, *The Economics of Development* (Homewood, Illinois: Richard D. Irwin Inc., 1975); Michael Todaro, *Economic Development in the Third World* (New York: Longman, 1985); Bruce Herrick and Charles Kindleberger, *Economic Development* (New York: McGraw-Hill, 1983).

45. Herrick and Kindleberger, *Economic Development,* p. 271.

46. Herrick and Kindleberger, *Economic Development,* pp. 271-272.

47. For example, Paul Baran, *The Political Economy of Growth* (New York: Monthly Review, 1952); Andre Gunder Frank, *Capitalism and Underdevelopment in Latin America: Historical Studies of Chile and Brazil* (New York: Monthly Review Press, 1969).

48. For example, Fernando Cardoso and Enzo Faletto, *Dependency and Development in Latin America* (translation) (Berkeley: University of California Press, 1979); Peter Evans, *Dependent Development: The Alliance of Multinational, State, and Local Capital in Brazil* (Princeton: Princeton University Press, 1979).

49. For example, Hamza Alavi, "The State in Post-Colonial Societies: Pakistan and Bangladesh" *New Left Review,* 74 (July-August 1972): 59-81; Colin Leys, "Capital Accumulation, Class Formation and Dependency: The Significance of the Kenyan case," in Ralph Miliband and John Saville, eds., *Socialist Register 1978* (London: Merlin Press, 1978), pp. 241-266.

50. Leys, "Capital Accumulation," p. 250.

51. Evans, *Dependent Development*, esp. Chapter 6, pp. 274-329.

52. Kevin Hewison, "The Development of Capital, Public Policy and the Role of the State in Thailand" (Ph.D. thesis, Murdoch University, Australia, 1983); Kraisak, "The Growth of Domestic Capital," pp. 135-146.

53. For an example of this approach, see Evans, *Dependent Development*, Chapter 6, pp.101-162; Kraisak, "The Growth of Domestic Capital," pp.135-138.

54. Richard Sklar, "Postimperialism: A Class Analysis of Multinational Corporate Expansion," *Comparative Politics* 9 (October 1976): 75-92.

55. David Becker, *The New Bourgeoisie and the Limits of Dependency: Mining, Class, and Power in "Revolutionary" Peru* (Princeton: Princeton University Press, 1983), Chapter 9, esp. pp.256-262.

56. For Becker, class formation is the process by which individuals become aware that they share specific interests; form social bonds on the basis of that mutuality of interest; organize to secure more effectively advantages for themselves; and collectively employ political assets to that end.

57. Works in this literature are, for example, Stephen Haggard and Chung-in Moon, "The South Korean State in International Economy: Liberal, Dependent, or Mercantile?" in John Ruggie, ed., *The Antinomies of Interdependence* (New York: Columbia University Press, 1983); Frederic Deyo, ed., *The Political Economy of the New Asian Industrialism* (Ithaca: Cornell University Press, 1987).

58. Frederic Deyo, "Coalitions, Institutions, and Linkage Sequencing—Toward a Strategic Capacity Model of East Asian Development," in Deyo, ed., *The Political Economy*, p.231.

59. Ibid., p. 232.

60. Montri Chenvidyakarn,"Political Control and Economic Influence:A Study of Trade Associations in Thailand" (Ph.D. dissertation, University of Chicago, 1979).

61. Ibid., p. 437

62. Narong Petchprasert, "Samakom Karnka Lae Ho Karnka Nai Pratet Tai" [Trade Associations and Chambers of Commerce in Thailand] (M.A. thesis, Thammasat University, Bangkok, 1975).

63. Narong, "Samakom," pp. 94, 166; Montri, "Political Control," p. 437.

64. Suthy Prasartset, "Some Aspects of Government-Business Relations in Thailand and Japan", published in *Papers and Proceedings of the Conference on Comparative Study of the Role of Government in Economic Development in Japan and Thailand* (Bangkok: Faculty of Economics, Chulalongkorn University, December 1982.)

65. Ibid., p. 4.23

66. Sawaeng Rattanamongkolmas, *Satanapab Botbat Panha Lae Naeotang Kaekai*

20

Kiaokab Kwam Ruammuu Pak Rattaban Lae Ekachon [Status, Role, Problems, and Solutions, Regarding Cooperation between the State and the Private Sector], a published report submitted to the National Economic and Social Development Board, 1986.

67. Philippe Schmitter, "Still the Century of Corporatism?" in Fredrick Pike and Thomas Stritch, eds., *The New Corporatism: Social-Political Structures in the Iberian World* (Notre Dame: University of Notre Dame Press, 1974), pp. 102-105; Leo Panitch, "The Development of Corporatism in Liberal Democracies," and Gerhard Lehmbruch, "Liberal Corporatism and Party Government" *Comparative Political Studies* 10 (April 1977): 61-90; 91-126.

68. Schmitter, "Still the Century," p. 102.

69. Schmitter, "Still the Century," pp. 102-103.

70. Schmitter, "Still the Century," pp. 102-105. For works on liberal corporatism, see *Comparative Political Studies* 10 (April 1977), and Peter Katzenstein, *Corporatism and Change: Austria, Switzerland, and the Politics of Industry* (Ithaca: Cornell University Press, 1984). For an authoritative work on authoritarian corporatism, see James Malloy, ed., *Authoritarianism and Corporatism* (Pittsburgh: University of Pittsburgh, 1977).

2

The Rise of Organized Business

The history of business associations in Thailand goes back as far as 1898 when Western traders opened the Bangkok International Chamber of Commerce.[1] The Chamber was then followed by the Fire Insurance Association of Bangkok in 1910 and the Siam Importers Association a year later. Membership of both associations consisted of European companies. The first business association created by local people, the Chinese Chamber of Commerce, came into being in 1908. It was organized by Chinese immigrants to regulate intra-community economic competition and to counter the influence of organized Western traders. Western associations drew little attention from the government as they were registered with, and directly responsible to, their home governments, according to the extra-territoriality enjoyed by Westerners in Thailand. However, business associations of Chinese immigrants were of concern to the Thai monarchy. While the royal government accepted the objectives of those Chinese associations as organizations for the promotion of the welfare and occupational interests of their members, it always suspected the associations of being involved in underground activities that were related to the efforts to overthrow the imperial government in Peking.[2]

Since the government was trying to absorb these Chinese into Thai society, it was unhappy with any development that would enhance their commitment to China. Moreover, in disseminating republican ideas, the associations posed a potential threat to the Thai monarchy. In 1914, the Association Act was thus introduced. Under this act the government was empowered to disapprove the registration or order the dissolution of any association deemed to endanger public peace and order.[3]

22

Until the period of absolute monarchy came to an end in 1932, there were no business associations of purely Thai citizens. Members of Chinese associations were mostly immigrants who were neither culturally nor legally Thai. The indigenous people were predominantly employed in agriculture and the public sector. Businesses in Thailand were controlled by European and, to a lesser extent, Chinese firms. Of the 235 leading trading houses in Thailand in 1933, only 38 belonged to Thais, presumably mostly of Chinese ancestry. Europeans and noncitizen Chinese owned 112 and 61 of these leading houses, respectively. (See Table 2.1.)

TABLE 2.1 Leading Trading Houses in Thailand, 1933 and 1940

Nationalities	1933	1940
European	112	103
Chinese	61	98
Thai	38	56
Indian	16	35
Japanese	8	7

Source: Kenneth Landon, *The Chinese in Thailand* (New York: Institute of the Pacific Relations, 1941), p. 141, as quoted in Montri, "Political Control," p. 203. Reprinted by permission.

Economic Nationalism, 1932-1957

The 1932 revolution which brought an end to the absolute monarchy stirred economic nationalism among the well-assimilated Sino-Thai and native Thai merchants.[a] A few months after the revolution, a group of these merchants formed the first business association of Thai citizens, the Siamese Chamber of Commerce.[4] The following year saw two other Thai business associations emerging: the Association for the Promotion of Siamese Trade and Commerce, and the United Merchants of Siam.[5] This development corresponded well with the policy of several post-1932 governments which

---

[a] By well-assimilated Sino-Thais I mean descendants of Chinese immigrants who held Thai citizenship and considered themselves politically and culturally Thai. It should be noted that some of these Sino-Thais began their political activities during the last few years of the absolute monarchy by asking the royal government to assist them in their efforts to compete with foreign, including Chinese, businesses. See Nakarin Mektrairat, "Song Krasae Pumpanya Nai Karn Patiwat Sayam Tosawat Ti 2470," in idem, *Kwamkid Kwamru Lae Amnat Karnmuang Nai Karn Patiwat Sayam 2474* [Idea, Knowledge, and Political Power, Regarding the Siamese Revolution of 1932], (Bangkok: Sataban Sayam Suksa: 1990), p. 94.

tried to use business associations of Thai citizens as a tool to loosen the grip of foreign control of the national economy.

In 1933 the Ministry of Economic Affairs outlined a nine-point program to nurture trade and industry in the country; one of the nine points stated that the ministry would "encourage the formation of a Siamese Chamber of Commerce."[6] However, government assistance to these associations was restricted to moral support. The first meeting of the Siamese Chamber of Commerce was opened by the state councillor of the Ministry of Economic Affairs.[7] The Association for the Promotion of Siamese Trade and Commerce had the president of the House of Representatives among its founders.[8]

These associations, however, did not enjoy material or legal support from the government. Most importantly, when the founding members of the Siamese Chamber of Commerce requested that their organization be registered as the Siamese Commercial Council with the intention of compelling all firms to join the council, the government turned down their request and insisted that their organization operate as a voluntary association.[9] Lacking substantial official support, business associations of Thai citizens went rapidly into decline as they had only small membership and limited financial resources, as compared with their European and Chinese counterparts.

European associations began to decline in the late 1940s.[10] Ethnic Chinese, capitalizing on their closer cultural and commercial ties with the indigenous people, increasingly replaced Europeans in various business sectors. Their emerging dominance of the Thai economy can be seen from the fact that in the late 1940s ethnic Chinese accounted for 70 percent of non-Thai capital invested in firms with a capital of at least US$ 50,000.[11] Much smaller in number, non-Chinese foreign firms preferred to join Chinese and Thai counterparts in relevant associations.

The development of Chinese business associations in this period may not be fully understood without a brief examination of the history of Chinese immigrants in Thailand and their reaction to the economic nationalist policy pursued by Thai governments since 1932, to which we now turn.

The Chinese in Thailand

The first Chinese settlement dates back several centuries. However, the Chinese population increased significantly only after Thailand opened its economy to international trade in the mid-nineteenth century. Ethnic Chinese constituted the core of the business and laboring classes in Thailand and by 1917 made up about 10 percent of the total Thai population.[12] Traditionally, the Chinese were rapidly assimilated into Thai society. Marrying local people was not uncommon among Chinese immigrants. Their children, in addition, spoke fluent Thai and some of them even entered the Thai bureaucracy, serving royal trading activities or engaged in tax farming. Consequently, it was reported in the nineteenth century that fourth-generation Chinese were unheard of in Thailand.[13]

Drawing on the analysis of G. William Skinner, three socio-political factors underlying the remarkable absorption of ethnic Chinese into Thai society may be cited.[14] In the first place, the Thai commitment to Theravada Buddhism posed a minor obstacle to their social integration with the Chinese, who are familiar with Mahayanna Buddhism. In comparison, Chinese assimilation was much more difficult in the neighboring East Indies and Straits Settlement, given the Islamic religious tradition of the indigenous people there. In the second place, prior to the first decade of the twentieth century, Chinese females almost never emigrated to Thailand, so that male immigrants had to marry Thai or Sino-Thai females.[15] In the third place, unlike the rest of Southeast Asia, Thailand managed to escape Western colonialism with the consequence that its ruling elite has always been composed of Thais. Ethnic Chinese, either to advance in their bureaucratic careers or to seek official permission for monopolies necessary for their commercial careers, had a strong incentive to integrate with native people. By contrast, in the colonial East Indies and the Straits Settlement, there could be little advantage for the Chinese in integrating with the society of the local population, while full acceptance in the elite societies of the Dutch or the British was impossible.[16]

Towards the last two decades of the era of absolute monarchy, however, a range of factors emerged which retarded the assimilation of ethnic Chinese in Thailand. To start with, in the 1918-1931 period, Chinese arrivals were unprecedently high while departures were relatively low. The result was an average annual surplus of immigration of 35,700 for the fourteen-year period. This is almost three times the rate for the preceding 36 years (1882-1917), which was 12,542 per year.[17] Secondly, Chinese no longer came in great numbers without their wives.[18] Between the early 1920s and the late 1940s the proportion of Chinese females in the immigration surplus increased from fifteen percent to 34 percent.[19] Finally, the events leading up to the overthrow of the Manchu rulers, the victory of the KMT-led nationalist revolution, and the Japanese aggression against China stirred nationalism among ethnic Chinese, who had been highly divided into speech or regional groups, with little national loyalty.[20] Rising Chinese nationalism in turn considerably slowed down the integration of ethnic Chinese into Thai society.

On the other side, the Thai elite came to be concerned about the loyalty of the ever-increasing ethnic Chinese population and its domination of the economy. Those with modern education also developed a spirit of Thai nationalism, patterned on the Western concept of the nation-state and nationalism. They began to see the Chinese as excessively money-oriented, devoid of civic and moral virtues, and as draining off Thai wealth in the form of remittances to their homeland. King Rama VI, writing pseudonymously, even compared the Chinese with an anti-Semitic caricature of the Jews, and dubbed them "the Jews of the Orient."[21] Still, these anti-Chinese feelings were translated into government policy only after the overthrow of the absolute monarchy.

Preservation of national independence, including economic independence, and improvement of the livelihood of the people were two of the six pillars of the platform of the group of military and civil bureaucrats who led the democratic revolution. Post-1932 governments, particularly those under Plaek Phibunsongkram (hereafter referred to as Phibun), a right-wing militaristic leader, defined these two pillars to be the increase in the government role in economic development and the promotion of indigenous Thai businesses.

Accordingly, the percentage of the annual government budget devoted to economic affairs was increased from 21 percent during the years 1922-1931 to 30 percent during the years 1932-1941.[22] In contrast with the preceding royal governments, which in the main had refrained from participation in commerce and industry, post-1932 governments erected several public enterprises, such as paper factories, an army textile factory, sugar mills and distilleries. Moreover, a series of legislative measures came into effect which either nationalized or reserved certain businesses only to Thai citizens or to firms in which government agencies or Thai citizens were major share holders. The list of such reserved businesses included oil refining and distribution, shipping, rice exportation, animal slaughtering, and even food hawking on government premises.

The adverse effect of economic nationalism on the Chinese was reinforced by unscrupulous crackdowns on the organized activities of Chinese communities. This occurred mostly during World War II when Phibun, being a Japanese ally, tried to curb Chinese anti-Japanese activities in Thailand. For that purpose, certain border provinces were declared strategic "prohibited areas" and all foreigners, mostly Chinese petty traders, were evacuated. In Bangkok, suspected Chinese schools, newspapers, and community organizations were closed.

Premier Phibun was in power for the first time from 1938 to 1944 in which year he was ousted by the House of Representatives. In 1948, through a coup, he resumed the premiership and remained in power continuously until 1957. His second premiership was again marked by extensive government participation in commerce and industry and economic nationalism, mostly against ethnic Chinese. The political harassment of ethnic Chinese also continued, but this time on different grounds. As China turned communist, Phibun, siding with the US in the Cold War, made several raids on allegedly communist Chinese organizations and leaders. Although his main targets seemed to be labor leaders, businessmen were also affected. For example, between November 10, 1952, and January 24, 1953, over 150 Chinese firms were raided.[23]

Chinese merchants chose not to react through political means which would have been overt and confrontational, fearing that doing so would have invited further repression. Besides accepting restrictions laid down by the officials or seeking naturalization, they tried to get around the restrictive laws in nonpolitical ways. Small businessmen either gave bribes to law enforcement officials or had their firms registered under the names of Thai citizens. However, large firms, which by nature required greater continuity and certainty, preferred to Thai-ify their corporations by inviting politicians or bureaucrats to join their executive boards. A 1955 survey by Skinner found that 60 of the 100 most influential Chinese leaders in Thailand served on corporation boards together with prominent Thais.[24]

Economic nationalism and a repressive political climate also led Chinese merchants in almost every trade to organize associations. Through them, businesses in the same line exchanged information and formulated concerted (but nonpolitical) action to respond to government regulation and harassment.[25] These Chinese-dominated associations also adopted Thai names to "make their activities less conspicuous and suspect."[26]

The Chinese Chamber of Commerce became the largest and most important of all Chinese business associations. Its membership included not only business firms and trade associations, but also language group associations and individuals. Indeed, the chamber worked as "the chief diplomatic and protective agency of the entire Chinese community,"[27] rather than the representative of exclusive business interests. For example, in 1943 when the Japanese army wanted to recruit Chinese workers for road construction, the chamber talked the Thai government into securing an agreement that the Chinese would to be employed rather than conscripted.[28]

To sum up, over the two decades following the end of the absolute monarchy, Chinese businessmen were preoccupied with the question of how to survive the nationalistic policy of the government. Various nonpolitical, low profile means were employed to circumvent the enforcement of government policy. Opposing any policy in the formulation stage, on the other hand, was avoided. Chinese trade associations also proliferated during these hard times. However, their main concern was not to lobby openly for or against a particular economic policy. As Chinese businessmen and Chinese associations constituted the overwhelming majority of the business community in Thailand, the overall picture for this period was that group-based, public policy-oriented activities of business were kept to a minimum.

Government Policy towards Associations

Public policy towards business associations in general over this 1932-1957 period was basically pluralistic. In the first place, it allowed only voluntary associations to operate. Secondly, associations were treated fairly equally by officials, without any one of them enjoying substantial recognition, privileges or material support from the government. Finally, no attempt by the government was made to use these associations as policy instruments in trade and industry until 1954 when an advisory Board of Trade was created.

The years between the end of World War II and 1954 were marked by a tremendous surge in Thailand's commodity exports. Competition in the export business was so severe that it resulted in the bankruptcy of a large number of firms. Unhealthy practices, such as the adulteration of export products and the breaking of contracts with foreign importers, worried officials, who were afraid that such abuses would damage the reputation of the country and hamper the inflow of much valued foreign exchange. To solve these problems, the Board of Trade was established to regulate commodity exports and to serve as advisor to the government in general economic matters.

All eight members of the interim board of directors of the Board of Trade were high officials appointed by the government. On the recommendation of the interim board of directors, however, the Board of Trade was soon registered as a private association composed of, among others, the Bangkok Chamber of Commerce (later to become the TCC), the Chinese Chamber of Commerce, the British Chamber of Commerce and the Indian Commercial Association.[29]

Authoritarian Capitalism, 1957-1973

Premier Phibun's domination of Thai politics came to an abrupt halt in 1957 when a successful coup was launched against him. After a brief interlude, Sarit Thanarat, the coup leader, took over the premiership. Unlike Phibun, who resumed elections and allowed for an elected House of Representatives after coups, Sarit abrogated the constitution and ruled without an elected legislature. Under his leadership a new course of development for Thailand was charted which has continued to the present. Encouraged and assisted by the World Bank and the US, Sarit abandoned nationalism and state-led industrialization, which had been the mainstay of Phibun's economic policy. Many public enterprises were either sold or leased to the private sector. The government's role was reduced to the provision of economic infrastructure and to the establishment of a legal and political order favorable to the growth of private enterprise, which was now regarded as the engine of development.

Sarit promised that all private enterprises, whatever their nationality, would enjoy similar rights. Once an investment project had been approved, the government guaranteed that it would not set up any enterprise to compete with it. Nor would the government nationalize private industrial enterprises. Approved projects enjoyed numerous privileges and benefits including exemption from (or reduction of) import duties on raw materials, protection from import competition, and exemption from (or reduction of) export duties. While these rights and privileges were designed to attract Western and Japanese investors, they benefited Chinese businessmen, too. Noncitizen Chinese businesses could now own land as this right was granted to all foreign businesses. Harassment of Chinese businessmen, particularly those in partnership with Western or Japaneses ventures, was all the more unlikely.[30]

Since Sarit's introduction of the new approach to development, the Thai government has seldom made any effort to replace Chinese or Sino-Thai businesses and business associations with indigenous Thai associations. The government has been content with gradually assimilating ethnic Chinese, allowing them to play a full economic role. While Sarit's government had a clear and systematic vision of how to promote private firms, apparent from the official First National Economic Development Plan (1961-1966), it did not have any equivalent vision for business associations. No explicit public policy towards business associations emerged during Sarit's era.

After the death of Sarit, Thanom Kittikachorn, his close associate, continued to govern Thailand autocratically. During Thanom's premiership, the government formulated the first systematic policy on business associations. This policy was implemented in two pieces of legislation enacted in 1966: the Chamber of Commerce Act and the Trade Association Act. The government alone was instrumental in the formation and the passage of these two acts. The Ministry of Commerce, which was responsible for the development of these acts, hardly solicited any opinion or information at all from the business community.[31]

The major purpose of the acts was to formalize and structuralize the existing system of associations. Business associations were divided into two kinds: 1) trade associations, members of which were firms or individuals engaged in the same trade or industry, and, 2) chambers of commerce, members of which were associations as well as firms or individuals involved in various trades or industries. Chambers of commerce were in turn divided into two kinds: those which were nationality-based and those which were territory-based. The former consisted of the TCC, representing Thai businesses, and other foreign national chambers, such as the Chinese Chamber, the American Chamber, the Indian Chamber. The latter included provincial chambers and the TCC, this time serving as both the Bangkok and the national chambers. The TCC and all foreign national chambers, in conjunction with participating trade associations and public enterprises, made up the Board of Trade, officially called the Council of Chambers of Commerce, which became the representative of all private business interests.

A mild form of nationalism was still an essential element of the acts. A territorial control was put on the associations of foreign nationals. If more than half of the total members of a trade association were foreigners, it was allowed to exist only in Bangkok.[32] A foreign chamber of commerce, likewise, could be established only in Bangkok.[33] Most importantly, the president of the TCC was ex-officio president of the Board of Trade. Chinese-background businesses, however, were not discriminated against in practice. The TCC was notably dominated by Sino-Thais holding Thai citizenship; and the acts did not seek to promote or create indigenous associations to compete with pre-existing ones which were dominated by ethnic Chinese.

In 1971 the status of organized business was further elevated when the government incorporated the promotion of its development into one of its five-year plans, the Third National Economic and Social Development Plan. Unlike the Trade Association Act and the Chamber of Commerce Act, the plan did not seek to structure or control business associations. On the contrary, it urged the government to encourage organized business to make recommendations regarding the formation of economic policies. Specifically the plan assigned the following tasks to the government:

1) Encouraging business to organize, especially in pivotal sectors such as exports, tourism and finance.

2) Encouraging the participation of business associations in various committees working on problems detrimental to national economic development.

3) Encouraging the establishment of a joint public-private committee in charge of the improvement of coordination between the government and the private sector.[34]

With the passage of the two 1966 acts and the Third National Economic and Social Development Plan, the Ministry of Commerce stepped up its promotional measures. An additional number of associations, not necessarily those concerned with the export of standard commodities, were given some privileges which were denied to nonjoiners. For example, the Thai Textile Manufacturing Association was granted special rights to import yarns and to allocate the textile export quotas. Fishmeal factories which wanted to be exporters had to join the Thai Marine Association, which was given the right to allocate the quotas for fishmeal exports.[35] This kind of encouraging measure, however, was applicable only to a few regulated trades or industries. For most trades or industries, government measures were confined to giving verbal encouragement and providing some facilities needed for the office work of the new associations.

Just as important, the official National Economic and Social Development Board (NESDB) invited representatives from the Board of Trade, the TBA, and the newly created ATI to join their planning and policy work. Between 1967 and 1971 these three institutions served on various NESDB subcommittees on the development of the private sector.[36] The Third National Economic and Social Development Plan, in addition, was the first of its kind which ever solicited information and opinions from business associations, mainly from the Board of Trade.[37]

Despite such recognition and the moderate encouragement given by the government, the growth rate of business associations was not substantially increased. From 1966 to 1973 an average of five associations were registered annually, compared with four in each of the preceding five years.[38] In addition, the ban on the formation of foreign business associations outside the capital city cut down the number of provincial trade associations which were predominantly Chinese. Meanwhile, the provincial chambers of commerce, designed to be a keystone in the national system of business associations, and potentially 70 in number, never exceeded the original two of 1966 until the late 1970s.

The passage of the Trade Association and the Chamber of Commerce Acts, however, encouraged the professionalization and Thai-ification of Chinese-dominated associations. They now had to keep a membership register and annual records, formulate bylaws and procedural rules, employ staff literate in Thai and operate increasingly in the Thai language.[39] According to a survey conducted by Montri Chenvidyakarn in the early 1970s, the majority of trade associations were largely Thai-ified: 63 percent of their members, 75 percent of their executive committee members, and 87 percent of their presidents held Thai citizenship.[40] The Chinese Chamber of Commerce, the traditional vanguard of all Chinese associations, also lost its preeminence to the Board of Trade and the TCC.[41] Given the official status of supreme business representatives and regularly charged with public responsibilities by the government, they came to be much more prestigious than their Chinese counterpart, even among Chinese business communities.

On the whole, by 1973 business associations still suffered from several weaknesses. Their members and leaders had relatively low education. Even among their presidents, only 43 percent had studied beyond high school, and nearly 15 percent had no formal education other than elementary school, if any.[42] Associations complained about the insufficiency of revenues collected from membership fees and their dependence on a few richer members and leaders. A good number of associations retained the traditional attitude of placing an emphasis on recreational, social and welfare functions. The representation of categoric interests to the government was not their central task. Most associations reported that they never or seldom participated in law-making, joined government committees, or assisted the officials in the supervision of business and trade.

It is fair to say then that business associations during this 1966-1973 period did not effectively function as interest groups in the manner found in liberal democratic regimes. Rather, the more active and successful ones worked as subsidiary policy instruments of the government. Montri Chenvidyakarn appropriately characterized the interaction between the government and organized business in those years as a form of "state (authoritarian) corporatism."[43]

It must be added that leading businesses continued to invite senior officials to join them as nominal executive directors or presidents throughout the period. Although nationalistic harassment ceased to pose a threat, keeping good ties with powerful politico-bureaucrats was still highly valued by business. In a society where favoritism and nepotism were more than tolerated, effective clientelistic ties could overcome government-caused inconvenience or delay, and deliver certain privileges and even contracts from the government.[b] In 1969 there were reportedly at least six top politico-bureaucrats each of whom had connections with 20-50 business firms. Another seven influential civilian and military bureaucratic leaders had connections with 10-18 firms each. On the whole, there were more than 80 senior military officers who were each connected to at least one firm.[44] For businessmen then, manipulating clientelistic ties with high officials for their particularistic interests was as important as, if not more important than, lobbying for or against categoric interests.

Weak as they might have been as interest groups, business associations were at that time much stronger than any other functional group. Independent farmers' associations or agricultural cooperatives were practically nonexistent. Almost all of them were created and/or sponsored, and closely controlled by the government for security and agricultural development purposes. Labor unions had been outlawed for fourteen years before the government allowed them to operate again in 1972. By comparison, business associations were largely independent of the government. Almost all of them had been organized by businessmen themselves. No public officials sat on the executive boards of business

---

[b] For this reason, until the 1970s even business firms with a "pure" Thai looking occasionally invited influential military-bureaucratic leaders to join their boards of directors. Interestingly, in 1956 Queen Rampaipanni (the widow of Rama VII, the last ruler of the absolute monarchy era) appointed Marshal Sarit Thanarat and Police General Pao Sriyanon, the two political heavyweights at that time, as directors of her company. See Sangsit Piriyarangsan, *Tunniyom Khunnang Tai (Po So 2475-2503)* [The Thai Bureaucratic Capitalism, 1932-1960] (Bangkok: Sangsan, 1983), pp. 260-263.

associations. Official control of their operation, internal regulation, and leadership selection, though harsh in theory, was mild in practice. No closures of associations or bans on their functions or leadership selections had been reported.

Moreover, by 1973 a range of associations successfully emerged as policy-oriented groups, chief among which were the Board of Trade, the TCC, the ATI, the TBA, the Thai Textile Manufacturing Association, and the Rice Traders Association. After over a decade of merely responding to official ideas and action, associations took the initiative in strengthening their organizations. For the Board of Trade and some leading associations, business strength was to be found in a stronger peak organization. Between 1972 and 1973 they discussed the creation of a new peak organization, to be called the Federation of Economic Organizations of Thailand. Whereas only chambers of commerce and not trade associations were required to join the Board of Trade, all kinds of business associations across the country would be compelled to join the new peak organization.[45]

Business also took up the idea of creating a joint committee officially representing the government and the business community which had been propounded in the Third National Economic and Social Development Plan but not yet translated into practice. In 1972 the Board of Trade and the ATI requested that the government set up such a committee to discuss economic and business problems from time to time.[46]

Neither scheme, creating a new peak organization with universal compulsory membership or initiating formal government-business consultation, was instituted, as the ten year rule of Thanom collapsed in the face of a massive student-led popular uprising in October 1973.

Open Politics, 1973-1976

The brief democratic years of 1973 to 1976 were not a fertile ground for the progress of formally organized and functional interest groups such as business associations. The abrupt opening of the political arena after almost two decades of an authoritarian rule led to the explosion of hundreds of student, peasant, and factory worker "demand groups." Like those Lloyd Rudolph and Susanne Rudolph describe in the Indian case, these demand groups were loosely organized, financially poor, and lacking in professional staffs.[47] They relied less on professional expertise and lobbying skill than on symbolic and agitational politics.

Between 1973 and 1976 there were 1,333 strikes and 322 demonstrations in the country.[48] As a result, governments in this period could not afford to formulate any long term, systematic policy, let alone consider various proposals made by leading business associations. Nor would it have seemed wise for the government to focus on the problems or grievances of functional associations, when coping with those of the demand groups was much more crucial to their immediate survival.

Montri Chenvidyakarn noted that during the three years of open politics, "trade associations in particular kept their profiles low . . . little was heard of their operations, their activities were rarely reported in the news media."[49] Labor unions were quite active during this period. However, most of them operated as a demand group rather than as a functional interest group—relying on strikes, political protests, and massive demonstrations. Though the political opening did not lead to stronger business associations, it created changes which indirectly affected government-business relations.

TABLE 2.2 Occupational Distribution of Members of the House of Representatives, 1933-1986 (Percentage)

Date of Election	Businessmen	Bureaucrats (Serving or Retired)	Others	Total	(1)/(2)
November 15, 1933	19.2	34.6	46.2	100	0.56
November 7, 1937	19.8	51.7	28.5	100	0.38
November 12, 1938	22.0	39.6	38.4	100	0.56
June 6, 1946	20.8	44.8	34.4	100	0.46
August 5, 1946	11.0	61.0	28.0	100	0.18
January 29, 1948	22.2	34.4	43.4	100	0.65
June 5, 1949	33.3	19.1	47.6	100	1.74
February 26, 1952	20.3	27.7	52.0	100	0.73
February 25, 1957	26.3	28.8	44.9	100	0.91
December 15, 1957	27.5	26.3	46.2	100	1.05
February 10,1969	45.7	20.6	33.7	100	2.22
January 26, 1975	34.6	12.3	53.1	100	2.81
April 4, 1976	29.4	22.2	48.4	100	1.31
April 22, 1979	37.2	18.4	44.4	100	2.02
April 18, 1983	38.3	10.2	51.5	100	3.75
July 27, 1986	24.8	6.9	68.3	100	3.59

Source: Adapted from Krirkkiat Pipatseritham, *Karn Plianplang Tang Setttakij Kab Panha Sitti Manusayachon Nai Pratet Tai* [Economic Change and Human Rights Issue in Thailand] (Bangkok: Thai Khadi Research Institute, 1985), Table 9-2, pp. 466-467, with the data for 1983 and 1986 updated by this writer.

TABLE 2.3 Businessmen in Thai Cabinets, 1963-1986

Premier	Beginning Date of Cabinet	Number of Businessmen	Total Number of Cabinet Members	Percentage of Businessmen
Sarit	February 1963	0	14	0.0
Thanom I	December 1963	1	18	5.6
Thanom II	March 1969	1	25	4.0
Thanom III	December 1972	3	28	10.7
Sanya I	October 1973	4	28	14.3
Sanya II	May 1974	3	31	9.7
Seni I	February 1975	8	30	26.7
Kukrit	March 1975	16	27	59.3
Seni II	April 1976	11	31	35.5
Thanin	October 1976	1	17	5.9
Kriangsak I	November 1977	2	33	6.1
Kriangsak II	May 1979	9	43	20.9
Kriangsak III	February 1980	5	38	13.2
Prem I	March 1980	17	37	45.9
Prem II	January 1981	12	40	30.0
Prem III	December 1981	17	41	41.5
Prem IV	May 1983	21	44	47.7
Prem V	August 1986	21	44	47.7

Source: Adapted from Krirkkiat, *Karn Plianplang*, Table 9-3, pp. 472-475, with the data for the period from December 1981 to August 1986 updated by this writer.

In the first place, with the surge in the public resentment of nepotism, corruption, and abuse of official power, all the hallmarks of the past military regime, clientelistic ties between high officials and businessmen were subject to strong public criticism. Meanwhile, the fragmentation and instability among the top military echelons made military patronage less productive and less reliable for private companies. The military-bureaucratic presence on the boards of large corporations thus declined. Importantly, the Bangkok Bank, the largest private bank in Southeast Asia, accepted the resignation of its exiled president, Marshal Prapat Charusathian, the second man in the deposed Thanom government; then, for the first time ever, the bank appointed a professional banker to its presidency.

The unprecedently liberal climate and the wide opening of electoral politics brought a legion of businessmen, not necessarily affiliated with business associations, into political parties, the House of Representatives, and various cabinets. Twenty-seven of the 51 members of the executive committees of three leading parties (Chat Thai, Kij Sangkom, and

Prachatipat) in 1974 were business people.[50] Following the 1975 election, people with business backgrounds became the largest group in the House, making up 35 percent of the total membership. The ratio between members of parliament with a business background and those with a bureaucratic background was at an all time high in favor of the former. (See Table 2.2.)

The proportion of cabinet members with a business background also increased tremendously during the 1973-1976 period. Particularly, more than half of the Kukrit cabinet, formed in March 1975, could be regarded as business persons. (See Table 2.3.) The strong presence of persons with career ties to business in both the legislative and executive branches of the government has continued, with a brief period in 1977-1978 as the exception. This marked change in the composition of the political elite appears responsible for the change in the political climate to one which, unlike the past, was highly supportive of cordial government-business consultation.

The Return of Authoritarianism, 1976-1978

The three years of democratic experimentation came to an abrupt end with the coup of late 1976. The country was placed under a repressive government supported by the armed forces, but led by a civilian bureaucrat, Thanin Kraivixian. This new government first appeared to be pro-business in that it harshly repressed the left-leaning student and labor movement. Later, it proved to be suspicious of, or at best indifferent to, all kinds of independent organized groups, including the middle class and business groups.

The Fourth National Economic and Social Development Plan approved by this government contained no section on the development of business associations. No further attempts to strengthen business associations and make more use of them in policy-making were initiated by this anti-communist and anti-labor government. Further, in trying to appear equidistant from all nonbureaucratic groups, Thanin at times rebuked business in public.

In one of his talks given to members of the Board of Trade and the ATI, he tactlessly criticized businessmen for being equally responsible, if not more responsible, for the widespread corruption among officials.[51] Only one member out of the seventeen members of Thanin's cabinet had a business background. The newly appointed legislature, in addition, was the exclusive domain of the military-bureaucratic elite.

Because of its anti-communist paranoia and contempt for nonbureaucratic groups, the Thanin government quickly and strongly alienated all but the ultra-conservatives. To save the deteriorating political situation, in October 1977 the same military group which had brought Thanin in removed him.

Kriangsak Chomanan, a pragmatic general, formed a government and headed for democratization.

The Thanin and the Kriangsak years, however, were not entirely unproductive for business associations. Barred from electoral politics, some top business leaders who rose to national prominence during the years of open politics returned to their associations. Between 1976 and 1978 the three flagship organizations, the ATI, the TBA, and the TCC, were endowed with prestigious and energetic leaders. A former deputy prime minister, Pramarn Adireksarn, headed the ATI, while a former minister of finance, Boonchu Rochanasathian headed the TBA. The Board of Trade and the TCC were also led by an assertive and widely respected business leader, Ob Vasurat, who happened to be a close friend and adviser to General Kriangsak.

Thus, when Thanin appeared indifferent to the development of business associations, these leaders turned to developing better cooperation among their associations. This was partly realized in June 1977 when the three flagship associations decided to form a loosely organized Joint Standing Committee on Commerce, Industry and Banking.[52] This committee consisted of the top leadership of the three associations and served as a forum to discuss problems of their mutual concern and to develop a common position.

At first the focus of the Joint Standing Committee was on representing the business sector of Thailand in the ASEAN Chambers of Commerce and Industry. The latter provided a forum for organizations representing the business and industrial interests of all ASEAN member nations to discuss economic and business problems of common concern, particularly those crucial to regional economic cooperation. Later, when Kriangsak's democratization was well under way, the Joint Standing Committee turned to domestic problems. In May 1978 it proposed that the government create a joint public-private committee to be charged with finding solutions to the problem of the trade deficit.

The proposal was well received by Kriangsak, who had been reportedly worried about the nation's economic and financial stability.[53] Thailand's trade balance since 1955 had been continuously in deficit with the deficits growing in line with trade volume.

Of particular concern to the government was that the deficit almost doubled in 1977, from US$ 600 million in 1976 to US$ 1.14 billion.[54] As a result, the current account deficit as a percentage of GNP increased from 2.7 percent to a record high of 5.7 percent by the end of 1977. (See Table 2.4.) Meanwhile, the international debt of the government also increased dramatically from an already high level of 56 percent of the international foreign exchange reserve of the country in 1976, to 95 percent within one year. (See Table 2.5.)

TABLE 2.4 Trade Deficits and Current Account Deficits as Percentages of GNP, 1960-1980

Year	1960-1969	1970-1972	1973-1975	1976	1977	1978	1979	1980
Trade Deficits	8.4	7.0	7.5	3.3	6.5	6.0	8.3	8.6
Current Account Deficits	1.8	2.3	2.5	2.7	5.7	4.9	7.5	7.2

Source: Adapted from Krirkkiat, *Karn Plianplang*, Table 7-1, p. 333.

TABLE 2.5 Government's International Debts as a Percentage of International Reserves, 1962-1980

Year	International Debts (US$mn) (1)	International Reserves (US$mn) (2)	(1)/(2) (Percent)
1962	153.40	507.25	30.24
1964	245.25	609.60	40.24
1966	263.05	863.80	30.45
1968	304.05	939.50	32.36
1970	325.95	766.50	42.53
1972	383.90	968.80	39.63
1974	511.70	1,564.25	32.72
1975	615.05	1,368.80	44.94
1976	832.50	1,484.40	56.08
1977	1,161.95	1,219.40	95.29
1978	1,816.30	1,358.70	133.68
1979	2,770.05	1,836.55	150.83
1980	3,659.50	2,055.91	178.00

Source: Adapted from Krirkkiat, *Karn Plianplang*, Table 7-15, pp. 379-380.

In June 1978 a consultative committee was formed to take care of the correction of the trade deficit and other urgent economic problems.[55] The committee was made up of senior officials and leaders of the three flagship business organizations with a deputy prime minister appointed to head it.

The idea of launching a joint committee to coordinate the activities of the government and the business sector, advocated by the Third National Economic and Social Development Plan in the early 1970s, was eventually realized. The committee met only a few times, mostly to listen to business complaints on public policy and administrative obstacles to the exportation of their products. However, a smooth working relationship between both sides rarely existed. For business, the government appeared not serious and not sufficiently urgent in implementing any solution advised by the committee.[56] Conversely, government representatives viewed their business counterparts as impatient and fond of accusation rather than consultation.[57] Consequently, the joint committee was frequently locked in stalemate and hardly any resolution which passed was ever effectively implemented.

Semi-Democracy, 1979-1986

At the end of 1978 the military leadership promulgated a new constitution, scheduled a general election and steered Thailand toward semi-democracy. The April 1979 election saw Pramarn Adireksarn, ATI president, and Boonchu Rochanasathian, TBA president, run successfully and their parties emerged as the two largest parties in the House of Representatives. However, with the support of some minor parties and the appointed Senate, which was dominated by the military, Kriangsak Chomanan was again chosen prime minister. Pramarn and Boonchu thus became major opposition leaders. Ob Vasurat, president of the TCC, did not run in the election; however, because of his friendship with Kriangsak, he was appointed minister of commerce.

The new government did not last long. Shortly after its formation, the cabinet had to make an unpopular decision to raise domestic oil prices in response to pressures created by the 1979 international oil shock. Inflation rose sharply, and considerably worsened the economic and financial stability of the country. Kriangsak was harshly criticized by the public and the mass media. Above all, middle-level commanders of the army, formerly the bastion of his rule, now withdrew their support. Added to that, his support in the House of Representatives and the Senate was also eroded. Thus, Kriangsak bitterly submitted his resignation in early 1980.

General Prem Tinsulanond, the army commander and minister of defense, was the overwhelming choice chosen to head a new cabinet. Unlike his predecessor, Prem put much more effort into securing the support of the House of Representatives. Major parties, not minor parties, were invited to join the government. Since most leaders of major parties were businessmen, almost half of Prem's cabinet members were persons with a business background. (See Table 2.3.)

Notably, Pramarn Adireksarn and Boonchu Rochanasathian became deputy prime ministers this time. Both men supported the desire of business to have a more effective role in government economic policy-making. Boonchu in particular held informal talks between cabinet ministers entrusted with economic affairs and leaders of the TBA, the TCC, and the ATI. He believed that holding informal discussions would be more productive than resuming a formal joint public-private committee.[58] Boonchu also openly championed the notion of "Thailand, Inc."[59] Briefly, he proposed that the future of the country lay in its increased competitiveness in the world arena—both in attracting foreign investment and in increasing exports. To succeed, he emphasized, the government and the business sector had to work as "colleagues in the same team or the same corporation when confronted with other countries all over the world."[60]

Government-business informal discussions, however, turned out to be not as fruitful as Boonchu had anticipated. Business leaders complained that the government team, even with Boonchu, a former TBA president, at its head, was not effective in translating their demands and opinions into policy action. The new leadership of the three flagship associations came to the conclusion that to make it work, a joint public-private committee at the national level had to be presided over by the prime minister, and its meetings should be formal and regularly scheduled.

Consequently, after Boonchu and his party withdrew from the government in March 1981, the three flagship associations under the banner of the Joint Standing Committee on Commerce, Industry and Banking lobbied Premier Prem for the creation of such a committee. In June Prem decided to accept their idea and the Joint Public and Private Sector Consultative Committee (JPPCC) with himself as its president was announced.[61] This committee was scheduled to meet every month and consisted of representatives from the TCC, the ATI, and the TBA as well as cabinet ministers in charge of economic affairs.

On top of that, during 1983-1984 the government started to sponsor provincial business organizations, especially provincial chambers of commerce. Apart from educating business leaders on the utility of business associations and providing them with some office facilities, officials employed the eligibility to join provincial JPPCCs as encouragement for business to organize. The government set a rule that it organized a joint committee along the lines of the central JPPCC, with the governor as its head, in any province which had a chamber of commerce, or provincial affiliates of the ATI or the TBA. As a result, there was a rapid growth in the number of provincial chambers of commerce. From four chambers in 1978, the numbered jumped to 28 in 1983 and by 1986 each of the 72 provinces had its own chamber. (See Table 2.6.)

TABLE 2.6 Growth of Provincial Chambers of Commerce

Year	Number of Chambers
1967	2
1979	4
1981	6
1982	10
1983	15
1984	39
1985	59
1986	72

Sources: Preecha Tanprasert, TCC vice-president, interview, October 16, 1987; Montri, "Political Control," p. 519; TCC Annual Reports, 1982, 1983, 1984, 1985, 1986.

Notes

1. G. William Skinner, *Chinese Society in Thailand: An Analytical History* (Ithaca: Cornell University Press, 1957), p. 170.

2. Narong, Petchprasert, "Samakom Karnka Lae Ho Karnka Nai Pratet Tai" [Trade Associations and Chambers of Commerce in Thailand] (M.A. thesis, Thammasat University, Bangkok, 1975), p. 30.

3. Montri Chenvidyakarn, "Political Control and Economic Influence: A Study of Trade Associations in Thailand" (Ph.D. dissertation, University of Chicago, 1979), p. 118.

4. Viraj Puengsunthorn, "Prawat Samakom Poka Tai" [History of the Thai Merchants Association], in *Nangsuu Perd Aakarn Samakom Poka Tai* [Commemorative Book on the Occasion of the Opening of the New Building of the Thai Merchants Association] (Bangkok: Krung Sayam Press, 1971).

5. Montri, "Political Control," p. 202.

6. Kenneth Landon, *Siam in Transition: A Brief Survey of Cultural Trends in the Five Years since the Revolution of 1932* (New York: Greenwood Press, 1968; originally published by University of Chicago in 1939), p. 62.

7. Ibid., p. 68.

8. His name is Chao-Phrya Dharmasakti-montri, see Montri, "Political Control," p. 202.

9. Viraj, "Prawat Samakom Poka Tai."

10. Montri, "Political Control," p. 157.

11. Suparb Yossundara, " A Preliminary Survey on Foreign Investment in Thailand," prepared for the International Monetary Fund, December 15, 1951, as quoted in Eliezer Ayal,"Thailand," in Frank Golay et al, *Underdevelopment and Economic Nationalism in Southeast Asia* (Ithaca: Cornell University Press, 1969), p. 329.

12. Skinner, *Chinese Society*, Table 8, p. 183.

13. G. William Skinner, "Chinese Assimilation and Thai Politics" *The Journal of Asian Studies* 16 (February 1957): 237.

14. Ibid., pp. 238-240.

15. Ibid., p. 238.

16. Ibid, p. 239.

17. Compiled and calculated from the data provided by Skinner, *Chinese Society*, pp. 172-173.

18. Landon, *Siam in Transition*, p. 87.

19. Skinner, "Chinese Assimilation," p. 238, fn.2.

20. Skinner, "Chinese Assimilation," p. 238.

21. Walter F. Vella, *Chaiyo: King Vajiravudh and the Development of Thai Nationalism* (Honolulu: University of Hawaii Press, 1978), p. 193.

22. Calculated from the data given by Chavalit Wayupak, "Karn Patiroop Settakij Nai Pratet Tai Po So 2475-2485" [Economic Reform in Thailand, 1932-1942], in Chattip Nartsupa and Sompob Manarangsan, eds., *Prawatsart Settakij Tai Chontuung Po So 2484* [Thai Economic History up to 1941] (Bangkok: Thammasat University Press, 1984), Table 1, pp. 610-611.

23. Skinner, *Chinese Society*, p. 335.

24. G. William Skinner, *Leadership and Power in the Chinese Community of Thailand* (Ithaca: Cornell University Press, 1958), p. 305.

25. Skinner, *Chinese Society*, p. 255.

26. Montri, "Political Control," p. 208.

27. Skinner, *Chinese Society*, p. 321.

28. "The Thai-Chinese Chamber of Commerce: From Setbacks to Steady Growth," in the Thai-Chinese Chamber of Commerce, *Handbook 1980* (Bangkok: no publication date), p. 58.

29. "Prawat Lae Nati Kong Sapa Ho Karnka Haeng Pratet Tai" [History and Functions of the Board of Trade], in The Board of Trade, *Yisipha Pi Sapa Ho Karnka Tai* [Twenty-fifth Anniversary Commemoration of the Board of Trade], (Bangkok: no publication data).

30. Kevin Hewison, "The State and Capitalist Development in Thailand," in Richard Higgot and Richard Robison, eds., *Southeast Asia: Essays in the Political Economy of Structural Change* (London: Routledge & Kegan Paul, 1985), p. 278.

42

31. Preecha Tanprasert, vice-president of the TCC, interview, July 16, 1987.

32. Section 15 of the Trade Association Act.

33. Section 14 of the Chamber of Commerce Act.

34. Government of Thailand, *Pan Pattana Settakij Lae Sangkom Haeng Chat Chabab Ti Sam, Po So 2515-2519* [The Third National Economic and Social Development Plan, 1972-1976] (Bangkok: NESDB, 1973), pp. 136-138.

35. Montri, "Political Control," p. 222.

36. Snoh Unakul, NESDB secretary-general, interview, August 4, 1987. Snoh led those subcommittees on the development of the private sector.

37. Snoh Unakul, interview, August 4, 1987.

38. Montri, "Political Control," p. 217.

39. Somboon Pataichant, manager of the Rice Exporters Association and a veteran in the community of business associations, interview, June 10, 1987.

40. Montri, "Political Control," Table 48, p. 250.

41. Boonsong Srifuangfung, president of the Chinese Chamber of Commerce, interview, August 14, 1987.

42. Montri, "Political Control," p. 252.

43. Montri, "Political Control," pp. 436-453.

44. Information in this paragraph is taken from David Morell,"Power and Parliament in Thailand: The Futile Challenge, 1968-1971"(Ph.D.dissertation, Princeton University, 1974), Appendix C, Table C-2, pp. 1026-1028.

45. Narong, "Samakom," p. 154 and Montri, "Political Control," p. 358.

46. Montri, "Political Control," p. 330.

47. Lloyd Rudolph and Susanne Rudolph, *In Pursuit of Lakshmi: The Political Economy of the Indian State* (Chicago: University of Chicago Press, 1987), pp. 252-254.

48. Chai-anan Samudavanija and Suchit Bunbongkarn, "Thailand," in Zakaria Ahmad and Harold Crouch, eds., *The Military-Civilian Relations in South-East Asia* (Singapore: Oxford University Press, 1985), p. 89.

49. Montri, "Political Control," pp. 450-451.

50. Visut Thamviriyawong, "Chonchan Nam Tang Turakij Kab Karnmuang Tai: Suksa Chapo Korani Karn Kao Ma Mi Botbat Tang Karnmuang Douytrong" [Business Elites and Thai Politics: A Case Study of Direct Political Participation], in Anothai Watanaporn, ed., *Karnmuang Tai Yuk Mai* [Modern Thai Politics] (Bangkok: Praepittaya Press, 1984), Table 1, p. 135.

51. *Kemtit*, March 28-April 3, 1977, pp.7, 11.

52. "Joint Standing Committee on Commerce, Industry and Banking," background paper for the Third Regional Meeting of the Joint Public and Private Sector Consultative Committee, January 26, 1986, Konkaen, Thailand, p .7.

53. M.L. Prachaksilp Thongyai, interview, August 18, 1987. M.L. Prachaksilp was a co-secretary of the joint public-private committee appointed by Premier Kriangsak in 1978.

54. *Asia Year Book 1979*, p. 313.

55. *Ruam Prachachart Turakij*, May 28- June 3, 1978, p. 6.

56. M.L. Prachaksilp, interview, August 18, 1987. There were two secretaries for the joint committee, one appointed by the government, the other by business.

57. Sataporn Kawitanont, secretary appointed by the government side to the joint committee, interview, November 17, 1987.

58. Boonchu Rochanasathian, interview, November 10, 1987.

59. He first advocated the idea of "Thailand, Inc." in a talk given at the Foreign Correspondents Club in Bangkok, on October 13, 1980.

60. Boonchu Rochanasathian, "Bansat Ruam Tai" [Thailand Inc.] in Boonchu Rochanasathian, *Kwam Kid Tang Karnmuang Kong Boonchu Rochanasathian* [Political Ideas of Boonchu Rochanasathian] (Bangkok: Image Publication, 1982), p. 7.

61. Government of Thailand, *Pramual Pol-Ngarn Kana Kammakarn Ruam Pak Rattaban Lae Ekachon Pua Kaekai Panha Tang Settakij (Ko Ro Au)* [Collections of Achievements of the Joint Public and Private Sector Consultative Committee (JPPCC)] (Bangkok: NESDB, 1986), Appendix, pp. 2-5.

3

The Principal Associations

A Brief Note

In Thailand there are two kinds of organizations working for the collective interests of business: trade associations and chambers of commerce on the one hand, and employers' associations on the other. As in many other countries, while trade associations and chambers of commerce in Thailand address a wide range of political and economic issues, they do not deal with employees or labor unions. Nor are they involved in the formation of the labor policy of the government. Both of these are functions of the employers' associations. Although the concern of this book is solely with trade associations and chambers of commerce,[a] a brief description of employers' associations is needed to give a complete picture of organized business.

Employers' associations have a much more recent origin than trade associations and chambers of commerce, as it was not until 1975 that they came into existence. In that year the government passed a labor relations law urging businessmen to organize employers' associations to handle wage disputes with employees or labor unions and to advise officials on labor policy. Under the sponsorship of the TCC and the ATI, a group of businessmen formed the first five employers' associations immediately after the law was passed.[1] In 1976 the Employers' Confederation was organized to function as the peak organization of employers' associations.

---

[a] Further, the term "business associations" as used in this study refers only to trade associations, chambers of commerce, and their peak organizations.

To handle wage disputes or advise public officials on labor issues, employers' associations have formed seven tri-partite committees with labor unions and the government.[2] However, as compared with trade associations and chambers of commerce, these associations have not been important policy actors. This has had much to do with the weakness of their opponents, organized labor. Labor unions were formed only after World War II;[3] and between 1958 and 1971, and again between 1976 and 1980, they were actually banned by the government.

It should be noted that while chambers of commerce and trade associations have proliferated since the early 1980s, employers' associations have not. In 1981 there were just ten associations representing employers in specific industries, one federation of employers' associations, and one confederation.[4] In 1985 the number of basic employers' associations had slightly increased to thirteen, representing eleven trades and industries, while the number of federations had remained the same.[5]

Equally noteworthy, no employers' associations or labor unions have been included in the JPPCCs, and to date there have been no discussions on labor matter by the JPPCCs. On the other hand, the seven tri-partite committees which do discuss labor policy have been accorded obviously lower priority by the government, as evidenced by the fact that none of them is placed at the cabinet level. The kinds of associations that this book is concerned with fall conveniently into two location-based categories: the peak business organizations and the trade associations, the majority of which are Bangkok-based; and the provincial chambers of commerce, which are located in areas outside Bangkok.

Associations in Bangkok

The description of Bangkok associations is given in the following order: peak organizations, foreign chambers of commerce, and trade associations. (See Chart 3.1.)

Peak Business Organizations

The most interesting thing about peak business organizations is that the Board of Trade is no longer the sole official spokesman for the whole business sector. Following the inception of the central Joint Public and Private Sector Consultative Committee (JPPCC), the three flagship associations—the Thai Chamber of Commerce (TCC), the Association of Thai Industries (ATI) and the Thai Bankers Associations (TBA)—became more important than the Board in terms of government-business policy consultation. However, the Board of Trade continues to play other major roles.[6]

CHART 3.1 Peak Business Organizations, Chambers of Commerce and Trade Associations in Bangkok

---

I. Peak Business Organizations
-The Board of Trade
-The Thai Chamber of Commerce (TCC)
-The Associations of Thai Industries (ATI)/The Federation of Thai Industries (FTI)
-The Thai Bankers Association (TBA)
-The Mining Industry Council
-Nonjuridical Peak Organizations

II. Foreign Chambers of Commerce

III.Trade Associations
-Agricultural Export Associations
-Industry Associations
-Tourist-Industry Associations
-Financial Associations
-Domestic Trade and Industry Associations

The Board of Trade. The most important function of the Board of Trade is to work with the Ministry of Commerce to maintain the quality of commodities and to set quotas, as well as minimum prices, for certain commodities which are to be exported within a specified period. In some cases where importers prefer not to deal directly with Thai exporters, or where the Thai government requires that transactions be made only through the Board, then the Board of Trade also serves as the negotiator for local traders.

Another chief function of the Board of Trade is to represent Thai business in international forums. For example, it holds annual meetings with Japan's Federation of Economic Organizations (Keidanren) and the Korean Chamber of Commerce and Industry to discuss obstacles to trade and investment between those countries and Thailand. Finally, though not formally represented on the central JPPCC, leaders or staff members of the Board join various government committees as either advisers or full members. As of early 1991 representatives of the Board of Trade served on at least 81 committees or subcommittees of the government.[7]

The Thai Chamber of Commerce (TCC). Founded in 1933 by a group of Thai citizens as the Siamese Chamber of Commerce, the TCC is one of the oldest business associations in the country. Like that of the Board of Trade, the development of the TCC has been much influenced by the government. The first three decades of its existence were marked by minimal membership and by severe financial problems. This can be attributed to the fact that few Thai citizens engaged in trade and industry, while the Sino-Thai businessmen preferred to work with the Chinese Chamber of Commerce. Only after the government, in 1966, made the TCC president ex-officio president of the Board of Trade did a large number of prominent business leaders begin to swell its membership.[8]

Traditionally the TCC limited itself largely to the tasks of issuing certificates of origin and running a college of commerce. Most problems and demands relating to the government and public policy which emanated from the TCC were dealt with through the Board of Trade. Since being appointed to the central JPPCC, the TCC has grown much faster than the Board of Trade. In 1977 the TCC had less than ten paid staff members, while the Board had about 30. In 1987, however, the number of TCC staff had grown to about 70, while the staff of the Board had only risen to about 50 members.[9] In terms of individual membership, between 1981 and 1986 the TCC and the Board enjoyed comparable increases of 24 percent and 26 percent respectively. (See Table 3.1.) However, in terms of institutional membership, which is a more indicative sign of peak organization status, the Board's membership virtually stood still, with 29 trade association members in 1981 rising to only 32 in 1986. By contrast, the TCC started with only six provincial chamber members in 1981; but the number had risen to 72 by 1986. (See Table 3.1.)

Like the Board of Trade, the TCC has been represented on numerous government commissions. At the end of 1990 representatives of the TCC sat on 56 government committees or subcommittees.[10] In the past the TCC was dominated by agricultural exporters. More recently, however, it has moved towards a more balanced representation. By 1987 TCC functions were organized around the subcommittees on finance, tourist industry, agriculture, transportation, exports and imports, and handicrafts.

TABLE 3.1 Membership of the Thai Chamber of Commerce and the Board of Trade, 1981-1986

	The TCC		The Board of Trade	
	Individual Members	Provincial Members	Individual Members	Association Members
1981	880	6	368	29
1984	918	39	474	30
1986	1089	72	465	32

Sources: Annual Reports of the Board of Trade and the TCC.

The Association of Thai Industries (ATI). Although specific industry associations, such as the Thai Textile Manufacturing Association, the Thai Printing Association and the Bangkok Rice Millers Association, have long existed, the ATI, speaking for industry as a whole, was only initiated in 1967. The founders of the ATI were leading industrialists who came to see that, despite its proclaimed goal, the government had not done enough to facilitate industrial development in the country. In addition, they perceived the Board of Trade and the TCC to be only spokesmen for agricultural exporters, rather than for industry as a whole.[11]

The ATI was rapidly accepted as the leading representative of industrialists. A survey by Montri Chenvidyakarn found that within six years the ATI had come to be regarded by government bureaucrats and trade association leaders alike as one of the two most influential business organizations, the other being the Board of Trade.[12] Initially the ATI was considerably handicapped in its peak organization role. Under the Trade Association and the Chamber of Commerce Acts, it had simply been a basic trade association, with a legal status no different from that of associations which represented particular industries. In other words, the ATI was not an association of associations as only firms or individuals could legally join it.

Despite these handicaps, after the creation of the JPPCC, the ATI, with its elevated status, attracted a much larger and a much more diversified membership. Between 1981 and 1985 the number of its members almost doubled, rising from 758 to 1377.[13] As of 1986 the ATI had 21 industrial sectoral committees and six provincial branches.[14] Between 1978 and 1980 leaders of the ATI and the Board of Trade tried to merge both organizations into a new Council of Chambers of Commerce and Industry, which would have become the only effective peak organization of the private business sector.[15] This, however, did not come to fruition. Thus, from 1980 onwards the ATI lobbied for a new law, finally enacted in 1988. This act elevated it to the status of the Federation of Thai Industries (FTI), the official spokesman for the entire private industrial sector, independent of, and equal in status to, the Board of Trade.

The FTI now has one of the largest permanent staffs among all business associations. In early 1991 it had 84 paid staff members.[16] Like the Board of Trade and the TCC, the FTI is extensively represented on government commissions. In late 1990 the FTI was represented on as many as 256 committees or subcommittees of the government[17]—which was more than any other business association.

The Thai Bankers Association (TBA). Legally, the TBA is also only a basic trade association. Of all three associations sitting on the central JPPCC, the TBA is the least bureaucratized. Founded in 1958 by a group of leading bankers, it did not even have a permanent staff until 1977; and as late as

1987 the TBA had only seven paid staff members.[18] This is not to imply that the association has been weak or inactive. Among peak business organizations, the TBA is the only one with fully inclusive membership; that is, all sixteen Thai-owned banks are members of it. These banks in turn represented about 94 percent of all bank assets in Thailand in 1979.[19]

Despite its low-key approach, participating in the public policy-making process has been a major function of the TBA. As early as 1962 legislation on the regulation of commercial banking activities was sent to the TBA for advice before it was enacted. By the end of 1990 the TBA had been represented on 81 government committees or subcommittees.[20]

Unlike other peak organizations, the TBA has not sought to expand into the provincial areas. An important reason for this is that all banks in the provinces are branches of those sixteen Bangkok-based banks which are already TBA members. However, TBA member banks have encouraged their field officers to form bankers' clubs to work closely with provincial chambers of commerce or ATI/FTI provincial branches.

The Mining Industry Council. Associations concerned with mining industries date back several decades. However, these associations, with the Thai Mining Association as their leader, came to realize that one way to attract government attention to their problems was to form an officially recognized organization which would combine all the mining industries.[21] After more than a decade of intermittent lobbying efforts, the government passed an act in 1983 which established the Mining Industry Council as the official representative of all mining-related industries.

Strictly speaking, the Mining Industry Council is not a peak organization. Most importantly, the council does not have institutional membership; only individuals or firms are eligible to join it.[22] In this respect it is similar to a trade association. In contrast with the latter, however, it is a statutory body.[23] Though the Council is not represented on the central JPPCC, the government has appointed it to the national Committee on Natural Resources Policy. The committee is headed by a deputy prime minister and is responsible for the formation of natural resources and mining policy.

Nonjuridical Peak Organizations. While the Board of Trade, the FTI, the TBA, and the TCC are registered with the government, a few other peak organizations, such as the Joint Standing Committee on Commerce, Industry and Banking, and the National Federation of Thai Textile Industries are not. As a result, they do not have juridical person status. The Joint Standing Committee, as has been mentioned, was formed by the TCC, the ATI and the TBA, and played an important role in the formation of the JPPCC. Since its birth in 1977, the Joint Standing Committee has not been a juridical person because it cannot be classified as either a trade association or a chamber of commerce, and registered with the government accordingly.

Nor has it been granted the status of peak organization, as have the Board of Trade and the Mining Industry Council.

Nevertheless, the Joint Standing Committee plays the role of an intersectoral peak organization. Its chief task is to help member associations reach common positions on key issues and represent them in international and national forums. All problems and issues which emanate from any of the three associations must now be agreed to first by this committee before being sent to the central JPPCC. The FTI, the TBA, and the TCC believe that in this way their policy contributions will be taken more seriously by the government, as they may be regarded as coming from the entire business community.[24]

Privately founded in 1975, the National Federation of Thai Textile Industries consists of five member associations: the Thai Synthetic Fiber Manufacturers Association, the Thai Textile Manufacturing Association, the Thai Weaving Industry Association, the Thai Garment Manufacturers Association, and the Thai Silk Association. The federation was first designed to represent Thai textile industries as a whole in the ASEAN Federation of Textile Industries. Of late, however, it has addressed domestic problems to the Thai government as well. The federation has a two-year term presidency which is rotated among the presidents of each of the participating associations.

One conclusion that can be drawn from the above discussion is that the structure of peak organizations has changed rapidly during the past ten years. The Board of Trade has not become what the government back in 1966 intended it to be, the only official peak business organization. Two of its members, the TCC and the TBA, and an outsider, the FTI, are now given a more important advisory role by the government. They are perhaps more respected by the business community as well. Several other independent peak organizations such as the Mining Industry Council and the National Federation of Thai Textile Industries, also exist.

Equally notably, there has been a substantial discrepancy between existing legislation and government practice. By law the ATI and the TBA were basic trade associations. However, in practice the government placed them, along with the TCC, at the level of peak organizations. Moreover, recent governments, in contrast with former practice, have accepted and worked with unregistered, nonjuridical bodies such as the Joint Standing Committee and the Federation of Thai Textile Industries.

Finally, the emerging system of peak organizations is far from consistent and inclusive. Firstly, the Mining Industry Council stands alone—it does not belong to either the Board of Trade or the Joint Standing Committee. Furthermore, representing a sector of industry (mining), it should have been made a part of the FTI, but it was not. Secondly, while the ATI was elevated to the formal status of a peak business organization, the TBA has not been so raised. Indeed, the TBA and the TCC formally remain members of the Board of Trade. Thirdly, while both the FTI and the Mining Industry Council have been raised to the same statutory status as sectoral peak organizations, the former may have trade associations as members, while the latter cannot. There have been talks in recent years about revising all existing laws, rules and policies governing various kinds of business associations so as to make them consistent with the changing reality of the situation. However, as yet, no really concrete moves have been made in this particular direction.

Foreign Chambers

Ten foreign chambers of commerce were in operation in 1990, the most significant of which were the American, the Chinese and the Japanese Chambers. Some foreign chambers, such as the American and the Japanese, restrict their membership to business persons, executives, or firms of their own citizenship.[25] Others, such as the Chinese and the German Chambers admit Thai individuals and firms as well. The German Chamber admits persons or institutions of any other nationality concerned with Thai-German trade and investment. Thus, these foreign chambers sometimes have Thai nationals as presidents or executive board directors; in particular, the Chinese and the Indian Chambers of Commerce are heavily dominated by Sino-Thais and Indo-Thais respectively.[b]

Foreign chambers are integrated into the Thai system of business associations through their membership of the Board of Trade. Although foreign chambers may directly contact Thai officials or agencies, they often submit their cases to the government through the Board of Trade or the Federation of Foreign Chambers of Commerce.[26] The latter is another example of a nonjuridical, though effective, federation of business organizations.

Some of these chambers are affiliates of the national chambers in their home countries. The American Chamber of Commerce, for example, is an "accredited federation member" of the Washington-based US Chamber of Commerce. The German Chamber of Commerce belongs to the Association of German Chambers of Commerce and Industry, which is the "mother house" of all German chambers of commerce both within the Federal Republic of Germany and overseas. Most chambers have close relations with their embassies. For example, the American ambassador to Thailand holds

---

[b] These two chambers were historically representatives of Chinese and Indian immigrants. A large proportion, if not the majority, of their membership and leadership now hold Thai citizenship.

monthly briefings with the board of governors of the American Chamber of Commerce,[27] and the ambassador occasionally expresses concerns and issues raised at such meetings to the Thai government.

Trade Associations

Most trade associations in Bangkok are central organizations. Of the total of 177 trade associations in existence in 1987 only eight did not seek nationwide membership. Distinctly Chinese associations have become uncommon. In 1987 there were only two "Chinese" associations: the Chinese Construction Association and the Bangkok Chinese Importers and Exporters Association. On the other hand, only two associations, the Thai-Owned Shops Promotion Association and the Thais' Industry Promotion Association, might be classified as dominated by "indigenous Thais." These four ethnic-based associations are in decline and an increasing number of their members are now Sino-Thais.

The overwhelming majority of trade associations in Bangkok are dominated by Chinese descendants who are now culturally and legally Thai. Non-Chinese foreigners play only a small role in trade associations. According to a 1981 directory, only eight out of the 131 Bangkok-based trade associations had non-Chinese foreigners on their boards of directors or executive committees.[28] From lists of directors or executive committee members of trade associations over the past five years as collected by the Central Registrar's Office, it can be estimated that only five out of 177 associations in 1987 had a significant number of foreigners in their leadership.[c]

While all chambers of commerce and peak business organizations are active, viable, and concerned about public policy which affects them, the majority of trade associations are not. A large number of these associations still function mainly as social clubs for colleagues in the same trade, or as venues for the welfare-oriented activities of their members. Some associations have no permanent staff. Meetings, planned activities, and elections are rarely held. Often, the leaders alone bear virtually all the administrative and financial burdens of the organizations which they represent.

Asked how many trade associations could be considered as very active and strong, desk officials at the Central Registrar's Office in late 1987 gave an

---

[c] These are the following associations: Pharmaceutical Products, Bangkok Shipowners and Agents, Siam International Mining, Thai-Japan Tourist, and Thai-American Trade and Investment Promotion. Either the presidents or the secretaries-general of these associations were foreigners, or more than 25 percent of their directors were foreigners.

estimate of 40-50. This is rather consistent with the number of associations that regularly submitted to the Central Registrar's Office their annual reports on activities, financial status and updates of their addresses and lists of members and leaders. Analyzing the January issues and June issues of Ruam Prachachart Turakij, an established business newspaper, I found that from 1985 to 1987 around 40 trade associations were regularly covered, i.e., were the subject of at least four news reports per month. Furthermore, my questionnaires sent between the July and October of 1987 were returned by only 56 of the 177 trade associations contacted. About 20 questionnaires were returned because the addressees had moved without notifying the Central Registrar's Office. Those which failed to return the questionnaires may simply have been uninterested or, more tellingly, lacking in staff capacity. (By contrast, similar questionnaires sent to peak business organizations were all returned; those sent to all 72 provincial chambers of commerce were returned by as many as 48 chambers).

All things considered, my estimate of active trade associations at work by the end of the 1980s was about 60, which was about one-third of the total. It should be noted, however, that there has been a steady increase in the number of such vibrant associations in the past few years. Besides, while older associations were first geared to social and welfare activities and only after shifted to policy-oriented activities, most of the associations which were founded after 1981 have placed an emphasis on public policy issues from the outset.[d]

Trade associations located in Bangkok may be divided in to five groups as follows:

Agricultural Export Associations. In late 1987 there were about ten associations in this category. The more active were those representing the major agricultural export businesses, such as the Rice Exporters Association, the Thai Tapioca Trade Association, and the Thai Maize and Produce Traders Association. These are among the oldest trade associations in the country. The Rice Exporters Association, for instance, has a history that dates back to 1919. The Thai Tapioca Trade Association has operated professionally since 1963. They are also among the most financially established associations. An obvious example is that in 1985 the Rice Exporters Association had assets which were substantially larger than those of the Board of Trade.[29]

---

[d] These associations are, for example, the Condominium Trade Association, the Thai Convention Promotion Association, the Association of the Members of the Securities Exchange, and the Association of Finance Companies.

The activities of trade associations in this group have usually been centered around the government's export regulations. Most exportation from Thailand has been conducted by the private sector. However, certain agricultural items, such as rice, maize, tapioca, mung beans and kenaf, have at times been under government monitoring for various reasons. Most importantly, the quantities of exported staple foods, particularly rice, have sometimes been controlled so as to prevent domestic shortage and "excessive" pricing, which might result in political instability. The price and the quality of several commodities have sometimes been regulated to discourage "excessive" competition and irresponsible practices, particularly the adulteration of products by exporters. Finally, some commodities, such as tapioca, have been regulated because importing countries have imposed quotas on them.

To enforce regulations, public officials have often enlisted the help of relevant associations. To begin with, in forming regulatory policies on various export items, public agencies have often sought opinions and information from the appropriate associations. Each year crop survey teams —sponsored by relevant associations—submit information needed for the official formulation of floor prices and exportable amounts of rice, maize, and tapioca. In addition, some associations work with the Department of Foreign Trade to allocate export quotas to appropriate traders. At times only government-designated trade associations, and not individual business firms, are allowed to enact transactions in certain commodities with importers.

Industry Associations. At the end of 1987 there were about 50 industry associations located in Bangkok. Since the 1970s industry has contributed to the national economy as much as, if not more than, agriculture. As mentioned in Chapter 1, the share of manufacturing in GDP rose from 14 in 1965 to 24 percent in 1988, while agricultural share declined from 32 percent to 17 percent. Even more significant is the rising share of manufactures in exports. In 1970 manufactured goods accounted for only 5.5 percent of Thailand's total export; by 1981 the export share had jumped to about 30 percent.[30] Accordingly, the government has been quite responsive to the problems and demands of manufacturers as represented by their associations. This is the case despite the fact that most industry associations were founded relatively recently and are not as strong—financially and organizationally—as their counterparts in the export of agricultural products.

Most active of all industry associations are those concerned with export-oriented industries. Many of them have focused on the improvement of the technological and managerial capability of their members so as to help them to meet the stringent demands of the international market. This has been achieved by a variety of means, such as publishing journals, holding seminars or conferences, seeking technical assistance from academics, and inspecting the manufacturing facilities of their members.

Associations representing large-scale, domestically oriented industries are also active. They have focused less on technical and managerial assistance to their members, and more on public policy. The Pharmaceutical Products Association and the Thai Pharmaceutical Manufacturers Association, for example, have been critical of the procurement policy which has given the government-owned pharmaceutical enterprises a tremendous advantage over private companies. The Thai Petrochemical Association has opposed the removal of the import surcharge on products which compete with their locally produced products. The Palm Oil Refiners Association has fought for a ban on the export of crude palm oil which is needed by the local refinery industry.

Tourist-Industry Associations. Associations representing businesses in this sector came into the limelight quite recently; not until the late 1970s had they gained substantial national attention. Nevertheless, they are now perhaps the most successful of all trade associations. As with industry, tourism has become so important to the economy that the government has to take special notice of its problems and demands. In the early 1980s tourism had replaced rice as the top foreign exchange earner, and by the mid-1980s remained ahead of textiles, the largest industrial export item. (See Table 3.2.)

TABLE 3.2 The Ranking of the Seven Top Foreign Exchange Earners over the Period 1981-1985

Ranking	1981	1982	1983	1984	1985
No.1	Rice	Tourism	Tourism	Tourism	Tourism
No.2	Tourism	Rice	Rice	Rice	Textile
No.3	Tapioca	Tapioca	Tapioca	Textile	Rice
No.4	Textile	Textile	Textile	Tapioca	Tapioca
No.5	Rubber	Sugar	Rubber	Rubber	Rubber
No.6	Sugar	Rubber	Maize	Maize	Integrated Circuits
No.7	Tin	Maize	Precious Stone	Integrated Circuits	Maize

Source: Annual Report of the Tourism Authority of Thailand, 1985.

The remarkable government responsiveness to tourism, much more than that to industry, is also a result of the articulation of its representative organizations. Chief among the five organizations are: the Association of Thai Travel Agents, the Thai Hotel Association, and the Thai Convention Promotion Association. Since the late 1970s the first two associations have undertaken several public relations campaigns to convince the government and the general public of the potentially immense contribution of tourism to both the employment level and the foreign exchange earnings of the national economy. Simultaneously, they have successfully requested a number of concessions from the government, such as a substantial reduction in the rates charged for public utilities used by hotels and for a bigger budget for overseas sales campaigns.

More than any other group, tourist-industry associations have cordial relations with their government counterpart, the Tourism Authority of Thailand (TAT). Each year they join with the TAT in conducting sales campaigns abroad. In 1984 these associations also cooperated with the TAT to form a new association to attract the booming business of international conventions to Thailand.

Financial Associations. By late 1987 there were ten financial associations located in Bangkok. The Thai Bankers Association has been considered in the section on peak organizations. Of the nine non-banking financial associations, six dealt with long-established insurance and pawn shop businesses. The remaining three were concerned with finance and securities —incipient yet promising businesses.

Associations representing insurance and pawn shop companies date back to the 1950s and 1960s. As of now only the insurance associations are active. The most important of them are the Thai Life Assurance Association and the General Insurance Association.

Since the late 1970s these two organizations have worked closely with the Office of Insurance of the Commerce Ministry. Increasingly the office has consulted these particular associations before it has proposed any bill or before it has imposed any rule or guideline regarding the regulation or the promotion of insurance business. Between 1983 and 1986 the General Insurance Association was consulted by the office on at least two bills. One was an amendment to the existing insurance regulation law, the other was the introduction of a third-party insurance system, a new opportunity for firms in this business.[31]

The Association of the Members of the Securities Exchange and the Association of Finance Companies are the two major spokesmen for the finance and securities trading businesses. These two organizations were founded only in the 1980s. Their predecessor, the Thai Finance and Securities Association, was established in 1973; however, financial and stock crises in Thailand in 1979 and 1983 brought bankruptcy to a large number of its members and severely damaged the reputation of the association. Thus, in 1981, firms dealing exclusively in securities trading began to leave for a new association specifically designed to represent that particular business. By 1985 the few remaining active members decided to dissolve the Thai

Finance and Securities Association. In its place, the surviving members of the abandoned association together with a group of leading firms formed a new Association of Finance Companies.[32]

Domestic Trade and Service Associations. More than half of the trade associations in Bangkok represent domestic trade and services. A large number of associations in this category have a long history comparable to that of the agricultural export associations. However, they are weak and less likely to draw public attention, being based as they are on small or medium and relatively unsophisticated businesses. Their activities, in addition, are geared mainly to the charity contributions or welfare promotion of their members. For years the Chinese Construction Association, for example, undertook no activities other than charity donation.[33] Between 1984 and 1986 half of the activities itemized in the annual reports of the Government Lottery Dealers Association were related to charity and the welfare of their members.[34]

Nevertheless, since the early 1980s a score of associations representing emerging large-scale trades and services have been frequently reported on in the media. Though less organized and bureaucratized than agricultural export associations and tourism associations, they are financially viable and well endowed with capable leaders and staff volunteers. These associations have, from the very beginning, focused on public policy and legislation issues. The Condominium Trade Association, for instance, has succeeded to some extent in reshaping laws governing the condominium business and those laws regulating multi-storey construction. Immediately following its inception in the mid-1980s, the Department Stores Association actively though unsuccessfully tried to persuade the government to permit the opening of duty-free sections in major department stores.

Provincial Associations

There are relatively few trade associations in the provinces, and their number has not significantly increased since the government created the central JPPCC in 1981. With the exception of tourism associations, these provincial trade associations are weak and inactive. Much more dynamic and active are provincial affiliates of the three national flagship associations. Of particular importance are provincial chambers of commerce, the story of which we describe in some detail now.

The Development of Provincial Chambers

Recent public measures towards provincial business associations, especially chambers of commerce, have been centered around the official concern for the development of provincial JPPCCs. Three years after the launching of the central JPPCC, the government also sought to organize similar committees in the provinces. To accomplish this, between 1983 and 1986 it held special annual meetings of the central JPPCC in three different regional centers. The meetings addressed regional problems and involved the wide participation of provincial officials and business leaders. Capitalizing on the widespread interest in these events, the central government directed provincial governors to form JPPCCs wherever there were local affiliates of the ATI, the TCC, or the TBA.

By the end of 1983 there were only fifteen provincial chambers and no ATI or TBA sub-organizations. Therefore, the central government instructed governors and commerce officials to assist the TCC in the creation of provincial chambers of commerce. Typically, the governor called a meeting of business leaders and educated them on the benefits they would derive from associational activities, especially their eligibility to participate in the provincial JPPCC. TCC officers would then explain to them how to register with the government, recruit members, and organize the chamber. Finally, the government might offer the new chamber office or secretarial assistance and the TCC would present it with a modest start-up fund.[35]

Provincial chambers, however, are not the exclusive creation of the government in cooperation with the TCC. On the contrary, my survey of 48 provincial chambers found that they rated the existence of a number of dedicated local leaders as more important than the persuasion or assistance of government or TCC officials in the creation of their chambers. The same survey also suggested that most chambers had founders who were from pre-existing trade associations or informal business groups which had been formed as social clubs or forums to mobilize needed credit for their members. (See Table 3.3.) Moreover, some of these founding leaders either had been or were simultaneously exposed to the philosophy and ideas on the roles and activities of chambers of commerce as being espoused by a group of non-government volunteers, the so called NIDA-IMET people, to which we now turn.

NIDA-IMET

While visiting Washington, D.C., shortly after the launching of the central JPPCC, Premier Prem requested that the US assist his effort to expand the role of the Thai private business sector in national development.[36] This request was warmly welcomed by the Americans because it fitted in with a new initiative of the Reagan administration which was to give more emphasis to the development of the private sector in aid-receiving countries. In late 1982 the Bureau of Private Enterprise of the Agency for International Development (AID) decided to give a grant of US$ 1 million

60

to start a private, US-Thai operated, Institute for Management Education for Thailand (IMET).[37]

TABLE 3.3 Selected Answers to Surveyed Questions as Given by 48 Provincial Chambers of Commerce

1. How would you rate the following factors as responsible for the creation of your chamber? (Choose only one answer.)

	Very Important	Important	Not Very Important
a. The existence of able and dedicated leaders at the time.	23	18	7
b. The persuasion and assistance of the TCC.	11	22	14
c. The persuasion and assistance of government officials.	14	17	16
d. The spontaneous awareness and understanding of a large number of businessmen.	6	17	24
e. NIDA-IMET's persuasion and assistance	14	19	13

2.The founding president and the leaders of your chamber are drawn from which of the following groups?
    a. Trade associations in the province.　(5)
    b. Chinese ethnic or charity organizations. (4)
    c. Informal business groups, organized for social activities or the mobilization of credit for members. (30)
    d. From other non-business groups. (2)
    e. Not from any particular group. (7)

Source: Conducted between August and October of 1987; 48 out of 72 questionnaires were returned.

Among the IMET projects was one proposed by a group of professors at the National Institute of Development Administration (NIDA). The project suggested holding annual off-campus short-course management training programs for leading provincial businessmen. In fact, there had been some business education up to college level in Thailand for decades. However, until recently, it was always regarded as a lowly field of study, not comparable to other fields such as medicine, engineering, or public affairs, which prepared students for professional or government careers. Even the children of businessmen themselves were not attracted to formal business education in their college years. Thus, while it is true that by the early 1980s a large portion of the younger generation of owner-managers who constituted the majority of the business class in Thailand (especially in the provinces), were highly educated, most had not been trained in the relevant subjects. For this reason provincial businessmen welcomed the NIDA-IMET program. Furthermore, not only did the program provide up-to-date knowledge of business administration, it also gave some practical tips for success. Finally, the program was short, lasting less than two weeks, and so was not disruptive to the regular work of the participants.[38]

The NIDA-IMET leadership soon came to consist not only of academics, but also of some leading businessmen and even public officials. Most of them were in their forties, apparently concerned with the public interest, and highly educated. Nikorn Wattanapanom, for example, held a doctorate in business administration from New York University and taught at the NIDA. Chumpon Pornprapa belonged to one of the richest business families in Thailand and also to one of the best educated. Sunthorn Srisattana was a senior official in the Ministry of the Interior who had long been interested in the role of the private sector in public affairs.

By career many of these people were in the public sector. Sunthorn was a bureaucrat. Teaching at the NIDA, a state-run graduate school, Nikorn also was a public official. Some of these individuals had even been involved in government commissions related to provincial business associations. Nikorn and Sunthorn sat on a commission for the preparation of the first regional JPPCC meeting in 1984.[39] Nonetheless, all of them worked as private volunteers on the NIDA-IMET project.

While the NIDA-IMET key men had high hopes for the provincial chambers of commerce, they saw their importance in terms of political development rather than the protection of business interest. In Nikorn's words:

> We are not worried about economic or business development. Thai firms and entrepreneurs are efficient and capable. Our country's main problem is the inefficiency and unresponsiveness of the bureaucracy. It is here that we think business associations can best contribute to the solution.[40]

In their belief, business associations would, appropriately led, become the core of a responsible and articulate private sector capable of forcing the government to be more responsive and efficient. Sunthorn, himself a bureaucrat, put it this way,

> Thailand's future is not in our fossilized, self-serving bureaucracy; it is, rather, in the more dynamic private sector. There is no hope that the state can rid itself of bureaucratic diseases without strong and consistent pressure exerted on it from outside.[41]

Nevertheless, in their view, not all kinds of business associations were willing and able to do so. By their very nature it was believed that trade associations would focus on highly specific occupational interests. By contrast, chambers of commerce would be in a better position to play an encompassing representative role, having members from all trades and industries.

With this idea in mind, the NIDA-IMET people taught participants how to improve their own businesses, and also brought to their attention the necessity of organizing as chambers of commerce, and of becoming involved in the making or debating of public measures that would affect them. They also suggested to their students that their chambers should not pursue only business interests. They stressed that chambers of commerce should strive to represent the whole private sector in the provinces.

Between 1983 and 1986, 372 businessmen were enrolled in the NIDA-IMET program.[42] Most were impressed with their instructors and satisfied with the new concepts and insights on management presented. Many, in addition, internalized their mentors' ideals on the missions and role of business associations. Of these, some had already been active in provincial chambers of commerce, others went on to found chambers in their own provinces.

Problems and Accomplishments

Given the short existence of provincial chambers, about half of which came into being after 1984, they have had to cope with basic organizational problems. First, a lot of them do not have permanent offices. My survey in 1987 found that 33 of the 48 chambers had their offices located in government buildings or in the houses or firms of their presidents. Second, their memberships are relatively small. A 1987 survey of eighteen selected provincial chambers, conducted by the Inter-Provincial Chamber of Commerce of Thailand,[43] found that in most cases they had between 100-200 members. The biggest of all, the Nakorn Ratchasima Chamber, had about 560 members.(Registered business firms, potential members of the chambers in most provinces, do not exceed 10,000.) Furthermore, since members are mainly small or medium-sized businessmen, membership dues can cover only a portion of the expenses of these provincial chambers. Based on that same survey of the eighteen chambers, over 60 percent of the chambers had membership dues which could cover less than half of their expenses during the years 1986 and 1987.[44]

Lastly, provincial chambers do not have experienced paid staff. Compared to Bangkok associations, their staff morale is relatively low and the rate of turnover rather high. Consequently, elected leaders have to bear a heavy administrative burden. This will become intolerable in the long run, since most leaders are owner-managers with heavy responsibilities in their own firms.

Despite these weaknesses, the accomplishments of provincial chambers have been impressive. Their activities thus far may be divided into three categories: contacting the government, service to the public and their members, and inter-provincial activities.

Contacting the Government. Provincial chambers now contact particular government agencies directly or go to provincial JPPCCs. The major themes of chamber-government contact have been business requests for better economic infrastructure, simplified and reduced taxation, improved investment climate in the provinces, etc. A large number of issues that chambers have brought to the government's attention are subject to local settlement, such as requests by the Chiangmai Chamber for a lift of the ban on large commercial traffic in their downtown areas during rush hours, and by the Rayong Chamber to restrict parking on the streets which obstructed entrance into the business premises of their members. Other requests or demands, however, are addressed to authorities well beyond the scope of local officials, including the governor. For example, the Chiangmai Chamber lobbied the Ministry of Communication to upgrade its provincial airport to an international level. The Nakorn Ratchasima Chamber not long ago set as a major goal persuading the Ministry of Communication to expand the highway leading to the province from Bangkok.

Locally manageable requests of provincial chambers have been fairly well responded to. Those involving higher authorities, however, have been largely put on long waiting lists for consideration or simply declined. Most provincial JPPCCs meet infrequently and irregularly. At one time, in Lampang, for example, for almost three years only three meetings were called. Even in Chiangmai, the second largest city after Bangkok, the JPPCC during 1986-1987 met only once every three months. Thus, most chambers were not particularly impressed by government responsiveness. My survey found that in 1987 half of the provincial chambers rated officials in their areas as slightly responsive or unresponsive. (See Table 3.4.) Accordingly, many provincial chambers came to the conclusion that they had to unite and push for more government attention. The details of these efforts will be dealt with in the section on inter-provincial activities.

TABLE 3.4 Responsiveness of Provincial Officials as Rated by Chambers of Commerce

Question: How responsive are senior officials in your province to your chamber's demands or problems?

a. unresponsive	(13)
b. slightly responsive	(11)
c. fairly responsive	(18)
d. very responsive	(6)

Source: same as that of TABLE 3.3

Services to the Public and Members. As with Bangkok business associations, provincial chambers of commerce have not confined themselves to working with the government alone. They have provided numerous services to the general public and to their members as well. Most publicized of all seems to be their organization of trade fairs or other festivities to stimulate local economies or to attract buyers, tourists, and investors from elsewhere. At present most chambers focus on providing services to members and businessmen in general, through which they hope to recruit new members. Chambers supply members with their monthly newsletters, which cover necessary information on business and related government activities in the provinces. Many chambers are attracting new members with identification cards which give them discounts when shopping at certain stores in their provinces or even in Bangkok. A few chambers, the Konkaen and Nakorn Ratchasima Chambers, for example, have experimented in carrying out necessary legal and government procedures, such as applying for or renewing certain licenses or permits, or representing members in minor business litigations for reasonable fees.

Inter-Provincial Activities. A striking feature of business association movement in the past few years has been a rapid rise in inter-provincial activities. Within a few years of coming into existence, provincial chambers jointly pursued several goals. Since late 1986 chambers of commerce from the northeastern provinces have pushed for a liberalization of trade across the borders with socialist Laos and Kampuchea. Since July 1987 southern chambers have publicized the problems of pervasive crime and violence in their home towns and have urged the government to quickly eradicate these problems. Even more noteworthy were the efforts by provincial chambers to consolidate their movement and to increase their bargaining power in relation to the TCC. These were achieved largely through cooperation between some energetic business leaders and the academics affiliated with the NIDA-IMET project mentioned earlier.

In 1984 these two sets of people started a voluntary organization called the Committee for the Development of Provincial Chambers. With its desire for independence in relation to the government, the committee searched for private sponsors, local and international. It quickly learned about a funding opportunity available through the Center for International Private Enterprise (CIPE) of the United States. The CIPE, which is an affiliate of the US Chamber of Commerce, was created by the National Endowment for Democracy (NED). The NED, created in 1983, is in turn a semi-private, nonprofit organization which receives annual appropriations from the US Congress. Its major goal is to "strengthen democratic institutions around the world through private non-governmental efforts".[45]

In 1985 the CIPE decided to give a US$ 97,000 fund to the Committee for the Development of Provincial Chambers to give training needed for the building of a strong network of provincial chambers in Thailand.[46] One of the first acts of the committee in that direction was to encourage provincial chambers to form the Inter-Provincial Chamber of Thailand as a non-juridical, loosely organized body, to facilitate activities among themselves.

Although the TCC, legally the peak organization of provincial chambers, wanted the Inter-Provincial Chamber to be an integral part of itself, the latter insisted on working independently. During 1986-1988 the Inter-Provincial Chamber of Thailand and the NIDA-IMET launched several seminars to disseminate among upcountry business leaders the philosophy and organizational know-how needed for the effective operation of chambers of commerce. The Inter-Provincial Chamber rapidly attracted a large number of followers through these educational programs. It also managed to pursue a few policies which were at odds with the TCC, for example, opposing the creation of the FTI, a scheme of which had already been approved by the TCC leadership.

Responding to the activism of the Inter-Provincial Chamber, the TCC tried hard to reach a compromise with provincial business leaders. An important strategy employed by the TCC for that purpose was to allocate many more seats on its board of directors to provincial chambers. Another crucial strategy was to step up its efforts to assist in the formation and operation of its provincial counterparts. These conciliatory moves conscientiously pursued by the TCC, coupled with an emerging rift within the Inter-Provincial Chamber, have led to the scaling down of independent and challenging activities of provincial chambers of commerce. The Inter-Provincial Chamber now keeps a low profile and its leaders work fairly closely with the TCC.

66

Notes

1. Employers' Confederation of Thailand, *Krobrob Sip Pi Sapa Ongkarn Naichang Haeng Pratet Tai 2529* [Commemorating the Tenth Anniversary of the Employers' Confederation of Thailand, 1985] (Bangkok: 1985), p. 39.

2. Ibid., p. 56.

3. Arnold Wehmhorner, "Trade Unionism in Thailand—A New Dimension in a Modernising Society" *Journal of Contemporary Asia* 13 (No.4, 1983): 482-485.

4. Employers' Confederation of Thailand, *Krobrob Sip Pi*, pp. 38-41, 58.

5. Samrit Meewongukos, ed., *Sayam Almanac 2528* [Siam Almanac 1985] (Bangkok: Sayamban, 1985), p. 569.

6. The Board of Trade has very recently regained its place in the economic policy community of the country due to the decision by the Chatichai administration in 1990 to put it on the central JPPCC in place of the TCC, which remains the national leader of provincial chambers of commerce.

7. Data obtained from the secretariat of the Board of Trade, February 1991.

8. Preecha Tanprasert, TCC vice-president, interview, July 6, 1987.

9. Data obtained from the TCC Research and Statistics Division, and the Research Division of the Board of Trade, October 1987.

10. Data obtained from the secretariat of the TCC, February 1991.

11. Taworn Pornprapa, a past president of the ATI, interview, August 13, 1987.

12. Montri Chenvidyakarn, "Political Control and Economic Influence: A Study of Trade Associations in Thailand" (Ph.D. dissertation, University of Chicago, 1979), Table 82, p. 376.

13. Chakrit Chulakasewi, ed., *Ha Pi Ko Ro Au : Hontang Haeng Kwam Samrej Kong Settakij Tai* [Five Years of the JPPCCs: Pathway to Thai Economic Success] (Bangkok: NESDB, 1986), p. 94.

14. Annual Report of the ATI, 1986.

15. *Ruam Prachachart Turakij*, August 27 - September 2, 1978, pp. 1, 12, and May 17-20, 1980, pp. 1, 12.

16. Data obtained from the secretariat of the FTI, February 1991.

17. Data obtained from the secretariat of the FTI, February 1991.

18. Prayong Watttanaprateep, TBA manager, interview, July 14, 1987.

19. Krirkkiat Pipatseritham, *Wikroh Laksana Karn Pen Chaokong Turakij Kanad Yai Nai Pratet Tai* [The Distribution of Ownership in the Thai Big Business] (Bangkok: Thammasat University Press, 1982), Table 4.2, pp. 58-59.

20. TBA, *Samakom Tanakarn Tai: Prawat Lae Kijjakam* [The Thai Bankers Association: History and Activities] (brochure, undated).

21. Data obtained from the Office of Information, the Mining Industry Council, July 1987.

22. Sections 12 and 13 of the Mining Industry Council Act.

23. Section 8 of the Mining Industry Council Act.

24. Prayong Wattanaprateep, interview, July 14, 1987.

25. Bylaws of both chambers.

26. Preecha Tanprasert, interview, July 16, 1987.

27. The American Chamber of Commerce in Thailand, "How the Chamber Can Benefit You" (brochure, undated).

28. Compiled from the data provided by *Thailand's Commercial Associations Handbook Directory (1982-1983)* (Bangkok: Sarn Prachachon Co., 1981).

29. The Rice Exporters Association had US$ 1.07 million assets, while the Board of Trade had US$ 0.81 million assets. See the 1985 Annual Report of the Rice Exporters Association and the 1986 Annual Report of the Board of Trade.

30. World Bank, Thailand: *Managing Public Resources for Structural Adjustment* (Washington, D.C.: World Bank Publication, 1984), Table 2.15, p. 32.

31. Annual Reports of the General Insurance Association, 1983, 1984, 1985, 1986.

32. The Association of Members of the Securities Exchange, *Turakij Laksap Nai Pratet Tai* [Securities Exchange Business in Thailand] (Bangkok: 1987), pp. 37-41.

33. Annual Reports of the Chinese Construction Association, 1982, 1983, 1984, 1985.

34. Annual Reports of the Government Lottery Dealers Association, 1984, 1985, 1986.

35. The amount of the fund was about US$ 800. The account in this paragraph is obtained from officials of the Ministry of Commerce, the TCC, the Ministry of the Interior and leaders of some provincial chambers.

36. Chakrit, ed., *Ha Pi Ko Ro Au*, p. 61.

37. John Bell et al,"End of Project Evaluation of the Institute for Management Education for Thailand, Inc., (IMET) Project," submitted to Office of Policy and Program Review, Bureau of Private Enterprise, AID, July 19, 1985, pp. 1-5.

38. Prayoon Chivasantikarn, president of the Lampang Chamber of Commerce and Boonlert Laparojkij, president of the Songkhla Chamber of Commerce, interviews, June 13 and July 25, 1987 respectively.

39. The (central) JPPCC's Order 6/2526.

40. Nikorn Wattanapanom, interview, June 11, 1987.

41. Sunthorn Srisattana, interview, June 10, 1987.

42. NIDA-IMET, *Krong Karn Sammana Pattana Nakturakij Channam Suan Pumipak* [A Seminar Project for the Upgrading of Leading Provincial Businessmen], May 12-22, 1987 (brochure, undated).

43. Data collected in July 1987 by the Project for the Development of Provincial Chambers of Commerce.

44. My calculation from the findings generated by the survey.

45. National Endowment for Democracy, *Statement of Principles and Objectives* (brochure, undated), p. 1.

46. Center for International Private Enterprise, "1986 Annual Report," pp. 20, 21, 30.

4

Associations and the JPPCCs

A study of government-business relations in the 1980s and the early 1990s must give attention to the Joint Public and Private Sector Consultative Committees (JPPCCs). Since 1981 several key problems of the business community have been resolved in these committees, which were created at the national level first and then later extended to the provincial level. The recent development of business associations, especially peak organizations and provincial chambers of commerce, has also been influenced by these JPPCCs. It is therefore important to understand the functioning of the JPPCCs and the factors underlying their emergence.

Coping with Business Problems

A major disappointment of the business community with the previous joint committee under the Kriangsak government was that their problems and demands were merely listened to—no action ever resulted. Since the committee was a consultative body, its resolutions were not necessarily heeded by the appropriate agencies or officials. At times, even when implementing agencies agreed to take action, no systematic and continuous secretarial assistance to follow up the matter was available. Worse yet, many of the problems met some unanticipated obstacles, which were not reported back to the committee. The ineffectiveness of the government, combined with the lack of well-prepared research on either side, caused discussions in the committee to degenerate into accusation and confrontation.[1]

As with Kriangsak's joint committee, the central JPPCC included business representatives and those cabinet ministers who were in charge of economic affairs. In marked improvement over the past, the premier presided over the committee, and shortly after its birth, the secretary-general of the national development planning agency (the NESDB) was appointed secretary of the committee.

While remaining in theory a consultative committee, the prestige and power of its president led implementing agencies to seriously consider its resolutions and to translate them into action more urgently than hitherto had been the case. The NESDB secretary-general, for his part, brought to the committee much needed research and secretarial support. In 1983 a subcommittee responsible for the screening of problems and issues for the JPPCC was also formed. This subcommittee was composed of the NESDB secretary-general, senior bureaucrats responsible for the implementation of economic affairs, and business representatives. Apart from doing preliminary research and setting the agenda for the monthly meetings of the committee, the subcommittee also monitored the implementation of JPPCC resolutions.

In theory, the JPPCC is a joint government-business organization working for solutions to important business and economic problems. Each side in the committee can make a request or suggestion to the other. In practice, however, it has turned out to be a venue for business to forward its complaints or requests to the government, rather than the reverse. From its inauguration to mid-1986, the central JPPCC held 46 meetings and reached resolutions on 34 key issues. Of these, fifteen were raised by the JPPCC secretariat, which is part of the government machinery, seventeen were raised by business, and two by both sides.[2] Moreover, many agenda items technically raised by the secretariat had in fact originated as business complaints or grievances, and thus were similar in theme to those formally raised by business.[3]

Problems and issues brought to the JPPCC by business seem to fall into three major categories: reducing bureaucratic red tape and delays, removing stifling laws and rules, and addressing the problems of excessive taxation. In comparison, those raised by the JPPCC secretariat include: strengthening the export capability of the economy, reviewing the overall taxation system with a view to enhancing foreign direct investment in Thailand, and setting up overseas sales-promotion tours to be led by the prime minister. Among the few issues and problems somewhat different from those raised by business itself were the launching of a credit program for small businesses, and encouraging the use in business of energy-conserving and environment-protective machinery and technology.[4]

Apart from national issues, the central JPPCC at times addressed itself to provincial problems. Between 1984 and 1986 it held three regional meetings in which the exclusive problems of the North, the South, and the Northeast were discussed. Furthermore, from late 1983 provincial JPPCCs were rapidly formed outside Bangkok. Organized along the lines of the central JPPCC, these committees are headed by provincial governors and are composed of other high officials as well as leaders of provincial chambers of commerce, or provincial affiliates of the FTI or the TBA. Each province may have only one JPPCC. In less than six years after the first provincial JPPCC came into being in 1984, all 72 provinces outside Bangkok had their own JPPCCs.[5] These committees have been designed to be a forum through which provincial economic and business problems are raised and their solutions formulated.

Promoting Associations

The immediate function of the JPPCCs, according to their advocates, was to tackle serious economic problems with the participation of business. However, from the very beginning, the government has also made the promotion of business associations another major function of the JPPCCs. The JPPCCs have encouraged the development of business associations in Thailand in different ways. For the three flagship associations and provincial chambers of commerce, the impact has been substantial and mostly direct. For most of the other associations, however, the impact has been indirect and modest.

Impact on ATI, TCC, TBA, and Provincial Chambers

Above all, the JPPCCs have given the ATI, the TCC, the TBA, and the provincial chambers regular access to an unprecedently high level of policy discussion of the government. The prestige and priority of these committees —signified by the presence of the prime minister and the provincial governors—combined with their displayed responsiveness towards business requests, have together provided a great incentive for businessmen to join, or to form a new association which would be entitled to participate in any one of the JPPCCs.

TCC membership grew from 778 in 1980, the year before the formation of the central JPPCC, to 1,066 in 1985, representing an increase of 37 percent in just five years.[6] ATI growth was even more impressive during the same period, as its membership more than doubled, rising from 605 to 1,317.[7] More recently, the ATI/FTI has expanded to the provinces as well. At the end of 1989 the FTI had nine provincial branches (officially called provincial clubs).[8] The most impressive growth record, however, belongs to the provincial chambers. In 1983, the year before the first regional meeting of the central JPPCC, there were only fifteen provincial chambers. However, by the end of 1986 the number of provincial chambers had jumped to 72 (the maximum possible). (See Table 2.6.)

Regular consultation on policy issues with the government in the JPPCCs has called for an institutional improvement of these associations. After the central JPPCC was created the number of policy research staff grew faster than any other section in both the ATI and the TCC.[9] Incipient provincial chambers, in particular, realized the vital nature of policy research work. As noted by the president of the Chiangmai Chamber, one of the most established of its kind:

> [Provincial] government-business cooperation is beset by the fact that the private sector has minimal information, compared with the government. . . . Without well-prepared information and statistics our [policy] arguments sound less convincing [to the public and the officials].[10]

The need to present well-informed viewpoints representative of their members to the JPPCCs has also encouraged these associations to make their organizational structures more differentiated. By 1985, the TCC had organized its activities around ten sectoral subcommittees.[11] At the end of 1989, the FTI had 25 industrial sectoral subcommittees (officially called industrial clubs).[12]

Mainly through USAID grants, the central JPPCC has financed the efforts of the ATI/FTI, the TCC and the TBA to upgrade their policy research and secretarial capabilities. Between 1983 and 1987, it received US$ 3.5 million from the USAID Project of "Private Sector in Development."[13] Part of this fund, about US$ 200,000, was allocated to a number of major research projects of the three associations.[14] These projects were largely studies of crucial problems affecting the private business sector, which were intended to be submitted to the central JPPCC for due action. They included topics such as a proposal for a marketing information center, the impact of the existing taxation system on industrial development, cooperation among the commercial banks for the improvement of business efficiency and public service, and the promotion of domestically produced intermediate inputs for manufactured exports.[15] Another US$ 200,000 from the fund was used to hire full-time policy advisors for the ATI, the TCC and the NESDB; these advisors assisted the organizations in analyzing major problems affecting business performance and issues pivotal to the improvement of government-business dialogue.[16]

In 1987 the Thai government received another five-year US$ 300,000 grant from USAID, under its rural industry and employment program, to be used for the development of the provincial JPPCCs and business associations.[17] With this fund the secretariat of the central JPPCC organized several meetings for public officials and business leaders in the same region in order to discuss the development of provincial JPPCCs.[18]

Impact on Other Associations

Significant as they are in connecting organized business to the government, the JPPCCs are not where most contacts between these two sectors occur. As before, most business associations still contact public agencies directly, rather than through the JPPCCs. My survey conducted in 1987 found that only a quarter of Bangkok-based associations admitted having some relation with the JPPCCs. (See Table 4.1.)

TABLE 4.1 Selected Answers to Questions Regarding JPPCCs Given by 57 Trade Associations in Bangkok

---

1) How would you describe your relationship or connection with the JPPCCs?

Close	Fair	Distant or Nonexistent
(10)	(5)	(42)

2) Do you agree that the existence of the JPPCCs has more or less beneficially affected your association?

Agree Strongly	Agree Moderately	Disagree
(15)	(34)	(11)

3) In what ways have the JPPCCs most affected your association?
   a. By allowing your participation in one of their organizations or channels. (11)
   b. By creating an atmosphere of increased public and government receptiveness to business problems and viewpoints. (29)
   c. Little or not at all. (10)
   d. In other ways. (5)

Source: The survey was conducted between August and October of 1987; 57 out of 177 trade associations returned the questionnaires.[a]

Although provincial JPPCCs are potentially more significant than their central counterpart as a government-business channel, at present they are still in their formative period. Despite this fact, a good many associations believed that the existence of the JPPCCs had led to a general atmosphere in which business requests or problems were more favorably responded to than had formerly been the case. This, they believe, is the major beneficial impact of the JPPCC system on them. (See Table 4.1.)

Some associations other than ATI/FTI, the TBA, and the TCC, have been given an opportunity to join various subcommittees of the central JPPCC. For example, until recently tourism and mining associations were invited to join relevant JPPCC subcommittees. Associations not represented on any

---

[a] Although the number of returned questionnaires was low as a proportion to the total number of questionnaires sent out, this survey may be interpreted as one undertaken on active associations, since the list of associations that returned the questionnaires largely coincided with the list of associations regularly reported in *Ruam Prachachart Turakij*.

74

subcommittee but which would like to work within the JPPCC system can file their cases with any of the three flagship associations, or with the secretariats of the central JPPCC or the various JPPCC subcommittees.

Since 1985 the central JPPCC has also organized conferences on particular topics in which concerned associations other than the ATI/FTI, the TCC and the TBA, including foreign chambers, are invited to join. Problems and opinions solicited from the meetings are passed on to the JPPCCs or to other relevant government agencies. By the end of 1986 nine of such conferences had been held on such topics as transportation and business, investment climate in the eyes of foreign investors, and capital market development.[19]

Chatichai and the JPPCCs

Much of what has so far been discussed as the achievement of the JPPCCs occurred during the eight-year-long semi-democratic period of Premier Prem. As mentioned earlier, in 1988 Thailand had its first wholly elected government since 1976, under the leadership of Premier Chatichai. It is therefore necessary to ask: How have the JPPCCs fared in the past few years under the new regime ?

An obvious change under Chatichai is that the central JPPCC has met less frequently. Compared to the virtual monthly meeting schedule during the early years of the Prem administration, under Chatichai the central JPPCC held five meetings in 1988, four in 1989, and only two in 1990.[20] Not surprisingly, it is widely held that Chatichai and the politicians entrusted with the economic affairs of the government have paid much less attention to the JPPCC system than did Prem and his men.

There are several explanations for the decline in the frequency of the central JPPCC meetings. One line of reasoning is grounded in the change of the nature of the regime. To be more specific, the exit of the non-elected elements—Prem and the technocrats in the cabinet—has created more opportunities for influential businessmen to present their problems, grievances, and demands (especially ones that are particularistic, as opposed to group-based) through political parties and politicians, rather than through the JPPCC system. Some knowledgeable political observers even believed that politicians in power have deliberately toned down the importance of the central JPPCC, in order that they may pursue the politics of spoils and patronage more effectively.

Of course, elected politicians are not necessarily corrupt nor are appointed technocrats necessarily honest. However, the common practice of vote-buying in rural areas by electoral candidates and the lack of a legitimate means for political parties to raise funds have largely accounted for considerable demand being made on politicians for them to amass illegal funds from under-the-table dealings with business. In this kind of new political environment, the JPPCC, which is noted for the transparent nature of its processes and its concern for broad interests, has, in the eyes of some high officials, somewhat diminished in importance and/or usefulness.

While the change of regime accounts a lot for the recent decline of the central JPPCC, one should also entertain the idea that the central JPPCC has met less frequently just because, after years of government-business efforts, few problems have been left for deliberation at the national policy level. This line of reasoning is consistent with the fact that even in the last years of Prem's premiership (1987-1988) the JPPCC met only five times annually.[21]

That political leaders now pay less attention to the JPPCC but more to the handling of particularistic problems and demands of business, may be conditioned as well by the change in the public perception of the state of the economy. As mentioned previously, during the Prem era, especially in its early years, government policy-makers and the public and the mass media alike, held that the country was in deep economic crisis. A serious awareness of the need to sacrifice parochial interests for the sake of the more broadly based or the nationally defined interests thus prevailed among top decision makers. With the coming of the double-digit GDP growth of the past few years, however, this kind of attitude was less likely to prevail.

While it is true that Chatichai, in comparison with Prem, has accorded lower priority to the central JPPCC, one should not jump to the conclusion that the whole system of communication between the government and organized business has considerably declined in significance. In fact, the central JPPCC meeting is but one part of the system and there have been signs of progress in other aspects of the JPPCC system. Firstly, the implementation of JPPCC resolutions by JPPCC subcommittees or by other public agencies continues to be pursued vigorously under the Chatichai government. Moreover, several state-business consultative commissions under various names have sprung up notably at ministerial and departmental levels.

Importantly, even the military, traditionally the bastion of conservatism and doubter of business loyalty to the state, has initiated a new National Defense College course. In this course military-bureaucratic leaders sit in the same class with prominent business figures (selected by leading business associations) to discuss various security and economic issues of the country. Reflecting the spirit of cordial state-business cooperation espoused by the JPPCCs, the supreme commander of the armed forces praised those businessmen who attended that course in 1989 as valuable "warriors of the Thai economic army," and asked all of them to work closely with the military for the prosperity and security of the nation.[22]

Last but not least, the Ministry of the Interior has of late spent much more in terms of both effort and resources in helping provincial governors and organized business to develop their JPPCCs. It is in the Chatichai administration that the JPPCC system has reached every province of Thailand. In fact, by early 1989 the JPPCC system in at least three provinces had been further extended to the district level.[23] (A district is an administrative unit placed one rung below a province; several districts make up a province.) Perhaps for these reasons, many chamber leaders or senior staff members, who had been very critical of the government's lack of support for their operation, have recently been satisfied with the ways the new administration have handled the provincial JPPCCs.[24]

In conclusion, there are both positive and negative signs for the development of the JPPCC system under Premier Chatichai. It is rather difficult to evaluate the overall picture. But, even if the JPPCC system as a whole has declined in policy significance, the decline has not been very significant.

Explaining the Rise of the JPPCCs

Given the central position of the JPPCCs in the working relationship between the government and organized business, it is necessary to explore some of the important factors that have contributed to their rise. The exploration should prepare the way for a subsequent assessment of the relative role of different actors—government and business, external and internal—in redesigning the system of business associations during the past decade. Such an assessment, in turn, is needed as part of an analysis of the role of organized business in political and economic development. An explanation of the emergence of the JPPCCs in terms of four major groups of factors is now in order: the rise in importance of the Sino-Thai business class, the economic crisis of the early 1980s, the government's need for political support, and external influences.

The Sino-Thai Business Class

The quest for an effective joint public-private committee is in a way the culmination of a steady growth of the business class and the successful integration of ethnic Chinese businessmen into the Thai culture and polity over the last three decades after the setback in the Phibun era. To start with, the private business sector has become the predominant force in the Thai economy. Between 1970 and 1979 private consumption was close to six times as great as public consumption, while private investment was almost three times of public investment.[25] We have already noted that among the 100 largest enterprises only nineteen were owned by the state, which held in turn only 36 percent of the total assets.

Local businesses, moreover, have not been swallowed up by multinational corporations. Among the 100 largest enterprises in the country in the late 1970s, 81 were private firms, and 52 of these were local. These local firms had combined assets five times those of the 29 foreign or multinational firms.[26] According to Kraisak Choonhavan, in the banking sector Thai banks owned 97 percent of the assets of the top 20 commercial banks in the country in the late 1970s.[27] Local ownership in crucial industrial sectors in the same period, though less towering, was still prominent. In the automobile and textile industries, for example, 44.5 percent and 45.3 percent respectively of the ownership belonged to local businessmen.[28]

Another major development is that local business has been dominated by large corporations, which, as asserted by Krirkkiat Pipatseritham, in the late 1970s comprised about 65 family groups, each group holding assets worth between US$ 32.7 million and US$ 6.1 billion.[29] The steady rise of the Sino-Thai business class and the emergence of large scale business operations may account for the recently improved financial and organizational capabilities of the business association movement, especially in Bangkok.

Added to that, the majority of ethnic Chinese businessmen have adopted Thai family names, acquired Thai citizenship, and received a Thai education. For example, as early as 1973, 63 percent of trade association members and 87 percent of their presidents held Thai citizenship.[30] A survey conducted in the late 1970s by Suthy Prasartset found that about three-quarters of the business leaders (general managers and presidents of the top 890 firms) were graduates of colleges or universities.[31] Since Chinese schools (where Chinese, in addition to Thai, is used as a medium of instruction) are allowed to operate only at the primary level, the finding suggests that the ethnic Chinese who constitute the core of the business elite have been substantially exposed to Thai culture through the educational system.

Many Chinese descendants, moreover, have served in high political and bureaucratic positions. Top politicians, such as Chamlong Srimuang, Bangkok's governor, Bhichai Rattakul, a deputy premier in the Prem government, and Premier Chatichai Choonhavan, have freely admitted their Chinese origin. Even Kukrit Pramoj, a living symbol of the Thai aristocracy and a former premier, claims to have a Chinese ancestry and observes some Chinese ceremonies.[32] A survey conducted during the early 1970s by Likhit Dhiravegin found that children of businessmen, presumably mostly of Chinese origin, constituted almost one-third of the bureaucratic elite (the special grade officers).[33] Among recent high bureaucrats with a prominent Chinese background have been Wicharn Niwatwong, permanent secretary of the Ministry of Commerce during most of the 1970s, Pao Sarasin, former chief of the national police force, Pairat Decharin, the current governor of Chiangmai (the most important province after the Bangkok metropolis) and Krirkkiat Pipatseritham, the present rector of the prestigious Thammasat University. Conversely, a substantial number of the offspring of bureaucrats have entered the traditionally Chinese-dominated business executive ranks. It was found that during the late 1970s one-fifth of the business elite were children of government officials.[34]

That the government has been more attentive to business problems and has allowed greater business participation in public policy discussion, may be explained in part by the fact that the private sector has become the predominant part of the national economy. Moreover, the notion that businessmen are foreigners can hardly be sustained as the ethnic Chinese have been assimilated into the mainstream of Thai culture; it is also true that a substantial number of business executives now come from a bureaucratic background. Equally important, the business community has not been denationalized by foreign capital. All these factors have served to exempt government-business collaboration from serious criticism.

The political democratization since 1973, save for the period between 1977 and 1978, also provided the flagship associations with politicians-cum-businessmen, such as Pramarn Adireksarn, Ob Vasurat and Boonchu Rochanasathian, who were powerful enough to succesfully advance the idea of a joint public-private committee to the governing elite. The heavy presence of persons with a business background in the legislature and the cabinet, a result of electoral politics, also created a hospitable environment for a close and cordial government-business dialogue. (See Table 2.2 and Table 2.3.) Still, had there not been a difficult situation when the request for a joint committee was made, the government might not have reacted promptly and the cabinet might not have accorded a very high status to the JPPCCs.

The Economic Crisis

The economic situation facing Thailand in the early 1980s was one of the worst since the depression which had paved the way for the overthrow of the absolute monarchy about 50 years earlier. Above all, the second world-wide oil shock pushed the cost of imported oil from 21 percent of the total value of imports in 1978 to 30 percent in 1980.[35] This sudden change exacerbated the problems of the trade deficit and external indebtedness, which the government had been trying to remedy since the time of Kriangsak. The trade deficit, which had been recorded as 6 percent of GDP in 1978, rose to over 8 percent in 1979 and 1980. The current account deficit also soared from 4.9 percent of GDP to more than 7 percent over the same period. (See Table 2.4.) The need to finance expensive oil imports, coupled with the rising interest rates on the world's financial markets, led to an alarming growth in the external indebtedness of the country, from an average of 14.3 percent per year during 1971-1975, to over 47 percent during 1979-1980. This rate of growth was more than triple the average rate of all less developed countries combined. (See Table 4.2.)

TABLE 4.2 Growth in External Indebtedness of Selected Less Developed Countries, Percent per Annum

Year/ Period	1971-1975	1975-1980	1978	1979	1980
Thailand	14.3	34.6	39.6	47.4	47.3
Philippines	13.4	26.7	22.9	15.3	16.6
Indonesia	31.6	11.8	11.4	1.4	10.4
All LDCs	22.3	19.6	24.6	13.9	14.3

Source: World Bank, Thailand: Managing Public Resources for Structural Adjustment (Washington, D.C.: World Bank Publication, 1984), Table 2.20, p. 40.

Much of this growth in external indebtedness was due to the increase of the public debt which more than doubled between 1978 and 1980. (See Table 2.5.) Government's increased international debt was, in turn, the result of the increase in public sector deficit. During 1979-1980 the annual ratio of the public sector deficit to GDP rose from 5.1 percent to 8 percent. Heavy public investment to make the country more self-sufficient in energy and the reluctance to pass the rising cost of imported fuel on to consumers both caused public enterprises to be responsible for nearly half of the public sector deficit during the period 1977-1980. (See Table 4.3.)

Associated with rising energy costs was the inflation problem. Between 1977 and 1979 the consumer price index grew in the range of 7-10 percent per year. In 1980, however, the annual growth rate of the index rocketed to 20 percent, the highest since 1974.[36] In addition, there was the problem of the slower growth of production in both agriculture and manufacturing. Bad weather condition led to an actual decline in agricultural production in 1979 ('growth' was -1.5 percent) and a slight growth rate (1.9 percent) in 1980. This compared unfavorably with the 4.8 percent annual growth rate during the years 1970-1979. At the same time, declining real income at home, especially agricultural income, and a deep depression in the West following the oil shock, pruned both domestic and export demand for manufactured goods. The annual growth rate of manufacturing output accordingly dropped by more than half, from an average of 10.3 percent of during the period 1970-1979 to a mere 4.8 percent in 1980.[37]

TABLE 4.3 Trends and Distribution of Public Sector Deficits, 1970-1980, as Percentages of GDP

Year/ Period	1970-1977	1977	1978	1979	1980
General Government					
Current Surplus	2.4	1.9	1.8	1.0	0.6
Investment	4.4	4.6	4.5	4.0	4.9
Deficit	-2.0	-2.7	-2.8	-3.0	-4.3
State Enterprises					
Operating Surplus	0.7	0.9	1.0	0.9	0.8
Investment	1.9	2.5	3.5	2.9	4.4
Deficit	-1.2	-1.6	-2.5	-2.1	-3.7
Total Public Sector					
Current Surplus	3.1	2.8	2.7	1.8	1.3
Investment	6.3	7.1	8.1	6.9	9.3
Deficit	-3.2	-4.3	-5.4	-5.1	-8.0

Source: World Bank, *Thailand: Managing Public Resources for Structural Adjustment*, (Washington, D.C.: World Bank Publication, 1984), Table 4.3, p. 67.

The Government's Need for Support

Added to these economic difficulties, the political situation was bleak. In April 1981, just two months before the central JPPCC came into being, Prime Minister Prem barely survived a coup attempt by a group of middle-ranking officers, known as the "Young Turks." Although coups are not uncommon in Thailand, this one was the most protracted of all in the last quarter of a century and could well have ended up in a bloody civil war, had the king, revered by most groups in Thailand, not thrown his support behind the government. The "Young Turks" had in fact been the group who pressured Premier Kriangsak to resign in 1979 and then became a major pillar of the Prem government for two years. In defeating them, Prem was —paradoxically—left vulnerable unless he could build up a new reliable military coalition. Thus, in the middle of 1981, the prime minister who constantly faced uncertainties in the legislature and the cabinet without his own party had to live with shaky military support as well.

It is possible that Prem decided to form the central JPPCC because he needed to enlist non-governmental assistance in rectifying the critical economic problems as well as to create an alliance with leading business groups to make up for the temporary loss of stable military support. It is very plausible, however, that other strategic governmental figures also had significant influence in his decision. To begin with, it should be recalled that about 30 percent of his cabinet members were persons with a business background. (See Table 2.3.) Moreover, as related by Taworn Pornprapa, ATI president at that time, it was Charn Manutham, a businessman serving in the cabinet, who played a key role in convincing Prem of the necessity of the JPPCC. Charn was in a good position as mediator between the business community and Prem. On the one hand, he was a serviceman-turned-businessman who had been a close friend of Prem since childhood; on the other, he had worked as adviser to the ATI and the TCC and was involved in their past efforts to drive for a formalized machinery of government-business consultation.[38]

Another governmental actor having influence on the JPPCCs was the NESDB. Throughout 1980 the NESDB worked on the Fifth National Economic and Social Development Plan, to be operative in the period 1982-1986. In January 1981 the final draft of the plan was reviewed and approved by economic cabinet ministers.[39] The plan suggested that a high policy-level joint government-business committee be installed to strengthen the role of the private sector in national development.[40]

Why did the Fifth National Economic and Social Development Plan call for a formalized government-business consultation? Part of the answer might well be in the international financial constraints imposed upon the country. As said earlier, a large part of the alarming external indebtedness was caused by increased public debt, which was in turn a result of the rising public sector deficits. If the country wanted to grow further without exacerbating its financial position, the public sector's investment and expenditure had to be pruned. More than at any other time, Thailand needed the private sector as the engine of growth. To support or assist the operation of the private sector, the government thus needed a reliable channel of communication with the business community.

The JPPCC system was also necessitated by the fact that Thailand, in reaction to chronic trade deficits, decided (in the Fifth Plan) to place an emphasis on export-oriented development. Snoh Unakul, the NESDB secretary-general in the Prem administration, explained that the JPPCC system was born out of an observation that, "any country which competes successfully ... in the international economic arena is also a country with a workable system of government-business collaboration."[41]

In an interview with me Snoh disclosed that a political consideration also, though not publicly admitted, was behind his advocacy of a public-private consultation committee. Snoh was first involved in an NESDB scheme to develop business associations in the 1960s. During 1967-1968 he was in charge of the first NESDB experiment on a joint government-business forum, i.e., the Subcommittee for the Development of the Private Sector.

Later Snoh also oversaw the formation of the Fifth Plan and served as the JPPCC secretary for about eight years.

Snoh has long believed that government-business relations determine the stability of a capitalist regime. In his own words,

> Historically, two kinds of capitalism existed: the decadent and the mature ones. Both kinds had a close government-business relationship. However, the decadent capitalism was characterized by corrupt dealing between officials and businessmen. The mature capitalism, on the other hand, had open consultation between legitimate government and business representatives. The decadent capitalism usually ended up in revolution, such as the cases of China and Russia.[42]

In Snoh's view, Thailand had been close to the decadent model of capitalism. Government-business relations in the past had served only those few who had massive financial resources or good personal connections with high officials. These relationships created resentment among the business community, as well as the general public, and could have led to political instability. Snoh's proposal for government-business dialogues was guided considerably by his conviction that a new system must be built in which under-the-table dealings were reduced by the availability of on-the-table consultation, by the government's responsiveness to the legitimate requests of business, and by the deregulation of the economy.[43] In sum, for Snoh, the JPPCC system was indispensable if Thailand was to have a stable, mature capitalism.

External Factors

Naturally, since the Thai economy is not autarkic, external factors have had influence on the development of the JPPCCs. The economic crisis that precipitated the creation of the central JPPCC was, to start with, largely a result of the 1979 world oil-shock and the ensuing "stagflation" in the West. Furthermore, the consolidation of the JPPCCs, has been assisted by American funds. The timing of the rise of the central JPPCC corresponded to the advent of Reagan's new emphasis on foreign economic assistance. Under the new Reagan administration, the AID has been directed to give a greater commitment to making the private sector, rather than the public sector, the key to the improvement of economic performance in the Third World. From fiscal year 1982 through fiscal year 1984, the agency spent US$ 900 million on the private sector of almost all countries in which it had missions.[44] Added to that, the new Bureau for Private Enterprise was established in the AID to advise field missions on private-sector projects as well as to launch innovative programs of their own.

The JPPCCs and business associations in Thailand have benefited from this new AID direction. To recapitulate, between 1983 and 1987, the AID mission gave a total of US$ 400,000 to improve the policy analysis of the NESDB and the three flagship associations represented in the central JPPCC. Since 1987 another five-year fund of US$ 300,000 has been given by the AID mission to improve the performance of provincial JPPCCs and provincial business associations. In addition, the Bureau for Private Enterprise gave a grant of US$ 1 million to establish the Institute for Management Education for Thailand (IMET). The IMET has improved the managerial capabilities of provincial businessmen, and has provided a solid foundation to the subsequent rise of business associations outside Bangkok.

Another US actor, a semi-private one as opposed to the AID, the National Endowment for Democracy (NED), has also played a role in the recent business association movement in Thailand. Through the Center for International Private Enterprise (CIPE) the NED has funded programs that assist business communities abroad to become a pluralist, democratic force.[45] From fiscal year 1984 through fiscal year 1986, the CIPE gave funds totalling US$ 6.7 million for this purpose. The efforts of the Inter-Provincial Chamber and the NIDA-IMET to build a strong network of provincial chambers of commerce in Thailand were facilitated by a US $97,000 grant from the CIPE.[46] In sum, between 1983 and 1987 the US contributed a total of US $1.5 million to the development of the JPPCCs and business associations in Thailand.

Although the US is the only source of external financial assistance, it is perhaps the Japanese experience, more than that of any other foreign country, that has inspired the recent business movement. As early as 1972, as mentioned in Chapter 2, a strong peak organization approach to business association development was advocated, albeit unsuccessfully, by the Board of Trade. This approach, according to veteran leaders of the Board of Trade, was motivated by the success of Japan's Federation of Economic Organizations (Keidanren).[47] Tellingly, the English translation of the name of the proposed new peak organization, Sahapan Ongkorn Settkij Haeng Pratet Tai, is exactly the Federation of Economic Organizations of Thailand.

The formation of the Joint Standing Committee on Commerce, Industry and Banking by the ATI, the TBA and the TCC in 1977 was also inspired by Keidanren. As told by Taworn Pornprapa, a key figure in the formation, leaders of the three associations came to appreciate the strength and unity of Japanese business under Keidanren. They also believed that a close association between the business sector and the government had helped the Japanese prevail in their negotiations with other countries.[48] It should be noted that both Taworn Pornprapa and Pramarn Adireksarn, ATI president at that time, had been heavily involved in joint ventures with the Japanese. Ob Vasurat, then TCC president, had had extensive experience of

84

negotiations with Keidanren and the Japanese government as a leader of the Thai private sector. The observations of these leaders on Keidanren and its relationship with the Japanese government might have been made through the above contacts with their Japanese counterparts.

Finally, the idea that the government and the business sector must work as if they were colleagues in the same corporation facing other nations in the intense international competition, as propounded by both Boonchu Rochanasathian and the NESDB, was also close to the practice of Japan and the East Asian NICs. The term "Thailand Inc.", coined by Boonchu, was also reminiscent of the term "Japan Inc." used by some American scholars to describe the collaboration between the government and the business sector in Japan.

Besides American funding and Japanese inspiration, the experience of Thai business representatives in the ASEAN Chamber of Commerce and Industry (ASEAN-CCI) was an important factor for the rise of the business association movement and the JPPCC system in the 1980s. In 1967 Thailand joined with Indonesia, Malaysia, the Philippines and Singapore to form the Association of Southeast Asian Nations (ASEAN). Four years later the ASEAN-CCI was formed with the objective of involving the private sectors of the member countries in regional economic cooperation.[49] The ASEAN-CCI consists of peak business organizations from all the ASEAN nations. It was in ASEAN-CCI meetings that Thai associations discovered themselves to be behind neighboring countries in terms of unity or coordination.[50] While the participants from other countries were chambers of commerce and industry, peak organizations that represent both trade and industry in respective countries, Thai participants consisted of the TCC and the ATI. The crucial point is that the TCC and the ATI had often contradicted each other at earlier ASEAN-CCI meetings. Chanond Aranyakananda of the TCC related the feeling of the Thai participants as follows:

We were quite embarrassed by our [TCC, ATI, TBA] weakness and divisiveness. It would be all right if the Japanese outdid us in this respect [the development of peak associations]. But, they [the ASEAN neighbors] were countries at our level of development, and yet they performed much better than we did.[51]

The decision to launch the Joint Standing Committee on Commerce, Industry and Banking in 1977 was thus motivated "in part by the desire of the TCC and the ATI to have a coordinating organization that could represent a unified view at the ASEAN-CCI."[52]

A major part of the discussion in ASEAN-CCI has been organized along the lines of separate industrial clubs such as textiles, steel, food, automobiles and plastics. Associations representing specific industries in each country were asked to participate in the respective clubs. It was here that businessmen from Thailand found they were also behind other countries in terms of trade associations. In several clubs, Thai participants were limited to the firm level, since there were still no associations representing such industries in their own country. A situation thus also existed in which a Thai coordinating body was needed to represent allied industries organized in the same club.

Some Thai business associations were created or strengthened during that time as a response to the need to be represented in various industrial clubs of the ASEAN-CCI. The Thai Plastic Industries Association and the ATI Plastic Industrial Subcommittee were created just for this purpose, although they are now important domestic policy actors too.[53] Another good example is the National Federation of Textile Industries. Initially, there was no supreme or coordinating body in Thailand holding the textile industry together. Instead, Thailand had five associations in the textile industry, each having specific concerns: yarn spinning, weaving, garments, silk manufacturing, and synthetic fiber manufacturing.[54] After these associations had joined the ASEAN-CCI's textile club in which discussions on problems of the textile industry as a whole often took place, they felt the need to have a coordinating body of their own to help them settle their differences so that they could be represented effectively in the club. The Federation of Textile Industries was accordingly established.[55]

External factors, important as they are, should not obscure the initiatives and capabilities of local actors. American funds, after all, came after the central JPPCC had been created. The JPPCC in addition, has a root that goes back as far as 1978 when Kriangsak initiated a joint committee. This was well before the advent of Reagan and his stress on the development of the private sector in aid-receiving countries. In most cases US funds were matched with substantial Thai funds. For example, the US$ 200,000 grant to major research projects of the ATI and the TCC was matched with equal funds from the two associations.[56] The US$ 1 million grant to the IMET was also matched by Thai funds of US$ 770,185 between 1982 and 1985.[57]

Equally significant, in the main it is not the American idea of pluralism that has guided the Thai institutional structure. Rather than staying aloof, the Thai government has a major role in the designing of the evolving business association system. On the other side, businessmen in general prefer a centralized, hierarchical system with strong peak organizations, not a decentralized system. Far from deterring government intervention, business actively seeks official status, assistance and—often—leadership.

Conclusion

Thus, the rise of the JPPCCs was due to the efforts of various actors. To begin with, the government for the first time has committed itself to build a nationwide network of cordial government-business consultation. It has elevated the status of the JPPCCs to a high place and has invested substantial administrative resources in strengthening their institutional capacities. The government has also helped the three national flagship associations to bring their constituent associations to join the work of the JPPCCs in one way or another. Official intervention in the development of organized business is most conspicuous in the provinces where public officers even call meetings of business leaders and prod them to organize and join provincial JPPCCs.

Unlike the past, the government has not been alone in its attempts to strengthen organized business and to redesign its institutional relations with the business community. Business leaders and associations have been a major partner in these attempts. Above all, it was the lobbying of the three flagship associations that triggered the formation of the central JPPCC. Moreover, businessmen, on their own initiative have created or improved peak organizations or federations which have become the foundation stones of the JPPCC system. The creation of the Joint Standing Committee on Commerce, Industry, and Banking, the Mining Industry Council and the elevation of the ATI to the FTI have been done with little or no government initiative.

All of these stood in marked contrast to what had happened in the previous eras. As mentioned earlier, the 1966 passage of the Trade Association Act and the Chamber of Commerce Act, the centerpieces of Thai legislation on organized business, was done solely by the effort of the government. Hardly any business leader or organization had been consulted on the acts beforehand. The Board of Trade, erected in the 1950s, came into being on the sole initiative of the government. The elevation of the Board and the TCC to the official status of peak organizations in the 1966 was an act of fiat. The business community had not been consulted of this elevation at all. Nor had it fought for the elevation. In summary, business associations over the past decade have come a long way as public policy actors in the development of a business representative system.

Government-business efforts to upgrade their relations have been facilitated by political and economic transformations which gathered momentum after the early 1970s, and just as importantly, by assistance and encouragement from sources outside the country. However, without significant socio-political changes in the country in the past quarter century and the initiative or capabilities of local actors, there would have not been grounds for external factors to exert meaningful influence on the recent business representative system.

With this background we are in a position to address the central question: To what extent have these associations become effective and autonomous interest groups, and how substantial and innovative have their contributions been to economic development?

Notes

1. M.L. Prachaksilp Thongyai and Sataporn Kawitanont, co-secretaries of the Kriangsak-appointed joint public-private committee, interviews, August 18 and November 17, 1987, respectively.

2. Government of Thailand, *Pramual Pol-Ngarn Kana Kammakarnruam Pak Rattaban Lae Ekachon Pua Kaekai Panha Tang Settakij (Ko Ro Au)* [Collections of Achievements of the Joint Public and Private Sector Consultative Committee (JPPCC)] (Bangkok: NESDB, 1986), pp. 7-30. Hearafter this work is referred to as *Pramual Pol-Ngarn, 1986.*

3. Conversation with officials of the JPPCC Division, NESDB in July 1987 and February 1991. This division is in charge of setting the agendas for the central JPPCC meetings.

4. Government of Thailand, *Pramual Pol-Ngarn, 1986,* pp. 7-30.

5. Data obtained from the Ministry of the Interior.

6. Chakrit Chulakasewi, ed., *Ha Pi Ko Ro Au: Hon Tang Haeng Kwam Samrej Kong Settakij Tai* [Five Years of the JPPCCs: Pathway to Thai Economic Success] (Bangkok: NESDB, 1986), p. 92.

7. Ibid., p. 94

8. Annual Report of the FTI, 1989.

9. Chanond Aranyakananda, TCC executive secretary and Acharin Sarasas, ATI secretary-general, interviews, July 6 and July 21, 1987, respectively.

10. *Matupum Raiwan Turakij*, special issue on the First JPPCC Regional Meeting, 1984, p. 13.

11. Annual Report of the TCC, 1985, p. 19.

12. Annual Report of the FTI, 1989.

13. Chakrit, *Ha Pi Ko Ro Au,* p. 61.

14. USAID/Thailand, "Thailand: Private Sector in Development," project number 493-0329, July 1982, p. 15.

15. Government of Thailand, *Pramual Pol-Ngarn Kwam Ruammuu Pak Rattaban Lae Ekachon Pua Kaekai Panha Tang Settakij (Ko Ro Au)* [Collections of Achievements in Public-Private Cooperation to Solve Economic Problems] (Bangkok: NESDB, 1987), pp. 55-56. Hereafter this work is referred to as *Pramual Pol-Ngarn, 1987.*

88

16. Government of Thailand, *Pramual Pol-Ngarn, 1987*, pp. 14-15; Government of Thailand, *Pramual Pol-Ngarn*, 1986, p. 75.

17. Government of Thailand, *Pramual Pol-Ngarn, 1987*, pp. 71-72.

18. Government of Thailand, *Pramual Pol-Ngarn, 1987*, p. 71.

19. Government of Thailand, *Pramual Pol-Ngarn, 1986*, pp. 76-83, and *Pramual Pol-Ngarn, 1987*, pp. 57-58.

20. Data obtained from the JPPCC Division of the NESDB.

21. Data obtained from the JPPCC Division of the NESDB.

22. Welcome Remarks by General Chaovalit Yongjaiyut, printed in Suthikiat Jiratiwat, ed., *Wittayalai Pongkan Ratcha-Anajak Laksut Karn Pongkan Ratch-Anajak Pak Rat Ruuam Ekachon Po Ro Au 1* [National Defense College, Special Joint Public-Private Course, Class 1] (Bangkok: 1989).

23. The three provinces are Chiangmai, Lampun and Konkaen.

24. These people are, for example, Amorn Wongsurawat, Winyu Kuwanan, Pratuan Ngarm-kham, Chanond Aranyakananda.

25. World Bank, Thailand: *Managing Public Resource for Structural Adjustment* (Washington, D.C.: World Bank Publication, 1984), Table 2.14, p. 30.

26. Akira Suehiro, *Capital Accumulation and Industrial Development in Thailand* (Bangkok: Chulalongkorn University Social Research Institute, 1985), Table VII-2, p. 7.10.

27. Kraisak Choonhavan, "The Growth of Domestic Capital and Thai Industrialization" *Journal of Contemporary Asia* 14 (1985): 137.

28. Kevin Hewison, "The State and Capitalist Development in Thailand," in Richard Higgot and Richard Robison, eds., *Southeast Asia: Essays in the Political Economy of Structural Change* (London: Routledge & Kegan Paul, 1985), Table 10.3, p. 274.

29. Krirkkiat Pipatseritham, *Wikroh Laksana Karn Pen Chaokong Turakij Kanad Yai Nai Pratet Tai* [The Distribution of Ownership in the Thai Big Business] (Bangkok: Thammasat University Press, 1982), Table 8.2, p. 328.

30. Montri Chenvidyakarn, "Political Control and Economic Influence: A Study of Trade Associations in Thailand" (Ph.D. dissertation, University of Chicago, 1979), Table 48, p. 250.

31. Suthy Prasartset, *Thai Business Leaders: Men and Careers in a Developing Economy* (Tokyo: Institute of Developing Economics, 1980), p. 58.

32. Paisal Sricharatchanya, "Happy Together," in *Far Eastern Economic Review*, February 18, 1988, p. 44.

33. Likhit Dhiravegin, *The Bureaucratic Elite of Thailand: A Study of Their Sociological Attributes, Educational Backgrounds and Career Advancement Pattern* (Bangkok: Thai Khadi Research Institute, Thammasat University, 1978), Table 3.3, p. 61.

34. Suthy, *Thai Business Leaders*, p. 36.

35. Krirkkiat Pipatseritham, *Karn Plianplang Tang Settakij Kab Panha Sitti Manusayachon Nai Pratet Tai* [Economic Change and Human Rights Issue in Thailand] (Bangkok: Thai Khadi Research Institute, 1985), Table 7-10, pp. 362-363.

36. Nipon Puaponsakorn, "Wipak Nayobai Settakij Chuang Sam Pi Ti Pan Ma" [A Criticism of the Economic Public Policy of the Past Three Years], in *Ruam Prachachart Turakij*, March 9, 1983, p. 4.

37. World Bank, *Thailand: Managing Public Resources for Structural Adjustment*, Table 2.7, p. 18.

38. Taworn Pornprapa, interview, August 13, 1987.

39. *Warasarn Settakij Lae Sangkom*, September-October, 1981, pp. 43-44.

40. Government of Thailand, *Pan Pattana Settakij Lae Sangkom Haeng Chat Chabab Ti Ha, Po So 2525-2529* [the Fifth National Economic and Social Development Plan, 1982-1986] (Bangkok: NESDB, 1981), pp. 418-419.

41. Snoh Unakul, a speech given on April 18, 1985, reprinted in Government of Thailand, *Rai-Ngarn Pol Karn Sammana Kana Kammakarn Ruam Pak Rataban Lae Ekachon Pua Kae Kai Panha Tang Settakij (Ko Ro Au) Nai Pumipak Krang Ti Song* [A Report on the Result of the Second JPPCC Seminar on Regional Economic Problems] (Bangkok: NESDB, 1985), p. 35.

42. Snoh Unakul, interview, August 4, 1987.

43. Snoh Unakul, interview, August 4, 1987.

44. AID, "Economic Growth and the Third World: A Report on the AID Private Enterprise Initiative" (Washington, D.C.: Bureau of Private Enterprise, AID, April 1987), p. 5.

45. National Endowment for Democracy, *Statement of Principles and Objectives* (brochure, undated), pp. 1,8.

46. Center for International Private Enterprise, "1986 Annual Report," pp. 20, 21, 30.

47. Preecha Tanprasert and Tapana Bunnag, interviews, July 6, and July 13, 1987 respectively.

48. Taworn Pornprapa, interview, August 13, 1987.

49. Pisan Suriyamongkol and Stephen Douglas, "Government-Business Relations in Thailand" *Thai Journal of Development Administration* 21 (July 1981): 465.

50. Ibid., p. 466.

51. Chanond Aranyakananda, interview, July 24, 1987.

52. Preecha Tanprasert, TCC vice-president, interview, July 6, 1987.

53. Siriporn Apirakkunwong, former manager of the Thai Plastic Industries Association, interview, June 25, 1987.

54. Indeed, the Thai Textile Manufacturing Association was set up as a representative of all industries allied to textile, but in practice it has largely spoken for only yarn spinners.

90

55. Songkram Chivaprawatdamrong, president of the Federation of Textile Industries, interview, August 5, 1987.

56. USAID/Thailand, "Thailand: Private Sector in Development," p. 34b.

57. John Bell et al, "End of Project Evaluation of the Institute for Management Education for Thailand, Inc. (IMET) Project," submitted to Bureau of Private Enterprise, AID, July 19, 1985, p. 30.

5

Associations as Interest Groups

Historically, interest groups in Thailand were very few in number, weak in their activities, and often created or closely supervised by the government.[a] Clientelistic relationships within the groups and between the groups and high officials were not uncommon. This, accompanied by the continued strength and flexibility of the military and bureaucratic forces in the Prem and Chatichai governments, leads to the question of whether or not business organizations, seemingly the most active and the strongest groups in the last decade, are fundamentally different from the interest groups of the past. In other words: To what extent are business associations more autonomous and effective than in the past?

To answer this question it is first necessary to explore the legal and institutional relations between the government and organized business. The aim here is to see if the present system of business representation contains corporatist elements which seriously undermine the autonomy of business associations.

Then several short but important cases will be used to demonstrate the success of business in initiating, transforming, or blocking public policies.

Finally, there will be a consideration of whether or not business associations are a formalized version of clientelistic networks, working mainly for the benefit of their leaders and high-ranking public officials. If that was the case, we are led to conclude that only a small change from the pre-1973 bureaucratic polity years has taken place.

---

[a] This chapter draws in part from Anek Laothamatas, "Business and Politics in Thailand: New Patterns of Influence" *Asian Survey* 28 (April 1988): 451-470. © 1988 by The Regents of The University of California. Used by permission of The Regents.

The Features of Corporatism

Several features of present government-business relations in Thailand fit a corporatist model quite well. First of all, official sponsorship and encouragement has played a major role in the development of business associations throughout the past decade. Official initiative in the formation of business associations is most heavily felt in areas outside Bangkok, where several governors or district officers typically call meetings of businessmen and urge them to form or join chambers of commerce in line with the central government's policy.[1] The creation of the JPPCCs also represents a vigorous attempt to institutionalize the relationship between the top leadership of the government and the business community.

Moreover, as Montri Chenvidyakarn has argued, the Trade Association Act and the Chamber of Commerce Act, the centerpieces of Thai legislation on business associations, contain many corporatist elements.[2] The Board of Trade, to begin with, is designated as the representative of the business sector and is to be consulted by the government. It is made up of the TCC, foreign chambers, and trade associations. Only one national chamber of commerce, the TCC, is allowed to operate and its president becomes the exofficio president of the Board of Trade. Likewise, provincial chambers are also limited to one in each province. Each must bear the name of the province which it represents, and each must be a member of the TCC. Foreign chambers are limited to one for each nationality and are encouraged to join the Board of Trade.

The Trade Association Act and the Chamber of Commerce Act empower the government to control the licensing and the registration of business associations throughout the kingdom.[3] The government-appointed registrar may refuse to register those associations deemed dangerous to the economy and/or to public order.[4] He or she may also deny any amendment to the regulations or the bylaws of an association.[5] The registrar may attend and, if it is deemded necessary, close a meeting of a suspect association.[6] If a person considered to be a threat to the economy or to the security of the nation is appointed to the board of directors of a trade association or chamber of commerce, the appointment may be nullified by the registrar.[7]

The Thai case, however, is far from an ideal case of corporatism. Significant pluralist features also exist. Above all, business persons and firms are not required by law to join any business association. Trade associations, though not chambers of commerce, are exempt from joining higher-level organizations. There is no limitation on the number of trade associations as there is for chambers of commerce, and a particular trade or industry is allowed to have more than one representative association. Associations are, in addition, free to contact public agencies directly, rather than being forced to go through a higher-level organization. Equally important, they may compete in a pluralistic style, for conflicts are not contained and bureaucratically solved by their superior organizations or by the government.

The textile industry, for example, is frequently fraught with conflict and infighting among five related associations representing different interests in the industry. The most serious conflict is between the "upstream" Thai Textile Association, which is the mainstay of the yarn spinners, and the "downstream" Thai Weaving Association, a situation that prevents the Industry Ministry from assigning an official representative status to a single association. All five associations are treated almost equally by the government, and this requires negotiations and compromises among the associations as they deal with both government textile policy formulation and its implementation. Similar problems exist in the tapioca industry, with conflicts occurring between "Bangkok" and "regionals" rather than between upstream and downstream.

Since the passage of the two acts more than 20 years ago, several changes in the structure of the political regime and public policy have brought about even more autonomy of, and competition among, business associations. To start with, the Board of Trade has not become (as the Chamber of Commerce Act had intended it to) the sole apex body of the economic sector as the majority of trade associations have chosen not to join its ranks. Two associations, the TBA and the ATI, have grown as strong as the Board of Trade and the TCC. The TBA and the ATI/FTI have been widely regarded as sectoral peak bodies, even though legally they were just basic trade associations.

A number of mining associations, after more than ten years of persistent effort, succeeded in persuading the House of Representatives to pass a law chartering the Mining Industry Council as the official representative of all mining industries. This council is, furthermore, not legally required to join the Board of Trade and hence becomes another independent, though statutory, sectoral peak organization.

Equally striking, there has been the emergence of unregistered, nonjuridical higher-level organizations, working independently of a statutory peak organization. Examples of these federations are the Joint Standing Committee on Commerce, Industry and Banking; the Inter-Provincial Chamber of Commerce of Thailand; the National Federation of Thai Textile Industries; and the Federation of Foreign Chambers of Commerce of Thailand.

Faced with the growth of nonjuridical entities, the government has shown tolerance and even acceptance. The government has worked closely with the Joint Standing Committee on Commerce, Industry and Banking, which was founded as a body coordinating the activities and policy viewpoints of the ATI, the TBA, and the TCC to be forwarded to the central JPPCC. Provincial JPPCCs also include unregistered, unofficially formed provincial bankers clubs as principal participants. Ko Ro Au Sampan, the official JPPCC newsletter, reports the activities of the National Federation of Textile Industries and the Inter-Provincial Chamber. Recently, the central JPPCC made it a policy to encourage trade associations involved with plant oil industries, animal food industries, and some related businesses to form a federation. As the relations among tapioca associations have improved, the Commerce Ministry is persuading them to form a federation as well.

Not only does the government allow business-initiated, often nonlegal, organizations to compete with the corporatist ones, it accepts those which perform better. Currently, the Board of Trade is the only official and statutory apex body of the whole economic sector. However, the nonstatutory Joint Standing Committee of Commerce, Industry and Banking is recognized by both the government and business as the more effective business representative. Since the early 1980s the government has accorded the most prestigious and powerful policy role to the Joint Standing Committee and its constituents (the ATI/FTI, the TBA and the TCC) instead of to the Board of Trade.

Finally, although the government is empowered to intervene in the registration, leadership selection, and internal regulations of business associations, this power is rarely exercised. In practice, associations are given a high degree of autonomy and freedom in their operation. Many of them do not regularly submit records of their activities, leadership name lists, financial status reports, or even new addresses to the official Central Registar's Office, and yet they incur no penalties.[8] Government intervention in the leadership selection of business associations is either extremely rare or nonexistent. In summary, although legal, institutional relations between the government and organized business exhibit corporatist features, it is basically true that business autonomy is substantial.

Political Effectiveness

One way to demonstrate the political effectiveness of organized business is to cite the success stories of various associations in obtaining public policies which they wanted. However, this kind of success alone may not reflect true effectiveness since such policies may have stemmed from the initiative of the government. To demonstrate that organized business is politically effective, it is necessary to show that the associations have been able to play an initiating role in public policy-making. Again, however, sometimes even successful initiation may not be equated with genuine effectiveness, for there may be a convergence of interests or complete agreement about what is needed between public officials and business. In such cases business initiative is followed up because of the consent of the government rather than because of any outside pressure that has been brought to bear on it. Thus, it is also necessary to find cases in which there was conflict—these can be used to demonstrate business success in transforming or blocking policies initiated by the government.

To sum up, business's political effectiveness is illustrated by selected short case studies which suggest business ability to (1) initiate, (2) transform, and (3) block public policies in recent years. These cases must involve significant policy issues. Just as important, it should be possible to distinguish between the policy initiator on the one hand and the policy follower or transformer or blocker, on the other. Accordingly, the cases to be examined here are deliberately chosen from those negotiated and settled mainly outside the JPPCCs, where government-business relations are highly interpenetrated.

Initiating Policy

As regards initiating policy, notable cases are the joint efforts by the chambers of the Northeast to liberalize trading with socialist neighboring countries, the chambers of the South fighting for the eradication of crime and violence, and the campaigns to promote gems and jewelry exports:

Liberalizing Border Trade. Trade across the borders with Laos and Cambodia had been a traditional mainstay of many provinces in the Northeast. After the 1975 communist victory, and particularly after the Vietnamese expansion into both countries, Bangkok severely restricted (and sometimes even banned) border trade. At times only a few customs check points were open for trading activities and commercial transportation; many export items were banned; and only government to government transactions were allowed.

Since early 1986 chambers of commerce in the border region have been pushing for the lifting of these restrictions. They first raised this issue at the Third JPPCC Regional Meeting. Responding to their requests, Premier Prem, who presided over that meeting, agreed to have "the Ministry of Foreign Affairs, the National Security Council, as well as the Ministries of the Interior and Commerce solve this problem."[9] Later, in 1987, led by the Udon Chamber and sponsored by a well known business newspaper, Ruam Prachachart Turakij, sixteen chambers organized a conference on Thai-Lao border trade to which numerous high officials were invited.[10] A few months after that, Thai-Cambodia border trade problems were also discussed at a conference in the southern part of the Northeast region, organized by the Ubol Chamber and participated in by many chambers in the region.[11]

Business requests for quick and massive trade liberalization were dismissed by several government agencies, including the military command and the Foreign Ministry, as militarily and diplomatically imprudent and economically impractical. However, in the last years of Prem's period as prime minister, the government began to pursue a policy of cautious but steady liberalization of border trade with its socialist neighbors. At least in part business lobbying appeared to be responsible for this modest policy shift.

With the advent of the Chatichai administration, which regards with great favor a diplomatic normalization with the Indochinese states, chambers of commerce have been in a better position to advance their cause. In mid-1989 the Prachinburi Chamber managed to meet with Cambodian Premier Hun Sen to discuss significant trade issues between Thailand's Northeast and Cambodia.[12] For their part the Sakol Nakorn and Ubol Chambers have held several talks with Laotian regional authorities to tackle trade problems with that country.

Crime and Violence in the South. For years the South has been plagued with problems of communist and Malay separatist insurgency, robberies and kidnappings, and abuses of power by law enforcement agencies. As a result, the region, which is well endowed with natural resources, has attracted relatively little investment and relatively few tourists. Even local business, according to the president of the Songkhla Chamber, one of the established chambers in the South, feels that the place is not safe enough to launch a large enterprise.[13]

In July 1987 fourteen provincial chambers of the region, in cooperation with Songkhla University, organized a conference on this issue. The conference was presided over by a deputy minister of the interior, and was attended by heads of the regional army and police force, as well as all governors in the South. The chambers, apparently in a move to dramatize the issue, called for an ultimate goal of making the region completely arms-free. Later, during the campaign period for the 1988 general election, these chambers also announced that they would strongly support those candidates who were sympathetic with their anti-crime cause.[14]

In response to these moves, high government officials pledged to do their best although they did not think a fundamental improvement in safety and order would be achieved in the near future.[15] Nevertheless, the public relation impact of the business campaign has been immense as evidenced by the fact that the slogan "creating an arms-free zone" initiated by the chambers was at one time even adopted by the national police chief for his nationwide campaign for the suppression of crime and violence.

Neither the drive for trade with Socialist neighbors in the Northeast nor the campaign against crime in the South is likely to obtain quick and dramatic results; however, they do illustrate the newfound confidence and assertiveness of business quite well. The first case involves an "intrusion" into military and security affairs, an area traditionally reserved almost exclusively for the military-bureaucratic elite. Even political parties and civilian leaders in the government seldom challenge the hard-line border trade policy long advocated by the military. The second case is a direct criticism of the enforcement of law and order, another area long regarded as being not the concern of the business community by both the government and the public.

Campaigns of the Gems Export Association. A third example of government action being taken as a result of business initiatives relates to the activity of the Thai Gems and Jewelry Traders Association. Until a decade or so ago, the gems and jewelry industry in Thailand was small and domestically oriented, despite the country's inexpensive raw materials and labor. In the early 1970s, however, international changes prompted foreign importers to look towards Thailand. Among these changes were political instability in Burma and Sri Lanka (which were among the top exporters of gems and jewelry in the region), rising labor costs in Western countries, and increasingly sophisticated Thai craftsmanship. In the new climate, Thai exports surged. However, some of the major Thai gems and jewelry firms were not satisfied. They realized that greater exports would be possible if a number of government-created obstacles were removed. Above all, the importation of rough stones and the exportation of finished gems and jewelry were highly taxed. Leaders of these firms, mostly young and well educated, formed the Thai Gems and Jewelry Traders Association through which they began to lobby for policies favorable to their exports.

They first went to the Ministry of Finance and requested the reduction or the abolition of the relevant import and export taxes. Next, they asked the Board of Investment, a public authority, to grant promotional tax and tariff privileges for their export items. Finally, they proposed the launching of joint international sales campaigns with the Department of Export Promotion.[16]

At first very few officials were aware of the export potential of gems and jewelry. "Some of us thought these enthusiastic businessmen were joking when they told us of their optimism," recalled an official at the Board of Investment.[17] Another major obstacle to government and public sympathy for these industries, according to a veteran business correspondent, was "a prevailing attitude that gems and jewelry were luxuries for a handful of rich people and had nothing to do with the welfare of the common people."[18] Perhaps this long and widely held assumption was the basis for the government's prohibitive taxation.

The association made an effort to show that gems and jewelry exports would bring employment to hundreds of thousands of ordinary people. Some statistics, which surprisingly were not previously publicly known, were marshaled to support the case. For example, the association argued that "the industry provided jobs for over 500,000 people," and that "about 70 percent of those employed were rice farmers who cut gems during their off season."[19]

After a while, partly convinced by these arguments, partly aware of the high priority their superiors now accorded to export promotion in general, the Ministry of Finance, the Board of Investment and the Department of Export Promotion yielded to the association's requests. In 1977 the duty on rough stones imported into the country was lifted. The business tax on finished jewelry manufactured in the country for export was also lifted in 1981, and more favorable promotional privileges were given to gems and jewelry exporters.[20]

The association managed to arrange a few exhibitions or sales campaigns abroad in cooperation with the Department of Export Promotion and the Ministry of Foreign Affairs. In 1987 the Third Biennial Gems and Jewelry Fair was graced by the prime minister and attended by buyers from 26 countries.[21] Of equal significance, in 1989 the associations pushed for government support for their launching of a special school that would continually upgrade the craftsmanship of Thai workers.[22] Finally, the association is currently helping its leading members to launch a new international exhibition and sales center in the Bangkok metropolitan area.

The export of gems and jewelry is now an undoubted success. By the end of 1986 this sector ranked as the fifth largest foreign exchange earner.[23] Thailand is now among the top gems and jewelry exporters of the world. The explanation of this success would be incomplete without taking the policy-initiating role of business into consideration.

Transforming Policy

The ability to transform or modify the content of government-initiated policy can be illustrated best by the success of provincial business leaders in eliminating the stipulation on compulsory membership from the FTI Bill. The objective of the bill was to elevate the status of the ATI to FTI, a statutory peak private industry organization. The bill was conceived by the ATI and approved in principle by the central JPPCC in 1983. One year later it was approved and sponsored by the cabinet.[24] Finally, in 1987 the government laid it before the House of Representatives.

Until the House passed the bill at its first reading, no associations other than those represented in the central JPPCC seemed to be aware of its consequences. News of the first reading, however, awakened provincial chambers to the setbacks this bill might bring to their organizations. They discovered that this Bangkok business-initiated legislation would compel all existing industry trade associations throughout the kingdom to become members of the FTI.[25] Provincial chambers feared that this legal advantage might lead local industrialists and industry associations to leave them, since their membership in chambers was voluntary.

Led by a newly founded coordinating body, the Inter-Provincial Chambers of Commerce of Thailand, provincial business leaders held press conferences and public seminars to disseminate their views. Each chamber also tried to lobby legislators from its own province.[26] Their plan was to defeat the bill at its second reading in the House. Provincial pressure was heavily felt throughout the House and parliamentarians who had initially expected the bill to pass easily began to fear that it might be defeated.

To avoid total defeat, ATI leaders asked for the help of the TCC, supposedly the peak organization of the provincial chambers.[27] Moreover, personal consultation with prominent leaders of the protest movement was sought.[28] The ATI was also believed to have exerted influence through two major ruling parties, the Chat Thai Party and the Social Action Party.

Pressured by both sides, which had equally strong political backing, the House could not but strike a compromise by passing the bill but eradicating the controversial section on compulsory membership. Although the bill was enacted, public policy on peak business organizations was substantially modified. One of the most important and far-reaching proposed pieces of government legislation affecting business associations ever to be introduced —compulsory membership—was deflected. The situation remains the same—no business associations have the advantage of compulsory membership, thanks to the provincial business protest.

Blocking Policy

An illustration of the capacity of business associations to block policy outright is a 1979 case in which tourist and hotel service associations successfully brought down a bill on the control and management of tourist services. The bill would have empowered the official Tourism Authority of Thailand (TAT), which until then had no authority other than promoting tourism in general, to set standards for services in hotels, restaurants, and travel agencies and to punish violators. News of this restrictive measure infuriated various tourism and hotel associations partly because, unlike past practice, the bill had been drafted by the TAT without consultation with the associations, and partly because it imposed what they felt were unreasonably harsh penalties for violators, including jail terms for what seemed minor violations.

The associations demanded withdrawal of the bill and applied pressure on the TAT in various ways. Symbolically, they declined its offer to discuss a possible adjustment of the content of the bill and canceled impending joint Europe-bound sales promotion trips originally planned with the authority.[29] It was also widely believed that the associations were considering the reduction or elimination of financial contributions to certain projects of the TAT.[30]

The authority eventually bowed to the demands of the associations, and it was not until three years later that a new, alternative bill was drafted. The governor of the TAT openly admitted the previous mistake of shunning prior consultation with business, while actively seeking "full business participation" in the drafting of the new bill.[31] By late 1990 the once controversial bill was on its way to the House of Representatives. Though its content was subject to further adjustment, it was acknowledged by both sides that unacceptable portions of the previous bill would never be included in the new version. The agency made it clear that the government would not establish commercial enterprises to compete with the private sector. Tourism promotion, not regulation, was to be the main direction of the agency. Regulation, if needed, would be mild and practical, and would be made after prior consultation with the associations directly concerned.[32]

A Growing Confidence

The above "objective" illustrations of the political autonomy and effectiveness of organized business are consistent with the "subjective" evaluation of government responsiveness to their needs and demands given by the leaders and officials of business associations. A majority of provincial chambers of commerce, to begin with, found that officials were somewhat responsive and effective in solving their problems. (See Table 5.1.)

TABLE 5.1 Government Responsiveness to Provincial Chambers

How responsive are senior officials in your provinces to your chamber's problems or requests?

a) Marginally or not at all responsive	(13)
b) Moderately responsive	(29)
c) Very responsive	(6)

Source: same as that of Table 3.3.

A survey was also conducted on Bangkok trade associations. Admittedly, the conclusions to be drawn from this survey are not quite a reliable picture of the total population, since only 56 out of 177 associations returned the questionnaires. However, this survey may be viewed as representing active associations, since the list of associations that returned questionnaires largely coincided with the list of associations that are regularly reported in Ruam Prachachart Turakij. The survey found that most of the associations that returned the questionnaires rate the government as somewhat or very responsive. (See Table 5.2.) Businessmen also believed that relative to ten years previously government responsiveness had improved somewhat. (See Table 5.2.)

TABLE 5.2   Government Responsiveness to Trade Associations

---

1. How responsive have government agencies been to your problems?
   a) Not very or not at all responsive   (3)
   b) Moderately responsive   (37)
   c) Very responsive   (14)

2. How effective has the government been in solving the problems you have raised?
   a) Not very or not at all effective   (6)
   b) Somewhat effective   (44)
   c) Very effective   (5)

3. Compared to what happened ten years ago, how would you rate the present responsiveness of government officials to your problems or requests?
   a) Equally or less responsive   (4)
   b) Moderately more responsive   (37)
   c) Much more responsive   (12)

Source: same as that of Table 4.1.

Just as important, business leaders seem to admit that, as a consequence of the improved responsiveness of the government, especially since the creation of the JPPCCs, their self-confidence has improved. Pong Sarasin, ATI president noted that:

> Indeed, several business problems have been relieved by the officials. . . . The [responsiveness] of the government at least made the private sector more self-confident. . . . Several problems, of course, have not been tackled as fast as businessmen had expected. But, the government, at least, began to understand, to have sympathy with, and recognize the importance of, the private sector.[33]

Likewise, at the provincial level Winyu Kuwanan, president of the Konkaen Chamber, observed a changed situation in his province:

> In the past, it was common to see bureaucrats as "important" people, and merchants as "insignificant people." Thus, whenever problems arose, we, merchants, dared not talk to the bureaucrats. The situation has changed recently. . . . Now, we are organized as a chamber of commerce, and a

provincial JPPCC has been erected. [As a result, we,] Konkaen merchants are now more articulate.[34]

In conclusion, judging from the legal and institutional relations of business associations with the government, from their policy interaction with public agencies or officials, and, finally, from their own subjective evaluations, business associations have become autonomous and effective interest groups.

The Weakening of Clientelism

The foregoing conclusion about the effectiveness and autonomy of business group action does not imply that action organized around personal ties (especially clientelistic ones) now plays only a minor role in Thailand. Though not as extensive or important as it was in the past, such ties are still significant.

Clientelism and Business Firms

Although many fewer firms than previously invite politically powerful individuals to join their executive boards, press reports suggest that clientelism continues to be a key to business success in Thailand. In 1987 Colgate-Palmolive (Thailand), a leading manufacturing and trading conglomerate, appointed to its board Pote Sarasin, a former prime minister and father to three of the country's most influential bureaucrat-politicians: Pong Sarasin, a deputy prime minister; Arsa Sarasin, the Thai Ambassador in Washington; and Pao Sarasin, the most promising candidate for the post of director-general of the national police force. Siam Motors, one of the country's largest automobile trading and assembling companies, now has a former governor of the official central bank, the Bank of Thailand, Nukul Prachaubmoh, as president of its executive board. At the Bangkok Bank, the largest bank in Southeast Asia, with one-third of Thailand's total private banking assets, Amnuay Virawan, former permanent secretary and minister of finance, heads the executive board. In 1985 Chaovalit Yongjaiyut and Pichit Kullavanich, the two contenders for the post of army commander, were included among the active high-ranking military officers holding shares in Mahachon Pattana, a company being set up mainly to do business with the government.

But exploiting clientelistic ties as a means of policy influence is not so important or decisive as it was in the past. Today, while a good many former officials are working for private companies, few active bureaucrats or politicians are on their boards of directors. Furthermore, those invited into companies are widely accepted for their managerial skills or experience, and thus are not valued solely for their political influence, as was the case in the past.

There have also been illuminating cases suggesting the difficulty of exploiting clientelistic ties in the face of increasing group action and the expectation among businessmen that the government should treat everyone equally. One such case which occurred in Bangkok during the early months of 1987 involved the transfer of purchase orders for 200,000 tons of rice from two major private exporters, Nakorn Luang and Thana Pornchai, to the Ministry of Commerce. This transfer was highly sensitive as the two companies had accepted the orders while the domestic prices of rice and paddy were very low, but the prices had since risen markedly. Accordingly, the transfer was widely seen as a favor granted by high officials to the two leading firms to save them from a huge loss; and, of course, administrators of the ministry were suspected of receiving kickbacks. The facts of the case are far from settled, but the relevant point is that as soon as other members in the Rice Exporters Association learned of the transfer, they acted swiftly to counteract this presumably scandalous transaction. The association's president demanded that, if the report were true, the government help other companies that were in the same situation.[35]

Another case of opposition to clientelism arose in Nakorn Ratchasima Province in 1986. In an unprecedented move, the chamber of commerce there forced local government agencies to make public all bidding on government construction contracts. Calls for bids also had to be posted in public, well in advance, so that every firm had the same chance to tender.[36] This move, supported by chamber members who were not influential contractors, was designed to prevent certain firms from securing a contract simply because of their clientelistic connections with high officials in the province. Thus, in both cases, clientelistic maneuvering between public officials and firms or individuals for particularistic benefits, an easy act in the past, was prevented or made more difficult by associational actions oriented toward equality among members.

Clientelism and the Operation of Associations

Traditionally, clientelism was pervasive not only in the operation of business firms, but—most probably—also in the operation of business associations. Writing in the aftermath of the 1973 uprising which led to the downfall of the longest ruling military regime, Prudhisan Jumbala observed that organized groups in Thailand, in marked contrast to Western pressure groups, had been very much permeated by "patronage relationship between the bureaucracy and extra-bureaucratic organizations as well as patronage within extra-bureaucratic organizations."[37] Thus, the increasing significance of business associations as policy actors nowadays should not lead one to rule out the existence of clientelism in these associations and their operations.

Although hard evidence is difficult to obtain, one can find some uses of seemingly clientelistic tactics by business associations even at present time. In the early 1980s, for instance, the Thai Rice Mills Association curried favor with the Army Commander, General Arthit Kamlang-ek, by inviting him to be its honorary advisor, and at the same time tried to cultivate a personal tie with a former premier, Kriangsak Chomanan, who was making a political comeback, by supporting him in his first election bid.[38] Both generals were known for their influence and prestige among politicians and bureaucrats. Another organization, the Rice Exporters Association, was known to have a very good relationship with high-ranking bureaucrats in the Ministry of Commerce because of its regular and generous donations to various charity and special rural projects favored by the permanent secretary or influential directors-general in the ministry. Lastly, it was widely believed that Dam Tiewtong, only a middle-ranking mining industrialist, was elected president of the newly-established Mining Industry Council in 1983 mainly because of his long-time personal ties with Commerce Minister Poonmi Poonasri.

Clientelism may manifest itself not simply in the tactics employed by associations in dealing with government officials. Some associations themselves may be only facades for the representation of the particularistic interests of their presidents and a few associates who control members of these associations through clientelistic ties. Provincial chambers are often seen by officials and the press as self-serving creations of locally influential business. Even in Bangkok occasional cases arise that are suggestive of such a clientelistic use of business associations. In the early 1980s, for example, many people believed that a decade of leadership of the Thai Fishery and Frozen Product Association by Pairoj Chaiyaporn, who was a business tycoon and an influential leader in the ruling Social Action Party, was based on his clientelistic control over the association. Another instance was noted in 1987 when a Thai Petro-Chemical Industry Association was created with its leadership and membership coming mainly from one company, the Thai Petrochemical Industry (TPI), and its affiliates.[39] This incident was seen by both the press and knowledgeable observers as a ploy by the TPI to counter the attacks of plasticware producers, who had organized under the banner of the Thai Plastic Industries Association. For years the TPI, which is to all its intents and purposes the only domestic producer of petrochemical raw materials needed for the manufacture of plasticware, had attempted to persuade the government to impose a heavy surcharge on imported raw materials of the same kind. TPI efforts, however, were frequently offset by the plastic industries group, so leaders of the company concluded that they needed an association of their own.

Perception of Clientelism and Reality

Analytical Confusion. The public perception of the foregoing cases may bear some truth, but the implications for the extensive presence of clientelism in business associations and their operations must not be overstated. As the above cases suggest, most reports about clientelism are merely interpretations of an event or situation and are not built on hard evidence. This shortcoming is often reinforced by analytical confusion among writers and observers. All kinds of personal relations that exist in the interaction between officials and business leaders are equated with clientelism, even though familiarity with public figures is always a great asset to enterprises and associations and is actively sought after, not only in Thailand but elsewhere as well.

In a strict sense, clientelism is "a vertical dyadic alliance, i.e., an alliance between two persons of unequal status, power or resources each of whom finds it useful to have as an ally someone superior or inferior to him."[40] The concept has been used to study the relationships between landlords or middlemen and agricultural workers in the rural areas, and powerful landlords and urban squatters in the cities—where substantial inequality in wealth, power, and status obviously exists. Clientelism can also be aptly used to describe the personal relations between government officials and businessmen in the heyday of the bureaucratic polity in Thailand, where socially humble and foreign—though wealthy—entrepreneurs coexisted with native bureaucrats or politicians who were socially and politically regarded as superiors.

It is perhaps true that in provincial areas clientelism continues to play an important role, since there is a wide gap in social status between officials and business leaders. However, in Bangkok, where that gap has narrowed to a great extent, what are loosely described as patron-client ties are often friendship or classmate ties. Thus, in the case of Dam Tiewtong, the president of the Mining Industry Council and Minister Poonmi Poonasri, a personal tie between them was more likely a classmate tie—from their days together at Chulalongkorn University—rather than a clientelistic tie between a "noble official" and a "humble, foreign merchant" as was characteristic of the bureaucratic polity era.

An analytical difficulty may exist also in the interpretation of the case of the TPI described earlier, or other similar cases where only one dominant company is willing to bear administrative and financial responsibility for the formation of an association. Critics often hold that unless an association is widely joined by "equals" who perceive common interests in the work of the association, it is not a "true" interest group.[41] The single firm or a few dominant firms taking the lead are consequently suspected of using the association as a pretext to create a clientelistic tie with smaller member firms on the one hand, and relevant public officials on the other.

There are alternative interpretations of these situations. Some leaders who take the initiative may have altruistic or other idealistic reasons for doing so. Moreover, following Olsonian "free-rider" reasoning, forming an association can be regarded as a "public good" in the sense that benefits from the functioning of the association may accrue as much to latecomers as to founding members.[42] If the number of potential beneficiaries is large, then firms tend to refrain from being founding members—waiting instead to join the association later. It seems to be true that an association is more easily formed if a few dominant firms exist. These firms, in taking the lead in forming an association, are simply pursuing their own self-interest in that they realize that because of their large size their returns from the association are likely to be considerable. If such is the case, they are willing to bear the costs associated with the founding of the association and to allow "free-riders" to enjoy the benefits generated by the association.

There is no reason to believe that this line of reasoning is less applicable than the prevailing clientelistic explanation. According to a key founder of the Petrochemical Industries Association, the TPI company was motivated by the large benefit it would receive should the association succeed in its lobbying against the plastic industries groups. Other members were not ignorant of this unequal distribution of benefit. But, they wanted to join it anyway, partly because they would receive that policy benefit too, but more probably because the founders promised to have the association invest in large-scale, modern laboratory and research facilities to be used by all members.[43] Being a giant establishment, the TPI company could afford to go it alone. For other relatively small-time potential members, however, the research and development benefits to be provided by the association were much more highly valued.

To conclude, this case involved much rational, instrumental calculation on the part of both founders and joiners. Both sides realized that there was benefit, though not the same for each. Negotiations and compromise also occurred. In one respect, that of the benefits to be derived from any public policy changes, the founders were the main beneficiaries. In another respect, that of the benefits to be derived from research and development activities, the joiners would be the beneficiaries. This behavior seems not to be a clientelistic model, in which the minor parties are seldom allowed to bargain and negotiate.

Reversed Clientelism. It should be noted as well that in recent years there have been instances of a reversed direction of dependence between public agencies or officials and business associations. A number of business associations in Bangkok have included in their top leadership persons of high stature, often those with prestigious bureaucratic or political backgrounds. Consequently, balance in terms of status between government officials, especially at the departmental level where most contacts occur, and the leaders of the associations is in some cases shifting in favor of the latter. Leaders of the TAT, for example, have expressed concern about cultivating good working relationships with leaders of tourist-industry associations for two prime reasons.[44] First, these associations contribute a substantial amount of money to joint public-private sales campaigns abroad, and second, which is more relevant to the point raised above, their leaders are politically influential—some of them are senators, former cabinet members, leaders of political parties, friends of the prime minister, and so on. Their goodwill toward the TAT and its leadership is thus indispensable to the organization's progress.

Changes in relative power and status are not always caused by changes in business personalities. As the burden of new and more complicated tasks for the budget-conscious government increases, departmental officials find that they need business assistance and cooperation—sometimes for financial support, sometimes for information, and sometimes for representational duties. This means that government departments and the private sector are becoming increasingly mutually dependent; both sides need each other. This has led to a new and more balanced relationship between government departments and business. The Thai Fishery and Frozen Products Association, for example, during the late 1980s contributed an annual sum of about US$ 20,000 to improve the inspection facilities of the Department of Fishery. It also made a lump sum donation, and planned to make annual contribution afterwards, to improve the computer facilities of the department of medical science.[45] All these facilities are needed to process the export products of members of the association, and it is therefore in their interest to help improve them. The Department of Medical Science and many other departments also have an interest in conforming to their superiors' call for better and quicker service to exporters so as to help the country obtain the badly needed foreign exchange.

To give another example, during the past few years the assistance of the Rice Exporters Association has been badly needed by the Commerce Ministry to cope with US protectionism. Since about 70 percent of the Thai work force are rice farmers, rice exportation is always the issue that worries the government most. The ministry needs the aid of the association to arrange meetings between US officials and Thai exporters in order to investigate the charge that Thai traders have received subsidies from the government to export to the US. Moreover, the ministry has asked the association to share the financial burden of this investigation, which is strictly speaking its own responsibility.[46]

As this shifting in power and status between public officials and businessmen continues, clientelism is less likely to occur. If it continues to occur, the direction of dependence might well be reversed. One cannot easily predict that the officials will always be the "patrons," and the businessmen always the "clients."

Inadequacy of Clientelism

Even in cases where clientelism is really at work, it is neither an adequate means of conducting business nor an irreplaceable one. The Thai Rice Mills Association, described earlier as having tried to develop clientelistic ties with various top military and political leaders, is also noted for its sophisticated, "modern" lobbying tactics. It spends considerable resources on crop surveys, research for policy position papers, and press coverage of its activities. A major reason given by a founding leader of the Thai Gems and Jewelry Association, mentioned earlier, was also suggestive of the inadequacy of clientelistic and under-the-table dealings:

> With tremendous foreign purchase orders coming in, the past practice of case-by-case under-the-table dealings, such as hiring airplane passengers to do the smuggling, or asking favors from high officials we have good ties with, or bribing minor customs officials, were considered inadequate and overly time-consuming. Businessmen had to find a new way to do things. They needed an association.[47]

Finally, Pairoj Chaiyaporn, long regarded as the "patron" in the Thai Fishery and Frozen Product Association, was "overthrown" a few years ago by a group of younger leaders who wanted to move the activities of the association away from the "exclusive" concern of one company and gear them to a wider range of interests.[48]

In brief, associations represent an important venue for businesses to pursue their collective, policy-oriented interests. There are reasons to believe that clientelism on the whole is decreasing in importance. Furthermore, its presence in the formation and operation of business associations is not as extensive as it was in the old bureaucratic polity era.

The Organizational Factor in Business Conflict

As interest groups, business associations not only contest with the government, but also compete with one another and with other functional groups. On the whole, interaction between business groups and other functional groups is minimal, since labor unions and farmers' associations in Thailand, except for occasional protests or demonstrations, are hardly at all engaged in the public policy process. However, as described earlier, recently business associations have been heavily engaged in conflict or competition among themselves.

Conflict has arisen between member organizations and peak associations, between those concerned with export-oriented products and those with import-substitution products, and between those dealing with input products and those with output products. Bases of conflict have also included differences in geographical locations and functional sectors. The emergence of associations has added a new dimension to business competition—the political, collective organizational dimension.

In the past business competition took place mainly in the marketplace between business individuals or firms. Of course, competition sometimes extended into the political arena. But, as mentioned previously, businessmen carried out this competition mainly by mobilizing the support of their bureaucratic patrons or, after the reestablishment of parliamentarism in the late 1970s, engaging in electoral politics. With the proliferation of organized activities of business, however, business associations became involved, providing a new and possibly effective means for smaller businesses to prevail over bigger businesses. With organizational strength and effective lobbying, small and medium-sized businesses can upset economic giants on significant policy issues. This point is well illustrated by the successful opposition of provincial businessmen to compulsory membership in the FTI which had been introduced by established Bangkok industrialists. The following two cases also underscore how business associations can help smaller firms in their battles against economically more powerful counterparts.

Drug Stores vs. Manufacturers[49]

Troubled by a new legislative measure which had forced them to hire university-trained pharmacists, several drug retailers across the country came to organize the Society of Drug Stores of Thailand in 1981. As the supply of professional pharmacists then was inadequate, their salaries were relatively high, and only pharmaceutical manufacturers and drug wholesalers could afford them. Retailers, mostly small and middle-income family firms, on the other hand, found that university-trained pharmacists were quite out of reach.[50]

One of the chief objectives of the society was therefore to send the retailers' children to a pharmacy school. However, most pharmacy schools in Thailand were state schools and admitted only those who passed a rigorous entrance examination. The leadership of the society thus came up with an innovative idea that a new pharmacy school, financially sponsored by the society, should be established in a private university in the North. This new school would have a special and sizable admission quota for the children of drug retailers. To raise money for this purpose, the society engaged in the wholesale business, with the cooperation of its members and pharmaceutical manufacturers. Under this scheme the society would make a massive purchase order from pharmaceutical manufacturers with a special 40 percent discount and then sell it to its members at a profit. The proceeds from this wholesale business would then go to the pharmacy school.

While most pharmaceutical manufacturers agreed to give a handsome discount to the society and refrain from making a direct sale to retailers for this special purpose, a multinational giant, the Schering Corporation, refused to do so. To the resentment of the society, Schering would give only a 15 percent discount. Worse yet, according to the society, this multinational manufacturer also sold directly to retailers at prices lower than those of the society.

To retaliate, the Society of Drug Stores called on its members to undertake a boycott against Schering. Specifically, they were asked to stop buying all Schering products, cancel pending orders, and defer paying Schering bills. As a result, Schering reportedly apologized to the society and pledged to adjust its original position. A pharmaceutical manufacturer commented perceptively on this incident, "The power of these drug stores really scares pharmaceutical manufactures . . . [if] even a German giant like Schering had to bow to them, whatelse could smaller manufacturers do.[51]

Textile Association vs. the Thai Melon

To fight the problem of the overproduction of yarn, the government had prohibited manufacturers from expanding their spinning operations for over a decade. From the early months of 1986, however, the continuously rising yen made Thai yarn very competitive on the world market. To the dismay of the Thai weaving and garment industries, the price of yarn at home had also rocketed. During the middle of the year, the Thai Melon Textiles, the country's largest spinning operation, sought government permission to install an additional 250,000 spindles for the exclusive production of yarn for export. While the weaving and garment industries understandably welcomed the Thai Melon's plan, the Thai Textile Manufacturers Association (TTMA), representing the spinning industry, strongly opposed it.[52]

Thai textile industries have been dominated by the seven largest conglomerates. Among them, the Thai Melon complex has been the predominant force. During the late 1970s and the early 1980s, its total assets were more than double those of the second largest conglomerate.[53] Moreover, if the new 250,000 spindles were installed, it would become one of the world's largest yarn producers.[54] Most member firms of the TTMA, however, had a bitter relationship with this textile giant. At times the Thai

Melon had refused to work with the rest of the association to curtail production or reduce price competition. Many TTMA members also believed that the Thai Melon illegally sold on the domestic market yarns that had been declared to be produced for export. Normally, yarns that are produced for export are entitled to special tax and tariff concessions and thus have a much lower cost, compared to yarns produced for the domestic market. Since most TTMA member firms were producers for the domestic market, they were afraid that should difficulties arise on the world market, the new export expansion of the Thai Melon might end up flooding the local market with supposedly export-oriented yarns.[55]

The protest of these smaller members was reinforced by some other leading yarn producers, such as Pongsak Assakul and Pramarn Adireksarn. Reportedly, these textile leaders were not prepared to undertake similar expansion and hence wanted to delay the implementation of the Thai Melon's plan until they were ready to catch up.[56]

Since the price of yarn continued to rise and other textile associations, particularly the Thai Garment Manufacturers and the National Federation of Textile Industries, disagreed with TTMA objections, in December 1986, the government allowed the expansion of yarn spinning for export purpose. However, the issue of the illegal selling of export-oriented yarns was extensively discussed by the policy-makers and measures to prevent it were devised.[57]

Furthermore, as soon as the new liberal textile policy was in effect, the TTMA urged that the government change its traditional policy which stipulated that to be eligible for tax and tariff concessions, only new machinery could be used for any expansion. The TTMA rationale for this policy adjustment was that used machinery was much cheaper and hence more affordable to most member firms. After a few months of deliberation, the government gave the green light to the TTMA proposal. Five months after the Thai Melon started to install its 250,000 new spindles, Pongsak Assakul, in the second-tier in the spinning industry, managed to add 40,000 second-hand spindles transferred from abroad to his plants.[58]

In brief, although the Thai Melon eventually managed to expand its capacity, it had to spend considerable time and effort. It was, in addition, closely watched concerning its handling of yarn sales in the domestic market. Through the TTMA, smaller firms "succeeded to some extent in keeping the Thai Melon from being the sole beneficiary of the new export opportunity."[59]

Certainly, a generalization that the existence of associations has considerably tipped the balance of power towards lesser member firms cannot be safely drawn from these few cases. However, the cases represent a trend in which collective efforts have become a new factor that must be taken into account to improve our understanding of intra-business conflict and its impact on public policy. Economic predominance does not necessarily lead to policy predominance. Political and organizational dimensions, brought in by the operation of business associations, do matter.

A Minimal Role in Electoral Politics

Representation in the legislature, the cabinet, and political party leadership by individuals from the ranks of organized business is not uncommon in Thailand. For example, Pong Sarasin, a deputy prime minister in the Prem administration, was a former ATI president. Boonchu Rochanasathian, Pramarn Adireksarn, and Ob Vasurat, the three business leaders who were instrumental in the creation of the central JPPCC, were several times cabinet ministers or deputy prime ministers.

In the 1986 general election seven out of more than 300 successful candidates to the House of Representatives were from provincial chambers' boards of directors.[60] It is also a common government practice now to appoint some distinguished leaders of business associations to the Senate, the prestigious but less powerful section of the bicameral parliament. In 1987 a former president of the TCC, Sompob Susangkarn, was a senator, as were the incumbent president of the Association of Travel Agents, Yaowalak Paengsapa, and the incumbent president of the Federation of Regional Tourist Business, Vijit Na Ranong.

In addition, some working or retired leaders of business associations have been active in political parties. In 1987 Boonchu Rochanasathian was the president of an opposition party. Pong Sarasin has been an important leader of a ruling party, the Social Action Party. Pramarn Adireksarn has been a senior leader of another ruling party, the Chat Thai Party.

Although several present and past leaders of business associations are at present in the government, political parties, or the legislature, few reports exist on institutional connections between business associations and electoral institutions. One reason for this is the prohibition of such associations from financing or engaging in any explicit—i.e., electoral—political affairs.[61] The Thai Rice Mills Association, for instance, was warned in 1986 by the special branch police (responsible for political and security affairs) not to engage in the electoral campaigning of a political party.[62]

Business leaders, with whom I have interviewed, have claimed that their pattern of electoral financing, if there is any, is mostly from business people as individuals to candidates as individuals. Business leaders active in political parties, in addition, never work there as official representatives of their associations. There is no definite pattern as to which associations hold a leverage on which parties. Typically, an influential association has leaders who cultivate relationship with politicians from several parties. When problems arise, the leadership will decide who in its ranks is the "right" man to be dispatched to deal with the concerned people in office.

Conversely, parties have shown little interest in business associations as institutions. The creation of the JPPCCs and the efforts to strengthen associations have proceeded without any initiative on the part of the parties. Instead, these major institutional changes have been brought about by associations and the "non-elected" elements of the government, i.e., the prime minister and the technocratic NESDB. Boonchu Rochanasathian, as a veteran leader of both political parties and organized business, admits that as of now no party seems to be aware of the significance of business associations in political and economic development. It is his observation that "when party men contact associations, they look for only short-term, personal benefits . . . and never devise any policy to develop business associations, or to bring about legitimate party-association cooperation.[63]

Thus far, the target of lobbying or other influencing activities of business associations has been mainly the executive branch of the government. Most associations have more contact with the executive than with the legislative branch, and that most of these contacts take place at the departmental level, which is the most immediate level for the policy implementation. (See Table 5.3.)

TABLE 5.3 Frequency of Government Contacts by Trade Associations

Respondents to the question:
Question: How often has your association contacted officials at the following levels?

	Often	Sometimes	Seldom
1. Ministerial level or equivalent	5	22	20
2. Permanent secretary level or equivalent	5	16	26
3. Director-general (departmental) level or equivalent	19	2	6
4. The parliamentary level -committees	5	9	28
-individual members	4	8	23

Source: same as that of Table 4.1.

114

This does not deviate much from the strategy employed by business, whenever possible, in the bureaucratic polity era. However, it is evident that nowadays contact between the legislature and business associations has increased significantly too. My analysis of summonses issued by the House to business associations for testimony or consultation indicates that during 1983-1987 an average of 4.45 persons a month representing business associations of some kind were summoned, compared to merely 0.13 during the democratic years 1975-1976, and 0.14 during the short-lived revival of the bureaucratic polity period 1977-1978. (See Table 5.4.)

TABLE 5.4 Frequency of Summonses Issued by the House of Representatives to Business Associations in Selected Periods (per Month)

Period	Frequency
October 2, 1975-December 30, 1976	0.13
January 1, 1977-June 22, 1978	0.14
May 1, 1980-October 31, 1980	0.33
July 1, 1982-November 16, 1983	1.86
November 17, 1983-June 11, 1987	4.45

Source: Compiled from the data given by the Division of Committee Affairs, the House of Representatives.

More importantly, the role of business associations in law-making has increased. As the economy becomes more differentiated and complicated, more sophisticated legislation is needed to handle new kinds of business and new situations. In recent years several new laws have been initiated by associations and departments of the government. In some cases, such as the law on third-party automobile insurance, the role of associations continues to be merely consultative. However, as business associations in the past few years have become more aggressive, laws drawn up solely by departments often face business opposition. Consequently, more and more departments have invited associations to join in the drafting. Such has been the case of the laws on the regulation of the construction industry, the value-added taxation system, and the regulation of the tourism industry.

In comparison, the role of political parties has been minimal in the formulation of these laws. Lacking interest and competency in these highly technical matters, they seldom take the initiative to introduce business laws. Furthermore, they are rarely consulted by associations before or during the process of drafting legislation.[64] The role of the parties and legislators in the House of Representatives is often limited to scrutinizing those bills sent in by associations and departments and passing them into laws.

Provincial Chambers and Political Visions

Virtually no association has any vision or plan about the development of political institutions. They are certainly cynical of various aspects of the current far-from-perfect democratic procedures and institutions. Yet, their actions never go beyond specific issues or problems of their immediate business concerns. Even peak business organizations, leaders of which are involved in politics, do not have much idea about using the associations to promote political development.

One reason for this, as mentioned earlier, is the law that limits political activities of business associations. Another reason may be that with the existence of the JPPCCs and the improved responsiveness of the executive branch of the government in the past decade, businessmen do not seem to feel that they need strong links to political parties and the legislature through which to exert their policy preferences.

Nevertheless, there was a possible exception in the Inter-Provincial Chamber of Commerce of Thailand. Key figures of this organization during 1986-1987 claimed to have a long term goal of steering provincial chambers towards the development of democracy.[65] These energetic leaders tried to spread among provincial chambers their notion of "democratic idealism," meaning that "politicians needed to be honest and well versed in policy issues and people should be able to make legitimate demands on the state."[66]

Leaders of the Inter-Provincial Chamber also believed that, if instilled with that idealism, provincial businessmen choosing to enter politics would serve as principled politicians. Extensive research-based lobbying activities of provincial chambers, on the other hand, in their view, "taught those remaining in the chambers to know what public measures they had to demand from politicians, and what kind of political behavior they needed to expect from them."[67] In other words, the Inter-Provincial Chamber planned to make "good actors as well as good spectators in politics" out of its activities with provincial businessmen.[68]

The long term plan of key leaders of the Inter-Provincial Chamber to lay a foundation for democratic institutions and procedures, however, has led them to shun direct involvement in politics and political parties at present. Nikorn, a respected mentor of the Inter-Provincial Chamber, explained, "[The task of] improving parties and politicians should be put off until we have enough qualified business people ... [only then] should we send these men in to guide parties and politicians along our lines.[69] Provincial chambers now simply lobby parties or politicians from time to time for what public measures they want. Their immediate impact on the development of electoral and legislative institutions is minimal.

Conclusion

Since this new evaluation of the role of business associations as interest groups is central to the argument that the Thai bureaucratic polity has been substantially transformed, it may be useful here to summarize the evidence of their autonomy and effectiveness in relation to the government as follows:

First, the three flagship associations have persistently urged the government to create and give a very high priority to the institution of close and cordial government-business relations.

Second, organized business groups are effective in influencing several substantive, as opposed to institutional, economic policies of the government as well. Although a large number of them are still not quite active, some—especially peak organizations and major trade associations in Bangkok—are able to initiate, transform, or block various public policies in an assertive manner that was unthinkable in the bureaucratic polity era. Not only do they influence, some associations even take part in the drafting of laws and rules governing business operation. No less important, provincial chambers, when united, also turn out to be significant policy actors.

Third, the presence of corporatist features in the business representation system does not seriously undermine the autonomy of business associations.

Fourth, the presence of clientelism in the formation and operation of business associations is not extensive and does not seriously weaken the importance of policy-oriented, group-based action by businessmen. The assertion that associations are only a formalized version of clientelistic ties among businessmen or between businessmen and public officials is hardly sustainable.

On the other hand, the contribution of organized business to the development of parties, the legislature, and electoral politics, is limited. While individual businessmen or informal business groupings are reported to be using or involved in parties and electoral politics, organized business shuns institutions or procedures that are explicitly political. Independent lobbying or participating in government commissions, as opposed to exercising influence on the government through parties and electoral politics, is its prevailing form of instrumental influence on public policy. Organized business is not yet a powerful force for democratization.

Notes

1. Preecha Tanprasert, TCC vice-president, interview, October 16, 1987. Preecha joined with governors and district officers in several campaigns to urge provincial businessmen to organize during the period 1984-1986.

2. Montri Chenvidyakarn, "Political Control and Economic Influence: A Study of Trade Associations in Thailand" (Ph.D. dissertation, University of Chicago, 1979), pp. 214-217.

3. Sections 7 and 8 of the Trade Association Act; Sections 7 and 8 of the Chamber of Commerce Act.

4. Section 10 of the Trade Association Act; Section 10 of the Chamber of Commerce Act.

5. Section 29 of the Trade Association Act; Section 36 of the Chamber of Commerce Act.

6. Section 34 of the Trade Association Act; Section 41 of the Chamber of Commerce Act.

7. Section 30 of the Trade Association Act; Section 37 of the Chamber of Commerce Act.

8. Conversation with officials at the Central Registrar's Office of Trade Associations and Chambers of Commerce, Department of Internal Trade, October 1987.

9. Government of Thailand, *Rai-Ngarn Pol Karn Sammana Kana Kammakarn Ruam Pak Rattaban Lae Ekachon Pua Kaekai Panha Tang Settakij (Ko Ro Au) Nai Pumipak Krang Ti Sam* [Report on the Third JPPCC Seminar on the Solution of Regional Economic Problems] (Bangkok: NESDB, 1986), p. 76.

10. *Ruam Prachachart Turakij*, May 2, 1987, pp. 8-9.

11. *Naeo-Na*, July 7, 1987, p. 7.

12. *Tarn Settakij*, June 19-24, 1989, p. 26.

13. Boonlert Laparojkij, interview, July 25, 1987.

14. *Ruam Prachachart Turakij*, July 13, 1988, p. 43.

15. *Ruam Prachachart Turakij*, July 18-21, 1987, p. 11.

16. Pornsit Sriorathaikul, president of the Thai Gems and Jewelry Traders Association, interview, October 29, 1987.

118

17. Conversation at the Board of Investment office, not for direct attribution, June 9, 1987.

18. Chumchun Poolswat, *Naeo-Na* business section chief, interview, June 9, 1987.

19. Pornsit Sriorathaikul, interview, October 29, 1987.

20. The Research Office of the Bangkok Bank, "Facets of the Thai Gemstone Trade" in *Thailand Business* (July-August, 1987), pp. 35-36.

21. *Thailand Investment News* (No.2, 1987), p. 1.

22. *Ruam Prachachart Turakij*, June 1-3, 1989, p. 2. ; June 11-14, 1989, p. 13.

23. Annual Report of the Board of Trade, 1986, Table 5, p. 45.

24. Government of Thailand, *Pramual Pol-Ngarn, 1986*, p. 19.

25. Section 17 of the FTI Bill (the 1987 cabinet draft).

26. *Ruam Prachachart Turakij*, July 29, 1987, p. 2.

27. Ruam Prachachart Turakij, July 14, 1987, pp. 1,4.

28. Nipon Wongtrangarn, leader and coordinator of the protest movement, interview, August 26, 1987.

29. *Ruam Prachachart Turakij*, March 24, 1979, p. 1.

30. Chumchun Poolsawat, interview, June 9, 1987.

31. *Ruam Prachachart Turakij*, May 1, 1982, p. 4.

32. Conversation with responsible officials of the Tourism Authority of Thailand and the Association of Thai Travel Agents during the period October-November, 1987 and in March 1991.

33. *Ruam Prachachart Turakij*, January 15, 1983, p. 7.

34. *Ko Ro Au Sampan*, January, 1986, p. 5.

35. *Tarn Settakij*, February 9-14, 1987, p. 1.

36. Interviews with officials of the Nakorn Ratchasima Chamber of Commerce, February 7-9, 1987.

37. Prudhisan Jumbala, "Towards a Theory of Group Formation in Thai Society and Pressure Groups in Thailand after the October 1973 Uprising" *Asian Survey* 14 (June 1974): 535-536.

38. Conversations with officials of the Thai Rice Mills Association, June 8, 1987.

39. *Naeo-Na*, July 2, 1987, p. 7.

40. Carl Lande, "Introduction: The Dyadic Basis of Clientelism" in Steffen Schmidt et al eds., *Friends, Followers and Factions* (Berkeley: University of California Press, 1977), p. xx.

41. For an example of this line of criticism see *Naeo-Na*, July 2, 1987, p. 7, "Samakom Plastic TPI Na Kan"[The TPI Plastic Industries Association looks funny].

42. Mancur Olson, *The Logic of Collective Action* (Cambridge: Harvard University Press, 1965).

43. Conversation with a TPI executive member and a founder of the Petrochemical Industries Association, July 1, 1987.

44. Conversation with officials of various tourist-industry associations and officials of the Tourism Authority of Thailand, November 1987.

45. Nipaporn Bunyanan, manager of the Thai Fishery and Frozen Products Association, interview, July 3, 1987.

46. Conversation with officials of the Thai Rice Exporters Association, June 10, 1987.

47. Conversation at the Thai Gems and Jewelry Traders Association, October 1987, not for direct attribution.

48. *Ruam Prachachart Turakij*, March 23, 1983, p. 4; March 26, 1983, p. 4.

49. The account given here is based largely on *Ruam Prachachart Turakij*, September 12, 1981, pp. 1, 12; September 16, 1981, p. 7; September 19, 1981, p. 4.

50. Conversation with some former leaders of the Society, July 17-19, 1987.

51. *Ruam Prachachart Turakij*, September 12, pp. 1, 12.

52. Songkram Chivaprawatdamrong, president of the Federation of Thai Textile Industries, interview, August 5, 1987.

53. Krirkkiat Pipatseritham, *Wikroh Laksana Karn Pen Chaokong Turakij Kanad Yai Nai Pratet Tai* [The Distribution of Ownership in the Thai Big Business] (Bangkok: Thammasat University Press, 1982), pp. 132-133.

54. "Thai Melon wants to install more spindles" in *Bangkok Post*, December 9, 1986, p. 28.

55. Kamnandang (pseudonym), "Suuk Prawatsart Nai Wongkarn Singtoh" [A Historical Conflict in Textile Industries], in *Naeo-Na*, December 2, 1986, p. 8.

56. Songkram Chivaprawatdamrong, interview, August 5, 1987.

57. Kamol Tantivanich, manager of the TTMA, June 30, 1987.

58. "Chae Rong-Ngarn Lob Nam Kao Kaen Pan Dai" [Exposures of yarn smuggling by factories] in *Naeo-Na*, June 10, 1987, pp. 5-6.

59. Kamol Tantivanich, interview, June 30, 1987.

60. Compiled from congratulatory telegrams sent by the TCC to successful candidates who were members of provincial chambers' executive boards.

61. Section 23 of the Trade Association Act; Section 30 of the Chamber of Commerce Act.

62. *Ruam Prachachart Turakij*, February 8, 1986, p. 13.

63. Boonchu Rochanasathian, interview, November 10, 1987.

64. Conversations with Representative Chaturon Chaisaeng of the House Committee on Economic Affairs, October 1987 and February 1991.

65. Interviews with Nikorn Wattanapanom, Sunthorn Srisattana, and Amorn Wongsurawat during late 1987 and early 1991.

66. Nikorn Wattanapanom, interview, June 11, 1987.

67. Amorn Wongsurawat, interview, February 9, 1987.

68. Sunthorn Srisattana, interview, June 10, 1987.

69. Nikorn Wattanapanom, interview, June 11, 1987.

6

The Economic Role of Associations

The Traditional Role

Traditionally, the most prominent role of business associations in the economy was the assistance given by the Board of Trade and the commodities associations to the official regulation of the agricultural exports of the country. In this role, however, business associations were sometimes seen in an unfavorable light. At times they were criticized as posing obstacles to newly established traders.

For example, in the late 1970s and early 1980s the Rice Exporters Association came under heavy attack from a new group of traders. In the view of these critics, the system of so-called "collective selling" which had been introduced by the association and the government operated so as to put newer firms at a grave disadvantage in relation to the longer-established firms. The system worked in such a way that exporters which acquired sales orders from abroad could fill only 10 percent of the orders. The rest of each order would then be allocated among members of the Rice Exporters Association in proportion to their recent export records.[1] The charge was that this rule unfairly favored established exporters who had already achieved high level of sales.[2]

Furthermore, agricultural export associations were suspected of collusion designed to produce unfair prices for farmers.[3] The government was aware of this possibility and hence prohibited trade associations and chambers of commerce from "excessively" suppressing or increasing the prices of goods or services, except when this was actually an enforcement of a government policy.[4]

121

However true the charge may have been in the past that business associations were bulwarks or beneficiaries of the controlled agricultural export policy of the government, it has become less true recently. Since the early 1980s the export of major commodities, with the exception of items put under quota restrictions by the importing countries themselves,[5] has been opened to much freer trade. Most domestically imposed quota systems have been removed and now firms may sell most items directly to foreign importers at whatever prices and in whatever quantities that can be agreed. Exporters no longer have to go to the government or relevant association first.

The exportation of rice, the most important agricultural export item, has been freed of the rule of "collective selling" and exporters no longer have to share their individually acquired sales orders with others.[6] The only restriction on new exporters is that they have to be accepted as affiliated members of the Board of Trade. This, however, has not posed any formidable obstacle to the newcomers; the number of rice exporters mushroomed after the abolition of the quota barrier system and the practice of "collective selling." In particular, several members of the domestically oriented Rice Mills Association, a traditional opponent of the Rice Exporters Association, have swollen the ranks of exporters.[7]

The way the liberalization policy was substantially achieved in the early 1980s also calls into question the credibility of a popularly held notion that agricultural export associations were the effective bulwark of export regulations, since these associations did very little to counter or resist the new policy. The key figure in the liberalization efforts was Commerce Minister Poonmi Poonasri. Along with several of his colleagues in the ruling parties, Poonmi was aware of the farmers' demands for higher agricultural prices following an unprecedently severe across-the-board decline in world prices. The minister and his colleagues realized that if the decades-old regulations governing exports were dismantled, this would both benefit and please farming communities in the rural constituencies.

Poonmi was supported by the technocrats who served as advisors to the government. In November 1981 these advisors urged the prime minister to urgently consider the liberalization of agricultural exports.[8] The World Bank, from which the Thai government often seeks advice, was also supportive of liberalization. In early 1981 a study sponsored by the Bank had called for the free exportation of virtually all agricultural commodities.[9] Finally, the liberalization proposal was enthusiastically supported by the press, who saw it as a means to redress the artificially low prices long received by farmers due to public intervention in the export process.[10]

Contrary to what one might have expected, the agricultural export associations kept silent during discussion of the policy. Even associations long regarded as highly influential, such as the Rice Exporters Association, did not block or deflect the liberalization move. A few associations, such as the Board of Trade and the Maize Traders Association, actually supported the liberalization as they believed that in such a depressed market situation free trade would make them more flexible and competitive.[11] It transpired that only career bureaucrats at the implementing stage resisted the change. Much publicized was the opposition of the director-general of the Department of Foreign Trade. In April and May, 1981 he rejected most proposals coming from various circles for the opening up of trade in maize and rice.[12] However, after a forceful intervention by several politicians, especially Minister Poonmi himself, the bureaucratic resistance died down, and the cabinet decided to go for the liberalization policy in the December of 1981.[13]

The traditional notion that the main role of the associations was their control of agricultural exporting does not hold true at the present time for another reason. By the late 1970s agricultural export associations had ceased to be the predominant force in the business community as well as in relations between the government and organized business. Their place had been taken by newly emerging peak organizations, export industry associations, tourist-industry associations, provincial chambers of commerce, and financial associations. With the combined use of political and economic collective work, these latecomers have assumed broader and, arguably, more acceptable roles in economic development. They have advocated and facilitated the country's shift to an export-oriented development strategy; they have urged and secured more government support for private business; and they have begun to assume a leadership role in provincial development.

The Advocacy of the Export Strategy

Recent "statist" writers on the so-called East Asian NICs have emphasized an autonomous and development-oriented state as the key to a successful export-oriented industrialization strategy.[14] According to these writers, efficient performance by private actors, especially labor and business, are highly praised and encouraged by the government. Nevertheless, public policy initiative and opposition by societal forces are generally kept small in these state-led NICs, and social manipulation or outright repression of labor's political opposition and collective bargaining are characteristic.[15]

More relevant to the concern of this study, even the policy role of business is considered to be relatively unimportant.[16]   Business organizations, including business associations, serve mainly as policy-enforcement tools of the state, rather than as channels through which business can exert some leadership or significant opposition to relevant public policy-making. In short, in the East Asian NICs, societal forces are not supposed to lead, but are supposed to be induced, harnessed, or even coerced, by "enlightened" governments to perform tasks required by the chosen economic strategy. In Thailand, by way of comparison, business associations have advocated and facilitated the transition to an export-oriented strategy since the late 1970s.

Until the Third National Economic and Social Development Plan came into effect in 1972, Thailand pursued an import-substitution strategy. Tariff protection, tax and duty concessions, and import and export quality controls were all adopted to promote the manufacturing of industrial goods sold on the domestic markets. Exports, on the other hand, were generally not subsidized. A number of agricultural export items, most importantly rice, were even subject to high export taxes and duties.

For a decade, between 1960 and 1970, the import-substitution strategy succeeded in providing a steady growth in manufacturing, averaging 11.9 percent annually.[17] However, it also created the problem of external balance of trade deficits, since imports, a lot of which were inputs needed in the production of substitute industrial goods, rose sharply, while exports grew at only a slow pace. Between 1966 and 1970 annual imports jumped almost 50 percent, while net services and net transfers rose modestly, and exports stayed virtually constant. As a result, the current account deficit rose almost ten times in that five-year period. (See Table 6.1.)

TABLE 6.1 Balance of Payments (US$ Million), 1966-1970

	1966	1967	1968	1969	1970
Exports, F.O.B.	664.3	663.9	635.9	685.9	685.4
Imports, C.I.F.	879.6	1055.7	1147.9	1229.1	1274.7
Trade Deficit	-215.3	-391.8	-512.0	-543.2	-589.3
Net Services	197.4	284.3	297.5	281.4	262.2
Net Transfer	46.3	57.6	74.4	57.1	48.6
Current Account Deficit	-28.4	-49.9	-140.1	-204.7	-278.5

Source: The International Bank for Reconstruction and Development, Current Economic Position and Prospects of Thailand, Vol.I, January 11, 1972, Table 4, p. 10.

To relieve the balance of payment constraint, a range of export promotion measures were introduced during the period of the Third and Fourth National Economic and Social Development Plans. This began with the revision of the Investment Promotion and the Export Promotion Acts in 1972, to provide a full tax exemption for inputs imported for the manufacturing of industrial exports. The following measures were also adopted: a refund of taxes levied in the production process; a discount on short term loans for manufacturers of exports; and an exemption from the business tax for manufacturers for export. Meanwhile, an Export Promotion Committee was set up to co-ordinate these promotional efforts.

Despite these efforts, the trade and balance of payment deficits continued to worsen. By the end of 1977 the financial position of the country had been further eroded by two additional factors: the escalating price of imported oil, and the massive defense expenditures of the preceding right-wing Thanin government. The percentage of the trade deficit to GNP, which had dropped to a satisfactory level of 3.3 percent in 1976, more than doubled in 1977. (See Table 2.4.) The public sector international debt also increased dramatically—from an already high level of 56 percent of the international reserves in 1976 to 95 percent in 1977. (See Table 2.5.) Alarmed by the rapidly deteriorating situation, in early 1978 the Kriangsak cabinet resorted to the traditional solution: curbing imports. Eighteen import items, including cars, were banned; higher tariffs were also imposed on 144 items considered "luxurious imports."[18]

Aware of the government's grave concern, the newly established Joint Standing Committee on Commerce, Industry and Banking, proposed that Premier Kriangsak create a cabinet-level joint public-private committee to take care of the trade deficit and other urgent economic problems. The chief lobbyist for the creation of this committee was Ob Vasurat, then TCC president, who happened to be a close friend of the premier.[19] In mid-1978 the proposal was accepted and such a joint government-business committee was formed with a deputy prime minister as its chairman.[20]

According to Taworn Pornprapa, then ATI president, from the beginning business representatives suggested to the committee that the emphasis should be placed on increasing exports—rather than curbing imports—to solve the trade deficit problem.[21] They also recommended that the government make it clear that export promotion was one of its highest priorities. These proposals were happily accepted by the government. However, when asked what further policies the government should pursue to improve the export performance of the country, business representatives replied with an unexpected answer. From the business point of view, as related by a co-secretary of the committee, "the existing policies were generally good enough; the problem was much more on the enforcement of the policies.[22] All sorts of practical obstacles to the export of Thai goods were then identified by business leaders. However, few public measures had been taken to overcome these obstacles by the time this committee was dissolved following the ending of the Kriangsak government in early 1980.

Between 1980 and 1981 an informal government-business forum was formed under the leadership of Boonchu Rochanasathian, in his new capacity as a deputy prime minister of the government. While the forum was intended to address all major economic and business bottlenecks, export promotion problems became its major concern.[23] Although export-related problems raised by business leaders since 1978 remained largely unresolved, the political and bureaucratic elites seemed to have reached a strong consensus that a set of urgent and comprehensive measures was needed to cope with them. Accordingly, when the central JPPCC replaced Boonchu's forum in mid-1981, these matters continued to dominate its early sessions.[24] Under the leadership of Premier Prem and the NESDB secretary-general, within a few years the central JPPCC managed to remove a wide range of implementation bottlenecks.

To begin with, customs formalities were drastically simplified. Customs check points for all export items were reduced from eight to three. Only a quarter of the items previously so required now needed to pass through the crime prevention check point. Customs processing at the Bangkok International Airport now could be done beyond normal office hours as well as on holidays (albeit at extra expense to exporters).[25] Export formalities were also largely simplified. For example, canned pineapple, one of the most controlled items, had previously had to go through 25 stations; in 1984 the overall number of stations was reduced to nine.[26]

In delineating the role of associations in bringing about the new strategy, one should also include the role of other important actors, particularly the Thai technocrats and the World Bank. In 1979-1980 a World Bank mission, in cooperation with leading Thai technocrats, issued a report urging Thailand to change its industrial development strategy to an exported-oriented one.[27] In 1981 an export emphasis was stated in the Fifth National Economic and Social Development Plan. Be that as it may, business complaints and demands which dominated various government-business meetings since 1978 contributed significantly to the formal adoption of the new strategy. Business associations were in the forefront of redefining the problem from one of policy formulation to one of policy implementation.

The Promotion of Specific Industries

Bureaucratic delays and inefficiency are not the only practical difficulties of an export promotion policy. Another major problem is: What trades, industries or services are to be promoted, and in what ways? Although public agencies have become more sophisticated in their economic analysis and although examples of successful export items from foreign countries abound, business initiative or advice is often needed to select items for promotion and then to work out concrete measures to assist the producers or suppliers.

Recently, in addition to conventional items (such as textiles and garments) and items introduced by experienced multinational corporations (such as electronic integrated circuits), several unconventional export items have been creatively identified and advanced by local businessmen through their associations. A leading example is the case of export gems and jewelry (described earlier). Tourist and hotel services for foreign visitors are another good example. As observed by the president of the Federation of Regional Tourist Business, originally it was unthinkable for the government to promote these businesses for two principal reasons: "First, they are services, rather than industries. Second, they were traditionally seen by the public and the press as luxuries and environmentally polluting, and having nothing to do with the common people."[28]

Since the early 1970s, however, the Association of Thai Travel Agents and the Thai Hotel Association have conducted successive campaigns to convince the government and the general public of the immense potential of tourism as an employment generator and foreign exchange earner.[29] They have also frequently made charitable donations and participated in cultural events, so displaying their social concern. Equally important, the associations lobbied successfully for the opening of courses in tourism in some state colleges and universities.[30]

Simultaneously, they made requests for government assistance, frequently on the ground that their businesses were export-oriented. A review of business newspapers finds that since the late 1970s their requests have included a substantial reduction of public utilities rates for hotels, faster and more courteous customs and immigration procedures at the international airports, a larger government budget for overseas sales promotion, and the creation of duty-free sections in large department stores to lure more foreign tourists.

Increasingly the government has responded favorably to these demands, since tourism is now regarded as an integral part of the Thai export-oriented strategy. The current Sixth National Economic and Social Development Plan prescribes the promotion of tourism as a principal means to generate foreign exchange and employment, as well as a basis for the creation of new urban centers.[31] Snoh Unakul had this to say about the role of tourism in the overall Thai economic strategy:

> Our pathway to a newly industrialized country status is quite unique. We will not emphasize only manufactured exports. Tourism and agro-industries also will be part of our export-oriented strategy. Thailand is not another Korea or another Taiwan in this sense.[32]

Another trade not conventionally conceived of as having export potential is printing services. Ten years ago it was not even on the promotional list of the Board of Investment. The main association which represents this service, the Thai Printing Association, was not at all concerned with political and economic activities. Until recently the emphasis of the association was on the welfare and recreational activities of its members. The emergence of a new leadership composed of highly educated young entrepreneurs in the mid-1980s has shifted the focus of the association towards the promotion of the export of printing services.[33]

Like those associations concerned with gems and jewelry and tourist services, the Thai Printing Association has tried to convince the Board of Investment to give export-oriented printing firms more tax and tariff concessions. The association also persuaded the Department of Export Promotion to display samples of Thai printing in its various exhibitions of Thai products held in several major cities abroad.[34] Recently it has also begun to lobby the government to reduce postal costs for export-bound printed materials.[35] Most importantly, in cooperation with the Printing Industry Subcommittee of the ATI/FTI, the Thai Printing Association has successfully attracted the attention of the central JPPCC to the achievements and problems of the service.[36]

In addition to lobbying for specific supportive public measures, a number of export-oriented associations have undertaken some economic activities to improve the performance of their members in the world market. Most common among these activities is perhaps sales campaigning. Associations extensively involved with this are usually those representing emerging fields or fields in which fortunes are sensitive to international image. A notable example is the annual international sales campaign undertaken by the Association of Thai Travel Agents and the Thai Hotel Association. Working hand in hand with the Tourism Authority of Thailand (TAT), both associations have organized many exhibitions abroad on Thai history, culture, tourist spots, and recreational facilities. In 1985 alone 34 exhibitions of this nature were held in several major cities of the world.[37] A few major firms, certainly, can do their own sales promotion, but the remainder still find it too expensive. Moreover, even established firms feel that without the associations and the TAT representatives it is not possible to draw the same amount of attention and confidence from potential visitors to Thailand.

Of equal interest are the innovative efforts by the Thai Printing Association. Every year the association publishes, with the most sophisticated technology available, a handbook on printing in Thailand. The main purpose is to inform potential foreign buyers of the quality, reliability, and relatively low cost of Thai printing. In addition, delegates of the association are sometimes sent to exhibit Thai products in book fairs held abroad. Most recently the association has organized interested members into a trading company, known as "IPEC." This trading company was set up to seek printing service contracts from abroad and then allocate them among members.[38]

Another noteworthy, though incipient, function pursued by industry associations is upgrading the technical capability in their fields to meet the stringent demands of the international market. The Thai Fishery and Frozen Products and the Thai Plastic Industries Associations, two notable examples, have published newsletters and journals which contain information on technology and the market situation. The Thai Plastic Industries Association is often praised by the Industry Ministry for its regularly held seminars on technology and techniques needed to improve Thai plasticware. A plan to open a technical library for its members was also under way by the late 1980s.[39] The Thai Fishery Association, on the other hand, each year organizes four to six conferences on the quality control of processed seafood required to satisfy foreign importers and inspecting agencies.[40] Moreover, it has made regular financial contributions to improve the efficiency of the public agencies responsible for the inspection of exported processed foods. In 1985, for example, the association bought a computer for the Department of Medical Science to be used in the inspection of its products.[41]

As of now there are no reports of technological research and development activities being carried out by business associations. However, plans for this are frequently raised. A couple of years ago the Thai Plastic Industries Association, for example, applied for a grant from the Japanese government to open a research laboratory for its members. In an attempt to improve their efficiency and to become more export-oriented, a few petrochemical industrialists in mid-1987 also formed an association with the goal of jointly investing in large-scale research and development facilities (also discussed in Chapter 5).[42]

Finally, as protectionism in developed countries increasingly poses a threat to Thai exports, some associations have played an important role in settling conflicts with governments and businessmen in those countries. The Thai Textile Manufacturing Association made a large financial contribution to the Thai government's litigation in the US against recent charges of subsidizing textile exports filed by American manufacturers.[43] The Thai Fishery Association often sponsors meetings between Thai officials and processors and inspecting officials of the importing countries to solve problems regarding Thai exports. In May 1985, for example, the association helped sponsor such a meeting with officials from Italy.[44] The Thai Food Processing Association also reportedly hired an American law firm to defend Thai exporters against the efforts by US tuna processors to gain the imposition of an import surcharge on Thai tuna.[45]

Thus, for the first time in the modern economic history of the country, leading local businessmen have—through the work of their associations—contributed significantly to the charting of a new development path. In the old days, by contrast, if there was any input from outsiders into the government's formulation of economic strategy or crucial policies, it was more likely to come from international or foreign agencies, especially the World Bank and the USAID, or from the foreign business community.[a]

Changing the Government's Economic Role

Since the early 1980s prominent business leaders have criticized the government's role in development. In a public meeting in 1981 Kukrit Pramoj, a former prime minister and leading businessman, made a trenchant criticism of what he perceived as the one-sidedness of the government's role,

> Economic growth thus far has been the result of the exclusive efforts and initiatives of businessmen, while the government has been indifferent and passive throughout. Had it been more supportive, more growth should have taken place. . . . [Only] when problems arise does the government step in, mostly to control [business operation] or to regulate selling prices, [though]. . . . This is unacceptable to businessmen since they have never received any support from the government.[46]

In a press interview, Chatri Sophonpanich, a leader of the Bangkok Bank and the Thai Bankers Association, cited official regulation as a major problem for Thai exports:

> A simple way to boost Thai exports is to do away with a myriad of government regulations. . . . These regulations have been continually added . . . . They have never been removed. . . . [These regulations] have led to the loss of [our] market [share] to competitors. They have increased the costs of exporters and delayed our deliveries to importers.[47]

Most importantly, business representatives on the central JPPCC have persistently raised the issues of bureaucratic red tape and delays, stifling laws and rules, and an exorbitant and outdated taxation system, which they regard

---

[a] Not surprisingly, the influence of foreign capitalist-related agencies on Thai decision-making is emphasized by writers of "dependency" perspective. For example, see Grit Permtanjit, "Political Economy of Dependent Capitalist Development: Study of the Limits of the Capacity of the State to Rationalize in Thailand" (Ph.D. dissertation, University of Pennsylvania, 1982). However, it is interesting to note that even a consultant to USAID also admitted that in comparison to external agencies, Thai business organizations traditionally played a very low profile in public policy making. See Wilson Brown, "The Private Sector Institutional and Cultural Environment in Thailand and Suggestions for Facilitating Private Sector's Role in Development" in USAID/Thailand, Thailand Private Sector in Development, project annexes, p. 72.

as a heavy burden placed on themselves and the economy as a whole by the government.

Bureaucratic Red Tape and Delays

An early concern expressed by business at the central JPPCC was about bureaucratic inefficiency. Initially, they raised the problems of unreasonably complicated and time-consuming customs formalities as a major obstacle to the export of Thai products. Later, government red tape and delays in other vital areas were also discussed. These included the handling of business applications for investment promotion, factory and product registration, and the processing of cargo shipping at the international airports.

The government, which had been proud of its bureaucratic tradition, appeared to be receptive to the idea that bureaucratic delays and inefficiency could pose a major obstacle to national development and undermine goodwill between public officials and businessmen. Prime Minister Prem, in his speech given in commemoration of the (central) JPPCC's first anniversary, agreed that it was necessary to adjust the working paces of the government and the private sector. He also held that, "if the private sector goes too fast while the government is left far behind, then imbalance will occur, conflict will arise."[48]

Several problems were thus effectively corrected. As noted earlier, customs and export formalities have been greatly reduced. The government also made it mandatory that official certificates of investment promotion and permission for factory and business operation be issued within 90 days by the concerned agencies, unless there were reasonable grounds for delay or denial.[49] Inspection and registration procedures for controlled products, such as processed food and pharmaceutical products, were also simplified and shortened. Finally, rigid and inefficient export shipping procedures at the airport were greatly improved. Customs processing of shipped items, as mentioned previously, could be carried out 24 hours a day, including holidays. Officials were also instructed to speed up the procedures for transferred cargoes and to complete them within three hours.[50]

Stifling Laws and Rules

A long term grave concern of business in Thailand has been the existence of several stifling laws and rules. Some of them are anachronistic and hence impractical or even embarrassing. For example, a law governing the hotel business which has been in effect for almost half-a-century demands that hotel owners have their fingerprints recorded by the police every year. Business tax laws and rules, long in use, also militate against emerging industries. Based predominantly on the structure of an agricultural economy, existing taxes fall on successive processors of raw materials and inputs and are calculated on accumulated values rather than on added values of the processed products.

Other problematic laws and rules are relatively recent in origin but overly restrictive. Most of them were enacted or decreed solely on the initiative of controlling bureaucratic agencies at the time when business and other extra-bureaucratic groups were not part of the policy-making system. These regulations are directed at monopoly and excessive concentration of wealth and economic power, profiteering, and environmental or health hazards.

Capitalizing on the priority accorded to export promotion by the new official development strategy, which was designed to rectify the deteriorating economic situation during the first half of the 1980s, business representatives pressed the central JPPCC for de-regulation. In response, the government has adjusted many regulatory policies and legislative acts, though a good many of its efforts are still in the process of being completed. Since 1982 the government has tried to liberalize the legislation affecting publicly-owned corporations. By 1987 a few other amendments had been sent to the House of Representatives. One sought to amend a law which put excessive and inflexible control over the manufacture of cosmetics.[51] Another would reduce the penalty for violation of the prohibition on profiteering and monopoly.[52] A new value-added taxation system was also approved by the government and was set to be introduced in the near future.

In addition, a few changes in rules which did not require a long legislative process to make them effective have been made. A notable example of these was the permission given to commercial banks to hold more than 10 percent of the shares in other business enterprises, as of December 1987.[53] Moreover, environmental zoning in certain areas, such as that around the ancient capital of Ayudhya, was adjusted to allow industrial expansion.[54] The Mining Industry Council, a vocal opponent of the government's environmental regulation, has been increasingly consulted by agencies in charge of environmental protection policy.[55]

Excessive Taxation

Of all the problems and issues brought to the central JPPCC by business, complaints about exorbitant rates or unfair collection of taxes, tariffs and duties, and requests for their rectification, probably rank highest in number. Since 1982 a subcommittee has been assigned to review and resolve these problems. During the first five years this subcommittee had to handle at least 55 major rectification requests.[56] Although most requests were aimed at piecemeal concession for special products, services, or trades, a few were comprehensive and systematic. By late 1987 the ATI had submitted at least two major studies and proposals, one calling for a reform in overall tax collection procedures, the other for an introduction of the value-added system, as said earlier.

As a whole, business proposals for concessions on taxes, tariffs, and duties were fairly well received by the government. By mid-1986, of the 55 requests received by the central JPPCC subcommittee on taxes and tariffs, 21 had been accepted but were still in the process of being implemented, twelve had been accepted and implemented to a certain extent, fifteen were under consideration for acceptance, and only seven had been rejected.[57] Refunds to industrialists for tariffs and duties levied on inputs imported for the manufacturing of exports were also increased and delivered more promptly. After a major reform in the Department of Customs in 1984, such refunds increased about 63 percent.[58]

Apart from the above responses to business requests, the government has also improved its supportive role by creating government-business committees or councils at the national level, similar to the central JPPCC, to enhance the communication between business representatives and responsible officials in certain fields deemed to be important by the government. During the past few years joint committees on tapioca, textiles, and mining and natural resources policies, to name a few, have been launched. In addition to these product-based committees, ministry-based committees have also been formed. Between 1986 and 1987 the Ministry of Agriculture and the Ministry of Public health had established ministerial level joint government-business committees to take care of problems and projects of concern to either or both sides.[59] Industry Deputy Minister Korn Tapparangsi explained the rationale of the committee on mining and natural resources policy, which may be applied to all other joint committees, as follows:

> The purpose of the committee is to bring flexibility and speed to the solution of private business problems. . . . [This committee] minimizes the procedural steps between entrepreneurs and the cabinet. [Problems] now go to the cabinet via only one stop, the committee.[60]

Another interesting development is that a few public bodies which are entrusted with the promotion or the support of a private industry, rather than for its control, have come into prominence. These include the Tourism Authority of Thailand (TAT) and the Department of Export Promotion. The best performance is probably that of the TAT. Although its origin dates back to the early 1960s, only in the late 1970s did the TAT begin to play a strong supportive role for the business sector. We have noted that the TAT annually joins with major business associations in the field organizing tourist promotion campaigns abroad. Moreover, it tries to persuade foreign business and media representatives to see Thailand's best tourist spots. In 1985 alone,

231 persons representing major foreign travel agencies and mass media were invited by the TAT for that purpose.[61] Equally important, the TAT takes a leading role in developing provincial tourist spots and holding cultural and historical festivals to promote provincial tourism.

In 1984 the authority and a few leading tourist and hotel associations formed a new trade association, the Thai Convention Promotion Association. This association aims to promote Thailand as a center for large-scale international conferences. The TAT has contributed almost half of the annual budget of the newly created association.[62] This makes it the first public agency to grant a subsidy to a business association.

The TAT is noted for its consultation with the business community. Not only does the authority allow business participation in the drafting of significant legislation or policy, but it also has two businessmen serving in its eleven-man executive board.[63] Leaders and functionaries in the Association of Thai Travel Agents and the Thai Hotel Association, with whom I have interviewed, claim that the TAT has won high praise from the business community for making tourism the number one annual foreign exchange earner several times during the past few years.

Efforts to improve the government's supportive role is also manifest in the involvement of the Foreign Ministry in trade and investment promotion. Traditionally, the ministry was preoccupied with security and political issues. Recent problems of protectionism in industrial countries and business complaints about the lack of government support in the search for overseas markets persuaded the government (in the early 1980s) to order Thai embassies to assume the new duty of supporting Thai exporters and inducing foreign investors and tourists to come to Thailand. Prime Minister Prem also set a precedent by joining with leading businessmen and representatives of business associations to visit foreign countries and to personally introduce Thai exports and tourism as well as to outline the favorable conditions for investment in Thailand. Between 1982 and 1987 nine trips of such a nature were undertaken.[64] Prem's example has been closely followed by Prime Minister Chatichai, his successor.

While it is premature to say that the government has played a supportive role to the satisfaction of business, it is certainly placing more emphasis on that role. Moreover, as is evident from recent remarks by top officials and by the content of some important official documents, the government has a sense of urgency in achieving a fundamental improvement of its supportive work for business operations. The Fifth National Economic and Social Development Plan (1982-1986) identified inefficient government support of the private sector as a major obstacle to Thai development. This plan also called for a lessening of official intervention in the economy and a revision of laws and rules that were obstructive to business performance. The Sixth National Economic and Social Development Plan (1987-1991) made an explicit statement that the government would place more emphasis on its supportive role than its regulative role in relation to private business operation. Snoh Unakul of the NESDB saw government administration as the most formidable obstacle to Thailand's international competitiveness, which was in turn the key to the success of the economy. To survive in the world market, Snoh insisted:

> We must increase the efficiency of our business and economic system. . . . We must emphasize competition, not protectionism. . . . The [most important] problem is government administration. If we do not improve it [first], we cannot correct any other thing. . . . Existing laws, rules, and procedures rid us of efficiency.[65]

Leadership in Provincial Development

The role of business in economic development policy-making is not played exclusively by Bangkok business associations. In recent years provincial chambers of commerce have entered the limelight and started to exert their leadership in provincial development. Historically, provincial businessmen received little attention from the state and their role in public policy-making was even more peripheral than that of their Bangkok counterparts. Provincial development, on the other hand, has attracted substantial attention from the government. To stem a nationwide rural insurgency movement led by the communists, between the 1960s and the 1970s governments invested considerably in provincial—particularly rural—economic development. However, provincial businessmen had a minimal role in this development which was initiated and controlled by rural development agencies of the government. Worse, businessmen were at times portrayed by the critical press and public officials as economic exploiters who drove poor villagers into communist hands.

However, through chambers of commerce, provincial businessmen have recently formed significant interest groups. Their activities have been extensively covered in the Thai business press. Well-known Thai business newspapers and magazines now have special sections devoted to provincial business in which the complaints and demands of chambers of commerce are frequently reported. Leaders of several chambers have suggested to me that the creation of the JPPCCs, the expertise and inspiration they received from NIDA-IMET educational programs, and a sense of solidarity among themselves have been prime reasons for their activism.

Most importantly, a desire to share leadership in local development has emerged among leaders of provincial chambers. In his 1984 inauguration speech, the founding president of the Lampang Chamber of Commerce pointed out to his fellow businessmen that,

> We used to rely too much on the government and the officials for the development of our province. We must realize that provincial authorities are all appointees from Bangkok, who come and go. They can hardly have a greater desire for the progress of the province than we do.[66]

In early 1987 the official journal of the Songkhla Chamber was devoted to the topic: "It's about time to show that we are the owners of the province." The editorial reads in part:

> It's about time local businessmen join hands to push for, not only their interests, but also the progress of the province. . . . [We should not] let the officials handle this [development] alone . . . [for] they are often preoccupied with other things. They are not well versed in everything. . . . Above all, who knows local needs better than we, local people, do? Bureaucrats who get transferred out every few years can hardly know local needs.[67]

Through political and economic activities, chambers of commerce have dealt with issues of provincial development, such as infrastructure, business climate, and the decentralization of administrative and economic power from Bangkok.

Infrastructure

Due to the poor economic institutions and infrastructure and the low supply of skilled manpower in the provinces as compared to Bangkok, several provincial chambers have asked the government to vigorously improve these deficiencies.[68] For example, in the North, the Chiangmai Chamber requested that the local airport be upgraded to an international airport and the Nakorn Sawan Chamber asked for a deep-water commercial port. In the Northeast, the Nakorn Ratchasima Chamber urged the government to expand the main highway which links the province to Bangkok. Several Northeast chambers have also expressed the need for an increase in telephone services in their provinces. In the South, the Krabi Chamber urged the government to establish a sophisticated fishery experimental station in the province. In the Central Plain, the Nontaburi Chamber called for a central market for vegetable and farm products.

Apart from asking the government to address these problems, some chambers have planned to operate enterprises that would augment the economic infrastructure in their provinces. The Sakol Nakon Chamber has considered providing public bus services, thus far lacking, in its town centers. The Chainat Chamber has discussed the feasibility of modernizing the provincial bus terminal. Most interesting and most likely to succeed is perhaps the Nakorn Pathom Chamber's attempt to launch a large-scale slaughter house with a modern sanitation system which will greatly improve the quality of pork, one of the principal exports of the province. The project has been granted financial assistance of about US$ 7.5 million from Japan and is well under way.[69]Legally, business associations are barred from engaging in any commercial activities.[70] To surmount this restriction, chambers simply initiate ideas and then encourage interested members to make a joint investment in needed infrastructure items.

As for human resource development, provincial chambers have organized educational conferences and seminars, at times in cooperation with the NIDA-IMET, for local businessmen. The following is an illustrative list of topics covered by their educational programs in the past few years: how to understand and file your new tax form; how to use personal calculator in your business; basic modern management for small firms; the impact of currency devaluation; basic investment and trade problems in our area; philosophy and the role of provincial chambers. According to Amorn Wongsurawat, an experienced president of provincial chamber, the purposes of these programs "were to familiarize local business people with public policy issues, to increase their sophistication in economic and business science reasoning and to arouse their public concern."[71]In addition, in cooperation with some universities, some leading chambers, such as the Konkaen, Nakorn Ratchasima, and Chiangmai Chambers, have opened formal short-course programs in business administration for interested members and outsiders. Graduates of these programs receive a "mini-MBA" degree.

More recently some chambers have also started educational seminars for farmers, who comprise the overwhelming majority of the provincial population. The Rayong Chamber, for example, organized a seminar on the topic "growing pineapples the profitable way" for about 200 farmers.[72] The Yasothorn Chamber, in cooperation with a local college, initiated an educational program on modern agricultural concepts and methods for farmers in the province.[73]

Business Climate

In recent years several provincial chambers have initiated activities to stimulate the local economy as well as to attract investors, buyers, and tourists from elsewhere to their provinces. Most publicized of these activities seems to be the organization of provincial trade fairs or other festivities. For example, in Samut Sakorn, a coastal province with an economy heavily dependent on marine and fishery products, a celebrated seafood fair was opened by Prime Minister Prem in 1986 when the chamber was merely two years old.

In the Central Plain region between September 1985 and September 1986, the Nakorn Pathom Chamber organized four provincial trade fairs to promote its most noted local products: fruit and processed pork. The fairs attracted many Bangkok and foreign visitors and produced total sales of over US$ 800,000.[74] In the North in early 1987 the Lampang Chamber took part in a revived ancient festival which featured a colorful procession and a spectacular sound and light show. The purpose of the festival was to highlight local history, preserve traditional arts and custom and, importantly, promote tourism.[75] More recently, in the Northeast, the Nakorn Ratchasim Chamber (at the invitation of the TAT) even despatched a troupe of local artists to perform in Singapore to attract tourists and investors to their province.[76]

Decentralization

Business leadership in provincial development is not limited to economic issues. Over the past few years provincial chambers have challenged Bangkok's predominance in the Thai political economy. Because of Thailand's heavy centralization of decision-making power, provincial businessmen often find that their requests for government permits, licenses, and registrations are unduly delayed and complicated. In various JPPCC meetings since 1983 chambers of commerce have requested that the making of official decisions be delegated to provincial authorities. As a result, the government now allows a number of business-related procedures to be undertaken directly in the provinces. For example, the provincial offices of the Industry Ministry, are now entitled to issue factory registration renewals. The ministry's effort to have machinery registration done directly in the provinces is also in progress.[77] Finally, a few mining industry permits are obtainable at the provincial offices of the ministry.[78]

More recently provincial chambers have targeted Bangkok business as well. Being small or medium-sized borrowers, provincial businessmen have always been charged higher interest rates than their Bangkok equivalents. With new strength in their inter-provincial movement, these businessmen challenged the traditional rule. In early 1987 several chambers sent letters to private banks as well as the central Bank of Thailand and the TBA, asking for the rectification of what they perceived as unfair and unequal treatment.[79] Another noteworthy provincial business challenge to Bangkok big business was their successful block of compulsory membership of the FTI in the latter half of 1987, described in some detail in Chapter 5.

Although their leadership of provincial development has not been firmly established and their actual successes in decentralization issues are still limited, provincial chambers of commerce are strengthening rapidly and can at least break the monopoly of public agencies on provincial development. Equally significant, they plan to strive for more effective decentralization of political and economic power from Bangkok.

After a major victory over the issue of compulsory membership in the FTI, Nipon Wongtrangan, president of the Pijit Chamber and a key figure in that fight, disclosed:

> The opposition to the FTI is, hopefully, but a prelude to a major change in the Thai political economy yet to come. Our long term goal, to be obtained in ten to twenty years, is to put an end to the practice of "Thailand is Bangkok." We will strive for a systematic transfer of power to the provincial areas.[80]

Although the above statement sounds overly optimistic, it is interesting to keep an eye on the future role of this potentially innovative force.

Limits to Business Influence

The preceding analysis of business leadership and its impact on political and economic development by no means implies that the government has become the captive of organized business. While the state has given much thought and made several concessions to business complaints, initiatives, and demands in most economic sectors, it has displayed a distinctive autonomy in financial and security exchange affairs. The following cases should illustrate this point.

Streamlining the Financial Businesses

Between 1983 and 1986 Thailand was stricken with a financial crisis which resulted from the mismanagement of a few family-owned banks and financial companies. Businesses run by families who owned these financial institutions were frequently awarded loans, regardless of their credit-worthiness. In addition to this, too large a portion of customers' deposits was carelessly invested in high return, but high risk areas—especially real estate. Problems arising from these unprofessional loan and investment policies were at times aggravated by dishonest directors or managers who plagued their own banks or finance companies with various forms of embezzlement. Nevertheless, these poorly managed financial institutions did not find themselves in really deep trouble until another challenging investment opportunity became available to them—stock brokerage.

A stock market sponsored and regulated by the government, but run by the private sector, has been in operation in Thailand since the mid-1970s. A few years after its inception the fledgling market underwent a series of high growth periods between the late 1970s and the early 1980s. The possibility of securing a lucrative return from this booming business led private financial institutions, particularly nonbanking finance companies, to invest heavily and recklessly on the stock exchange. Some finance companies even engaged in the rigging of the stock market for quick profits.

By 1983 the impact of these abusive practices began to be felt when a few mismanaged finance companies suffered serious liquidity problems. Frantic cash withdrawals by depositors brought these companies to the brink of bankruptcy and posed a threat to the whole financial sector. The stock market was also affected since most finance companies rushed to sell to ensure their own liquidity. As a result, the prices of most listed securities plunged.

In response to this crisis, the government created stabilization funds from which trouble-ridden financial institutions could borrow. More significantly, it also introduced legislative measures to streamline the businesses themselves. The 1983 legislative amendment on nonbanking financial businesses forbade finance companies to award loans to their directors,[81] and required that a person assuming a position in the directorship or management of a finance company must meet professional and educational standards set by the Bank of Thailand. Finance companies that failed to issue regular financial statements at a specified time, or to maintain a specified amount of cash reserves, or to contain business loss within a specified limit, might be ordered by the Bank of Thailand to discontinue their operations.

Two legislative amendments in 1985 on banking and nonbanking financial businesses introduced even more stringent measures.[82] A major highlight of these amendments, according to Supachai Panitchpak, a senior official entrusted with the control and investigation of financial institutions, was to give preemptive power to the Bank of Thailand. They required, for example, that "suggestions" issued by the Bank of Thailand to troubled financial institutions that they change their management, raise the amount of their registered capital, or merge with other companies to avoid problems of too little liquidity and bankruptcy, had to be obeyed as if they were resolutions of the shareholders.[83]

The stock market, on the other hand, was restructured by the 1984 amendment of the Security Exchange of Thailand Act. Above all, manipulation of the market became a criminal offense. The amendment also required that the directors (and their spouses) of the stock market and the stock trading companies make public reports of their securities trading on the market.[84]

It must be noted that most amendments mentioned above were introduced as emergency decrees (Pra Raj Kamnod) issued by the executive branch of the government. Under Thai law, unless the House of

Representatives fails to ratify them afterwards, such decrees have the same force as acts passed by the legislature in the normal way. Business associations were allowed little role in the drafting of these amendments as the chief initiators of these emergency laws were public agencies. The 1983 amendment to the legislation on nonbanking financial businesses was instigated by the Bank of Thailand.[85] The Bank of Thailand and the Ministry of Finance also designed the amendment to the legislation on banking business in 1985 without any consultation with the influential TBA.[86] Especially noteworthy is the fact that no cabinet members other than the prime minister, the finance minister and one of his two deputies, all of whom were nonparty men, knew of this amendment until it was sent to the cabinet. Even the other deputy minister of finance, who came from a political party and had a business background, had not been informed beforehand.[87]

The 1984 amendment to the Security Exchange of Thailand Act was the only one of its kind that was sent to the House of Representatives for approval before becoming effective (Pra Raj Banyat). However, even in this case the Association of the Members of the Security Exchange had not been consulted. According to the association's vice-president, the government had kept secret the details of the amendment until it was sent to the House.[88]

These newly introduced legislative measures have been rigorously enforced. Two member banks of the TBA had their directorships purged and both were put under the close administrative control of the Bank of Thailand between 1984 and 1986. Between December 1983 and September 1985 the government revoked the business licenses of twelve finance companies.[89] Many more companies, while still in operation, were put under the administrative control of the Bank of Thailand. This was partly responsible for a marked decrease in the membership of the Thai Finance and Securities Association, representing nonbanking financial businesses at that time. By early 1985 only 43 companies remained in the association, compared with 101 in 1981.[90] Because of this, the remaining members decided to disband the association.

Thus, in restructuring the financial and capital sectors, the government did not seek the active participation of the relevant associations; rather, official regulation and control of companies or banks actually led to the demise of a principal association in these sectors.

Stabilizing the Balance of Payment

The capacity of the government to make economic policy without business input if it so chose was also demonstrated in its efforts to stabilize the international balance of payments of the country between 1983 and 1984. After a few years of recession the Thai economy grew rapidly in 1983, with a major adverse side-effect: a more than doubling of its trade deficit. As a result, the current account deficit as a percentage of GDP jumped from 2.7 percent in the previous year to 7.1 percent, while the debt service ratio, as a percentage of total export values, increased from 16.6 percent to 19.5 percent. (See Table 6.2.)

TABLE 6.2 Balance of Payments (US$ Million), 1979-1983

	1979	1980	1981	1982	1983
Trade Balance:	-2,304	-2,829	-3,022	-1,571	-3,871
Exports	5,235	6,448	6,902	6,835	6,306
Imports	-7,539	-9,277	-9,924	-8,406	-10,177
Service Balance	158	544	284	382	727
Transfers (Net)	60	208	169	183	277
Current Account Balance	-2,086	-2,077	-2,569	-1,066	-2,867
Current Account Deficit (% of GDP)	7.7	6.2	6.9	2.7	7.1
Debt Service Ratio (% of exports)	14.6	14.8	14.8	16.6	19.5

Source: World Bank, *Thailand: Managing Public Resources for Structural Adjustment*, (Washington, D.C.: World Bank Publication, 1984), Table 2.1, p. 34.

Reading these as signals of the dangerous financial position of the country, the Bank of Thailand in December 1983 tried to curtail imports by imposing a ceiling on L/C credit given to importers. In January 1984 it also ordered commercial banks to curb the expansion of the total credit lines given to customers in general to an annual rate of 18 percent, a marked reduction from the uncontrolled rate of 32.4 percent of the previous year.[91]

The credit limit policy brought difficulties for a large section of the business community. Payments made by bad checks all over the country in the first four months of 1984 amounted to US$ 1.07 billion, nearly three times the US$ 388 million of the same period in the previous year.[92] Small businesses were particularly hard hit as the average interest rate in the unofficial market in February 1984 was reportedly as high as 36 percent, compared to the official rate of 17-19 percent.[93] Middle and upper middle businesses were also affected. Most members of the National Federation of Textile Industries and the Thai Rice Mills Association, for example, suffered heavily from the 18 percent credit control, according to their presidents.[94]

While big businesses were believed to be least affected by the measure, there were indications that they too did not see it in a good light. For example, the Board of Trade and the TCC asked the government several times to discontinue the 18 percent credit policy, in "both formal meetings and, especially, informal discussions with senior officials including the prime minister."[95] In a JPPCC meeting the TBA also reportedly requested that the government loosen its grip on the 18 percent credit policy.[96]

It was not business association opposition, but a confidential memorandum by Deputy Prime Minister Bhichai Rattakul to Prime Minister Prem, that brought an end to the controversial policy in August 1984.[97] That memorandum cited the relative success of the policy in keeping the trade deficit under control alongside the disproportionately negative effects of the policy on small and middle businesses as the reason for the government to end the 18 percent credit policy. The fact that Bichai had a business background and was well connected with major associations may suggest that business influence eventually worked. This claim of business influence through Bichai, however, is yet to be substantiated. More important is that the government had even so been able to resist business resistance for almost a year. Further evidence of the autonomy of the government is obtainable from another incident occurring just months after the discontinuation of the 18 percent credit policy.

In November of that same year (1984) the government came up with another "surgical" measure, a 15 percent devaluation of the baht. This devaluation was the third undertaken by Prem and was one of the largest in decades. It was also a decision that was courageously taken, considering that it came just two months after the ending of the credit control policy. The finance minister, furthermore, had told Parliament early that year that there would be no currency devaluation within twelve months. However, as soon as the devaluation decision was made public, it was the military rather than the business community which made a bold move to contest it. The supreme commander of the armed forces made a fiery attack on the government decision on television. He also joined with a few other top military leaders in publicly making a request for a cabinet reshuffle. The reasons for their dissatisfaction were that the supreme commander had not been informed beforehand of this decision and that the budget for weapons purchases from abroad had shrunk considerably in real terms after the devaluation.

During this critical moment the business community kept silent, although there was a report that some top businessmen swiftly sold their international currencies in anticipation of a government reversal of its devaluation decision to avoid a showdown with the military.[98] The government, however, was adamant and the military finally conceded. The decisiveness of the government even under military threat might account for the absence of business efforts to resist or deflect this devaluation afterwards.

To sum up, in restoring the country's balance of payments, government autonomy was displayed. Decisions that ran against the immediate interests of a large section of the business community were made secretly by a handful of policy-makers. Associations were neither informed nor consulted beforehand; nor could business resistance effectively oppose or deflect the government decisions. Even the intimidating military could not change the course of the government; the government appeared to be autonomous in its relation with its armed forces as well.

Conclusion

Thus, organized business has played a positive role in the recent economic development. In a marked departure from the past, leading business figures working through their associations have taken part in the charting of a new development strategy, an export-oriented one, for the country. On top of that, specialized associations have organized political and economic activities to promote the export of their products or services. Furthermore, associations have been vocal proponents of a more supportive role of the government in relation to business operations. They have also asked for a reduction or rationalization of government regulations and the tax system. Finally, in the provincial areas where extra-bureaucratic groups were traditionally weakest, emerging chambers of commerce have striven for a leading role in local development.

Despite the general increase in the economic role of business associations, the government has apparently retained its autonomy in the financial, monetary and security exchange areas. Unlike other sectors, associations in these sectors have not been able to exert much influence on public decision-making. The government has not solicited business opinions or sought the consent of business in deciding critical issues or in restructuring business operations in these sectors in difficult times.

Notes

1. *Ruam Prachachart Turakij,* January 27, 1979, p. 2.

2. *Ruam Prachachart Turakij,* January 17, 1981, pp. 1, 12; September 26, 1981, p. 2.

3. This is a major criticism of business associations made by Narong in his study. See Narong Petchprasert,"Samakom Karnka Lae Ho Karnka Nai Pratet Tai" [Trade Associations and Chambers of Commerce in Thailand] (M.A.thesis, Thammasat University, 1975), pp. 130-137.

4. Section 22 of the Trade Association Act; Section 29 of the Chamber of Commerce Act.

5. A major example is tapioca exporting to the EC countries.

6. *Ruam Prachachart Turakij,* December 9, 1981, p. 6.

7. Nipon Wongtrangan, vice-president of the Thai Rice Mills Association, interview, June 8, 1987; *Ruam Prachachart Turakij,* July 15, 1982, p. 4.

8. *Ruam Prachachart Turakij,* November 21, 1981, p. 1.

9. *Ruam Prachachart Turakij,* April 25, 1981, pp. 6, 7.

10. See various editorials, articles and comments in *Ruam Prachachart Turakij* during the latter half of 1981 for example.

11. *Ruam Prachachart Turakij,* April 1, 1981, p. 2; April 25, 1981, p. 1

12. *Ruam Prachachart Turakij,* April 1, 1981, p. 2; May 16, 1981, p. 1.

13. *Ruam Prachachart Turakij,* December 9, 1981, p. 6.

14. For example, Frederic Deyo, ed., *The Political Economy of the New Asian Industrialism* (Ithaca: Cornell University Press, 1987); Leroy Jones and Il Sakong, *Government, Business, and Entrepreneurship in Economic Development: The Korean Case* (Cambridge: Harvard University Press, 1980).

15. Chalmers Johnson, "Political Institutions and Economic Performance: The Government-Business Relationship in Japan, South Korea, and Taiwan," in Deyo, ed., *The Political Economy,* pp. 149-151.

16. Leroy and Sakong, *Government, Business and Entrepreneurship,* pp. 66-69; Frederic Deyo, "Coalition, Institutions, and Linkage Sequencing—Toward a Strategic Capacity Model of East Asian Development," in Deyo ed., *The Political Economy,* pp. 230-232.

17. World Bank, *Thailand: Managing Public Resources for Structural Adjustment* (Washington, D.C.: World Bank Publication, 1984), Table 2.2, p.7.

18. *Asia Year Book 1979,* p. 313.

19. M.L. Prachaksilp Thongyai, a co-secretary of that joint public-private committee, interview, November 17, 1987.

20. *Ruam Prachachart Turakij,* May 28-June 3, 1978, p. 6.

21. Taworn Pornprapa, interview, August 13, 1987.

22. Sataporn Kawitanont, interview, November 17, 1987. Sataporn was a secretary to that committee who was appointed by the government side.

23. Boonchu Rochanasathian, interview, November 10, 1987.

24. Snoh Unakul, JPPCC secretary, interview, August 4, 1987; see also *Ruam Prachachart Turakij,* "Rattaban Nad Ekachon Tok Toh Sang Uppasak Karn Song Ok" [Government and business continued to talk about obstacles to export], September 9, 1981, p. 12,

25. Suwannee Samrong, "Kanton Lae Pitikarn Song Ok Kon Lae Lang Karn Prabprung" [Export procedures and formalities before and after the improvement], in *Settakij Lae Sangkom,* July-August, 1984, p. 25.

26. Ibid.,p. 43.

146

27. World Bank, *Thailand: Industrial Development Strategy in Thailand* (Washington, D.C.: East Asia and Pacific Regional Office, 1980).

28. Vijit Na Ranong, interview, July 19, 1987.

29. Seree Wangspaichit, a deputy governor of the Tourism Authority of Thailand, interview, November 19, 1987.

30. Prapat Suthaves, ATTA manager, interview, November 12, 1987.

31. Government of Thailand, *Pan Pattana Settakij Lae Sangkokm Haeng Chat Chabab Ti Hok (Po So 2530-2534)* [The Sixth National Economic and Social Development Plan, 1987-1991] (NESDB: 1986), sections on: The Plan for the Development of Production System, Marketing, and Employment Generation; The Plan for the Development of Urban and Special Areas.

32. Snoh Unakul, interview, August 4, 1987.

33. Kongsak Lopongpanitch, secretary-general of the Thai Printing Association, interview, September 29, 1987.

34. Kongsak Lopongpanitch, interview, September 29, 1987.

35. *Chodmai Kao*, January-June, 1987, p. 3.

36. Kongsak Lopongpanitch, interview, September 29, 1987; Chakramont Pasukwanij, interview, January 3, 1991.

37. Annual Report of the Tourism Authority of Thailand for 1985, p.28.

38. Kongsak Lopongpanitch, interview, September 29, 1987.

39. Siriporn Apirakkunwong, former manager of the Thai Plastic Industries Association, interview, June 25, 1987.

40. Nipapan Bunyanan, manager of the Thai Fishery and Frozen Products Association, interview, July 3, 1987.

41. Annual Report of the Thai Fishery and Frozen Products, 1985.

42. Conversation with a key founder of the Petrochemical Industries Association, July 1, 1987.

43. Kamol Tantivanich, manager of the Thai Textile Manufacturing Association, interview, June 30, 1987.

44. Annual Report of the Thai Food Processing Association, 1985.

45. *Ruam Prachachart Turakij*, March 10, 1984, p. 1.

46. *Ruam Prachachart Turakij*, April 22, 1981, p. 12.

47. Chatri Sophonpanich, interview, in *Ruam Prachachart Turakij*, January 6, 1982, p.3.

48. Chakrit Chulakasewi, ed., *Ha Pi Ko Ro Au: Hontang Haeng Kwam Samrej Kong Settakij Tai* [Five Years of the JPPCCs: Pathway to Thai Economic Success] (Bangkok: NESDB, 1986), p.20.

49. Ibid., p. 21.

50. Government of Thailand, *Pramual Pol-Ngarn, 1986*, pp. 33-34.

51. Government of Thailand, *Pramual Pol-Ngarn, 1987*, p. 12.

52. Government of Thailand, *Pramual Pol-Ngarn, 1987,* pp. 40-41.

53. Government of Thailand, *Pramual Pol-Ngarn, 1987*, p. 37.

54. Government of Thailand, *Pramual Pol-Ngarn, 1987,* p .2.

55. Annual Reports of the Mining Industry Council, 1983-84, and 1985.

56. Analyzed from data given in the section on the achievements of the subcommittee, published in Government of Thailand, *Pramual Pol-Ngarn, 1986,* pp. 36-68.

57. Analyzed from data given in Government of Thailand, *Pramual Pol-Ngarn, 1986*, pp. 36-68.

58. Government of Thailand, *Pramual Pol-Ngarn, 1986*, p. 31.

59. Government of Thailand, *Pramual Pol-Ngarn, 1987,* pp. 126-127 and pp. 148-149.

60. Korn Tapparangsi, interview, in *Sapa Karn Muang-Rae*, June 1987, p. 79.

61. Tourism Authority of Thailand, Annual Report 1985, p. 31.

62. Savali Siripol, marketing executive of the Thai Convention Promotion Association, interview, October 30, 1987.

63. Annual Report of the Tourism Authority of Thailand, p. 9.

64. Government of Thailand, *Pramual Pol-Ngarn, 1987*, pp. 7-8.

65. Snoh Unakul, speech reprinted in *Ruam Prachachart Turakij*, August 14, 1985, p.9.

66. Prayoon Chivasantikarn, president of the Lampang Chamber of Commerce, interview, June 13, 1987.

67. *Ho Karnka Changwat Songkhla*, February, 1987, p.3.

68. Information in this paragraph is taken from various issues of *Ko Ro Au Sampan.*

69. *Ruam Prachachart Turakij*, January 14, 1987, p. 11.

70. Section 22 of the Trade Association Act; Section 29 of the Chamber of Commerce Act.

71. Amorn Wongsurawat, interview, February 9, 1987.

72. *Ho Karnka Changwat Rayong*, November, 1987, pp. 1, 7.

73. *Ruam Prachachart Turakij*, May 2, 1987, p. 10.

74. Compiled from the data given in the Annual Report, 1985-1986 of the chamber.

75. *Ho Karnka Changwat Lampang*, December 1986, p. 1.

148

76. *Ho Karnka Changwat Nakorn Ratchasima*, October 1987.

77. Government of Thailand, *Pramual Pol-Ngarn, 1986*, pp. 105, 107.

78. Government of Thailand, *Pramual Pol-Ngarn, 1987*, p. 107.

79. *Ruam Prachachart Turakij*, February 28-March 3, 1987, p. 13.

80. Nipon Wongtrangan, president of the Pijit Chamber and a leader of the Inter-Provincial Chamber, interview, August 26, 1987.

81. The 1983 Decree on the Amendment of the 1979 Act on Financing, Security Exchange and Credit Foncea Businesses, Section 8.

82. The 1985 Decree on the Amendment of the 1979 Act on Financing and Credit Foncea Businesses and the 1985 Decree on the Amendment of the 1962 Act on Banking Business.

83. *Dok Bia*, February 1986, pp. 101-102.

84. *Ruam Prachachart Turakij*, July 13, 1983, p. 1.

85. Rerngchai Marakanont, interview, in *Dok Bia*, February, 1984, p. 94.

86. *Ruam Prachachart Turakij*, November 6, 1985, pp. 1,13.

87. *Ruam Prachachart Turakij*, November 16, 1985, pp. 1, 13.

88. *Ruam Prachachart Turakij*, July 13, 1984, p. 1.

89. The Association of Finance Companies, *Turakij Ngern-Tun Nai Pratet Tai 2529* [Financial Business in Thailand, 1986] (Bangkok: no date), pp. 45-46.

90. The Association of the Finance Companies, *Turakij Ngern-Tun Nai Pratet Tai 2529*, p. 10.

91. Rattakorn Asdorntirayut, *2527 Pi Haeng Prawatsart Karn-Ngern* [1984: An Historical Year in Monetary History] (Bangkok: Dok Bia Press, no date), p. 1.

92. A confidential memorandum by Deputy Prime Minister Bichai Rattakul to Prime Minister Prem, dated August 17, 1984, reprinted in *Ruam Prachachart Turakij*, August 29, 1984, pp. 20,21,23. (The figures were converted to US dollars by this writer.)

93. *Ruam Prachachart Turakij*, February 1, 1984, p. 1.

94. "Patikiriya 18 percent Kon Ko Ku Kao Wa Yang Ngai" [Reaction to 18 percent credit control, how borrowers think], in *Ruam Prachachart Turakij*, August 29, 1984, p. 20.

95. Chanond Aranyakananda, TCC executive secretary, interview, July 24, 1987.

96. Rattakorn, *2527 Pi Haeng Prawatsart Karn-Ngern*, p. 66.

97. Reprinted in *Ruam Prachachart Turakij*, August 29, 1984, pp. 20, 21, 23.

98. Rattakorn, *2527 Pi Haeng Prawatsart Karn-Ngern*, p. 5.

7

Liberal Corporatism: The Thai Model

As the conclusion of this book, the final chapter presents a theoretical analysis of the political and economic impact of business associations as well as their relations with the government over the past decade. It also puts the Thai government-business relationship in comparative perspective. The major purpose here is to answer the following questions: Is Thailand still a bureaucratic polity? Does pluralism or corporatism better describe the government-business relationship? What implications does the Thai case have for the study of Third World development?

The Decline of the Bureaucratic Polity

We have noted that during much of the period between 1932 and 1973 Thailand was a classic bureaucratic polity. The country was under the rule of military governments or electorally derived governments which relied heavily on the support of the armed forces. Most premiers and cabinet members of both kinds of governments were either serving or retired military or civilian bureaucrats. Political parties, whenever allowed to operate, were often either the creation or were under the patronage of leading politicians-cum-bureaucrats. Interest groups were few in number and weak in action. Extra-bureaucratic forces were thus unable to control or guide the government which was marked by "the domination of the official class as a ruling class."[1] Major policy decisions were made by the military-bureaucratic elite who occupied both the political and administrative positions of the government, almost without input from nonbureaucratic groups.

Although the Thai economy was organized along the line of capitalism, the influence of organized business on the policy formation of the government was minimal. Businessmen could affect public policy only

149

defensively and in a covert, particularistic manner; and the effect was felt in the implementation stage rather than in the formulation stage of policy. The prevailing forms of the instrumental influence of business were the outright giving of bribes, and more importantly for big business enterprises, the creation of clientelistic ties with military-bureaucratic leaders. Saying this is not to deny the structural influence of business on the policy-making of the government in those bureaucratic polity years.

Charles Lindblom, a pluralist writer, has observed that in a capitalist society, business is in a very privileged position to extract policy concessions from the government because "jobs, prices, production, growth, the standard of living, and the economic security of everyone" as well as the consequent government stability depend on the performance of businessmen.[2] "A major function of government, therefore, is to see to it that businessmen perform their tasks."[3] However, in a capitalist system businessmen cannot be simply commanded to perform by the government. Rather, they must be induced or encouraged with various incentives, such as tax concessions, subsidies, loans, inexpensive labor costs, the provision of necessary infrastructure, and the existence of a sound socio-political environment.[4]

Writing in a Marxist tradition, Fred Block has also pointed out that in a capitalist economy, the state is structurally compelled to pursue policies favorable to the capitalists because of the latter's overwhelming control over the investment process and over various types of wealth and institutions in the society.[5] No less important is the fact that "a market economy creates periodic economic crises" which "threaten social dislocation and social rebellion."[6]

In summary, according to both Lindblom and Block, the government is impelled to grant businessmen a great many of policy benefits due to their strategic importance to the growth and stability of the capitalist economy. Following the logic outlined above, one may argue, as Kevin Hewison does, that the absence of channels and institutions through which business might influence the government policy-making process—most relevant here being the absence of strong business associations—does not mean that business exerts no influence on public policy.[7] Hewison correctly pointed out that the notion of bureaucratic polity introduced by Riggs overlooked the economic-structural constraints that "pariah entrepreneurs" could impose on the government even when the bureaucratic polity was at its zenith.[8]

Be that as it may, the structural influence of Thai business was probably not substantial during the pre-1973 period, since the economy was still in an early stage of capitalism. As late as 1970, agriculture, which was dominated by self-employed small farmers, employed about 80 percent of the Thai population.[9] Just as important, according to a World Bank mission, until Marshal Sarit came to power in the late 1950s, only 2 percent of industrial enterprises were classifiable as large, i.e., with more than 50 employees.[10]

Of the total 306 large industrial enterprises, 40 belonged to the government;[11] these government-owned enterprises were the most modern of the country's large enterprises.[12] In terms of investment, during the period 1952-1957 the proportion of gross fixed investment made by the government in relation to that made by private business ranged from 47 percent to 62 percent.[13] (Later, by contrast, in the 1970-79 period gross fixed investment by the government accounted for only 28 percent of the total investment.)[14]

In addition, the structural influence of business is determined to a great extent by the culture or ideology prevailing in the society. To the extent that public officials and the general public alike firmly believe that private property is inviolable, that entrepreneurs are also delivering goods for the public when they make a profit, and that government should not participate in commercial or industrial activities, then economic structural influence works effectively in the interests of business. Such was not the case during the time of the bureaucratic polity. Economic nationalism, which led to the establishment of extensive public enterprises and the occasional harassment of Chinese entrepreneurs, was a major official doctrine from the early 1930s to the late 1940s. In the 1950s, while economic nationalism subsided, anti-(Chinese) communism was another convenient justification that officials could employ to deter activities considered to be abuses of economic power, or simply to extort money from businessmen. The vulnerability of Chinese businessmen when confronted with the Thai authorities, and the low regard accorded to them by the public, were put dramatically by a Thai newspaper in the 1950s as follows:

> It is easiest in the world to bleed Chinese in our country. Merely preferring a charge of being communist or having communist tendencies is more than sufficient for members of the police to obtain huge sums of money from them as they please.[15]

In brief, although the assimilation of ethnic Chinese into Thai society from the long historical standpoint proceeded steadily, until the 1970s there was still a notable distinction between Chinese entrepreneurs and the indigenous Thais. This hindered the acceptance of the belief that in the final analysis the interests of business are also the interests of the public.

Moreover, even when the structural influence of business has been substantial, it has not substituted for instrumental influence. Without business inputs in public policy-making, officials may not know accurately what business needs. At times the government and the business community may strongly disagree on what they perceive to be the best policy to serve the interest of business. Evidently, despite his pro-business policies, Premier Thanin, who presided over a revived but short-lived bureaucratic polity

152

between 1976 and 1977, ended up alienating a large section of the business community. In other words, though Hewison was justified in entertaining the possibility that the Thai bureaucratic polity may have been a "capitalist state" in the sense of a state "for" the capitalists, it surely has not been a state run "by" the capitalists. This makes a real difference and the Thai capitalists have shown during the past decade that they are no longer complacent about having the capitalist state run exclusively by the bureaucrats. Businessmen need organizations and channels to present their views to the government or to reach a compromise with it whenever disagreement occurs if their interests are to be served.

It should be noted too that the business community is not a homogeneous entity. Different public policies have different consequences for the interests of particular sectors or industries. Consequently, competing business groups need their own organizations to determine viewpoints within their own ranks and to contend or compromise with other groups if they are to secure a desirable public policy on any particular issue. Bob Jessop, an unorthodox Marxist scholar, has even claimed that business associations are a necessary venue for a dominant capitalist faction to convince other factions, as well as the state, of an overall strategy that the economy should have in a particular period.[16]

All of these said, the findings of this study support the claim that the Thai bureaucratic polity is in rapid transition. Business associations, both in Bangkok and the provinces, have become assertive and articulate interest groups. Sino-Thais who have been well assimilated into Thai culture have constituted the core of trade associations, provincial chambers of commerce, and their peak organizations. Foreign businessmen or executives play a small role in business associations, except in nationality-based foreign chambers of commerce. Since foreign chambers of commerce are not active or publicized, business associations are generally regarded as indigenous organizations and are well accepted by the Thai polity.

Since the late 1970s organized business has advised, initiated, transformed, or blocked important economic policy and legislation of the government. Above all, business associations have played a leading role in the formation of the central JPPCC, which has become the center of government-business relations. Associations have been instrumental in proposing an export-oriented strategy for the country as well. Successive tax and tariff reductions as well as removals of bureaucratic delays and inefficiency to cut costs for local businessmen competing in the world market have also been prompted by the requests of organized business. Even provincial chambers of commerce have become important policy actors. Though inexperienced and less endowed with resources, these newly established organizations have exerted their influence on public policy-making. Through informal groupings and through the Inter-Provincial Chamber, chambers have expressed their concern for regional and provincial development. They have proposed measures to decentralize some economic and political decision-making from Bangkok. Of equal interest, they demanded greater autonomy in their relations with the government and the central business associations. Given their enthusiasm and rapid pace of development, these provincial chambers have the potential to become significant contenders with their Bangkok counterparts for public attention and resources.

Viewed in this light, the Thai polity can hardly be termed a bureaucratic polity—at least as an overall characterization. While the public decision-making process in certain other policy areas, such as the military, may continue to be bureaucratically controlled, clearly in the economic realm major decision-making has ceased to be the monopoly of the bureaucracy. To begin with, most economic ministers are now career politicians with a business background, rather than active or retired high-ranking bureaucrats as before. More important is that organized business has exerted significant influence on public decision-making. Not only can businessmen influence public policy through their strategic position in the capitalist economy or through their clientelistic ties with high officials, they can also affect the policy directly as organized groups.

The Emergence of Liberal Corporatism

Since several, if not the majority, of the business associations have become assertive and effective nonbureaucratic policy actors, what model best fits the current relations between the state and organized business in Thailand? Two models of policy interaction deserve particular attention: pluralism and corporatism.

As explained earlier, in a pluralist model the government plays a minimal intervening role in the formation of societal groups, or in structuring the relations between itself and the groups, or among the groups themselves. Groups work more as independent policy advocates than as the policy instruments of the government. They are generally organized into an unspecified number of multiple, voluntary, nonhierarchically ordered categories and compete for desired public policies or legislative measures on a formally equal footing since public agencies seldom recognize or assist particular groups. Although most writers of the pluralist view do not go so far (as critics from the corporatist camp often hold) as to assume that public officials have no interests or convictions of their own, they emphasize interest groups as the major source of, or influence on, public policies.

An alternative to pluralism is corporatism. While corporatism admits the influence of interest groups on the policy and legislation of the government, it stresses the initiative and autonomy of the government. Writers of the corporatist perspective hold that not only can public officials deflect or resist

154

societal demands, they can also design or influence legal and institutional relations between the government and groups as well as relations among the groups. Ideally, groups are organized in a very hierarchical fashion and then linked to the government. Group competition is thus expected to be limited since major conflicts will be solved by higher, particularly peak, organizations and public officials. Finally, corporatism holds that interest groups work not simply as policy advocates, but often also as executors of some public duties. In return, they are provided by the government with legal recognition, financial support, and permanent access to the authorities and processes of the government.

The current government-business relationship in Thailand seems to fit a corporatist model better than a pluralist model. Rather than playing a minimal role, the government has been active in the creation of the JPPCCs and the promotion of peak business organizations and provincial chambers of commerce. Four peak organizations—the Board of Trade, the TCC, the Mining Industry Council, and the FTI—have been given a statutory status by the government. The number of representative bodies in certain categories —nationality-based chambers, provincial chambers, the peak association of mining industries, and the peak association of the whole industrial sector—is officially limited. Equally relevant, only three major associations, the TCC, the TBA, and the ATI/FTI, and their provincial affiliates have been represented on the JPPCCs.

On top of this, several business associations, especially peak associations, do not function simply as public policy advocacy groups. Rather, they often work as partners of public agencies in the implementation of certain policies or rules and regulations. The Board of Trade and agricultural export associations have assisted in the public regulation of the export of agricultural products. Tourism associations have co-sponsored official international sales promotions. Industry associations have been increasingly drawn into public efforts to defuse trade protectionism against Thai manufactured goods in Western countries.

The Thai government is also aptly viewed as capable of acting autonomously in relation to organized business if it chooses to do so. In establishing the JPPCCs, strategic actors in the government, especially Premier Prem and Secretary-General Snoh, did not simply react to business requests. Instead, they had an interest in utilizing organized business to solve grave economic problems, to stabilize the political situation, to improve the efficiency of the bureaucracy, and to a lesser extent, to minimize illegitimate clientelism between government officials and businessmen. Equally important, although the government has been responsive to numerous demands of business in various commercial and industrial issues, it has not sought business participation in making critical financial decisions and has even worked against the interests of certain financial associations.

The Thai government-business relationship, however, is not full-blown corporatism. A high degree of autonomy and free competition are allowed to business associations. Except in special cases, individuals and firms are not legally required to join business associations. Only chambers of commerce, but not trade associations, are compelled to join higher-level organizations. While special recognition and access to government machinery are given to certain peak organizations, business associations are free to contact or lobby either government agencies or personnel directly. They are not forced to go through higher-level organizations or officially recognized associations. When conflicts arise, business associations are allowed to compete with each other directly for desired public attention and resources, rather than being compelled to have the conflicts solved by higher organizations. Indeed, peak organizations or federations of associations occasionally have great difficulty in introducing policies or imposing rules on their members. The TCC, for example, could not force provincial chambers of commerce to abandon their fight against compulsory membership in the would-be FTI. Nor could it prevent provincial chambers from forming another coordinating organization of their own, the Inter-Provincial Chamber of Thailand.

Despite these qualifications, the new reality is best understood as a form of corporatism because the government has an extensive role in promoting business associations and in structuring government-business relationships as well as intra-business relationships. Government involvement in the development of business associations since the introduction of the semi-democratic regime has not declined; it has indeed increased considerably. Parallel to that, rather than opposing public interference, business has called for even more official recognition and sponsorship as well as for a permanent advisory place in public policy-making. It is obvious, then, that neither party has been guided by the pluralist ideal of public noninterference in the associational life of the civil society.

What kind of government-business corporatism does Thailand have? This question may be answered by referring to the nature of business relations with other functional groups on the one hand, and with the government on the other. As far as the relations of business associations with other functional groups are concerned, the present corporatist arrangement is bilateral and not multilateral. That is, the parties in the arrangement are limited to the government and business. Only business associations, not farm groups or labor unions, are represented in the nationwide JPPCC system.

As with organized business, government relations with farm groups and labor unions are marked with corporatist features. Until recently very few farm groups were spontaneously organized. Instead, most of them have been initiated in various forms, such as cooperatives and agriculturalist groups, by public agencies for agricultural development or anti-communist purposes.

156

Moreover, they are hierarchically organized and closely supervised by the government. All cooperatives, for example, are required to join the Cooperative League of Thailand. This league is a quasi-public body, serving as the contact between the government and cooperatives; five public officials, appointed by the government, sit in its twelve-member executive council.[17] The law also explicitly states that agriculturalist groups must be under the sponsorship, support, and supervision of the government.[18]

Though few labor unions have been recently initiated or created by the government, their internal operation and leadership selection are under close official supervision. No general meeting of any labor union is lawful without the participation of public officials; and leaders of unions are occasionally dismissed by the government.[19] Furthermore, labor policy and wage dispute settlement are the province of government committees—albeit with the participation of labor representatives.[20]

The more relevant point, however, is that instead of bringing all major functional groups into the same system of policy consultation and interest mediation, the government has established institutional relations with each functional group separately. There has been little interaction among different bilateral arrangements. Only a number of tri-partite committees bring business into contact with another functional group, i.e., labor. However, by and large these tri-partite committees deal only with the settlement of wage disputes.

To date only the corporatist arrangement between the government and a business association has enjoyed substantial government support and secured an important place in public policy-making. Farm groups are almost never consulted by public officials on major economic matters. Labor unions are occasionally consulted, but largely on matters relating to the practicality of wage policy only. With the predominant role of business associations in the determination of economic public policy, compared with other functional groups, Thailand's government-business relationship is closer to the Japanese "corporatism without labor"[a] than to the European multi-partite corporatism.[b]

---

[a] Although agricultural groups are part of Japanese corporatism, only business groups have an important role in the making of government economic policies. See T. J. Pempel and K. Tsunekawa, "Corporatism without Labor: The Japanese Anomaly," in Philippe Schmitter and Gerhard Lehmbruch, eds., *Trends Towards Corporatist Intermediation* (Beverly Hills: Sage Publication, 1979), pp. 231-270.

[b] Labor unions and/or farmers' associations, in addition to business associations, are usually included in the corporatist arrangements found in Western countries. See, for example, Peter Katzenstein, *Corporatism and Change: Austria, Switzerland, and the Politics of Industry* (Ithaca: Cornell University Press, 1984).

However, is the present Thai government-business relationship liberal (societal) corporatism or authoritarian (state) corporatism? According to Philippe Schmitter, liberal corporatism may be defined as a system in which "the legitimacy and functioning of the state [are] primarily or exclusively dependent on the activity of singular, non-competitive and hierarchically ordered [societal groups]."[21] In other words, whereas the government role is indispensable, societal groups play the central role in creating and legitimizing liberal corporatism. They therefore enjoy considerable autonomy and play an effective policy-making role. In Schmitter's words, they are "autonomous and penetrative" in relation to the state.[22] Liberal corporatism is said to be found in "political systems with relatively autonomous, multilayered territories; open, competitive electoral processes and party systems."[23] It is believed to be "the concomitant, if not ineluctable, component of the postliberal, advanced capitalist, organized democratic welfare state."[24]

Authoritarian corporatism, by contrast, is a system which is imposed by the state on societal groups. The political autonomy and policy effectiveness of societal groups are limited. In other words, they are "dependent and penetrated,"[25] since they are often "created by and kept as auxiliary and dependent organs of the state."[26] Authoritarian corporatism is held to be found in anti-liberal, capitalist developing countries in which "territorial subunits are tightly subordinated to central bureaucratic power; elections are nonexistent or plebiscitary."[27]

Regarding Thailand, Montri Chenviyakarn has argued that up to the late 1970s, while organized business had a peripheral role in the public policy process, the relationship between the government and business associations was essentially that of an authoritarian (state) corporatism.[28] Following Schmitter, one of Montri's major though implicit criteria in defining the Thai system up to that time as authoritarian corporatism was its close association with the authoritarian, bureaucratic polity.[29] The other criterion was the dominant role of the government both in the development and in the control of civil associations.[30] A very important function of Thai corporatism as viewed by Montri was to weaken or control nonbureaucratic groups while allowing them some token participation in public affairs. Until much later, even business associations were closely controlled so that they could "exert relatively little influence over government policy and actions."[31]

After more than a decade of constitutional rule, extensive public efforts to promote business associations, and increased activism on the part of organized business, it is necessary to raise the question: Is authoritarian corporatism still a valid description of government-business relations? To answer this question, one should note several changes in the Thai polity. First of all, the current corporatism is no longer associated with an authoritarian regime. Certainly, Thailand is less than a fully fledged democracy, mainly because coup attempts still occasionally happen and the support of the armed forces or the monarchy can be as important as that of political parties for the survival of a government. Nevertheless, the Thai polity in recent years has been far from authoritarian in disguise. In establishing a multi-party system and holding competitive general elections, without the existence of an official ruling or military party, the system has allowed for a high degree of political contestation. In principle the system allows for the parties victorious in the polls to form a cabinet with all its members drawn from the ranks of the elected politicians. Of the two Houses, the Senate, whose members are mostly high military and civilian bureaucrats appointed by the government, has limited formal power, as compared to the elected House of Representatives.

In addition, since the late 1970s Thai citizens have enjoyed a relatively high degree of political rights and civil liberties. According to Raymond Gastil,[32] Thailand has performed well by international standards in terms of the observation of political rights and civil liberties. Gastil rated countries from (1) to (7) according to the varying degrees of political rights or civil liberties they allowed their populations. Countries rated (1) gave them most, while those rated (7) gave them least. [33] (See Table 7.1 and Table 7.2.)It appears that by 1980 Thailand performed better than South Korea and Taiwan,[34] and by 1984 it surpassed all other ASEAN countries in terms the observation of political rights and civil liberties combined.[35] Even Malaysia and Singapore, two ASEAN countries with an unbroken electoral tradition since independence, have been outranked by Thailand in this respect.

TABLE 7.1 Ratings of Selected Countries in Terms of Their Observation of Political Rights

Country	1978	1979	1980	1981	1982	1983	1984	1985
Thailand	6	6	4	3	3	3	3	3
S.Korea	5	5	4	5	5	5	5	4
Taiwan	5	5	5	5	5	5	5	5
Singapore	5	5	5	5	4	4	4	4
Malaysia	3	3	3	3	3	3	3	3
Philippines	5	5	5	5	5	5	5	4
Indonesia	5	5	5	5	5	5	5	5
Brunei	6	6	6	6	6	6	6	6
India	2	2	2	2	2	2	2	2
US	1	1	1	1	1	1	1	1

Source: Raymond Gastil, *Freedom in the World: Political Rights and Civil Liberties 1985-1986* (New York: Greenwood Press, 1986), pp. 59-71. Reprinted by permission.

More specifically, freedom of association and expression is honored in Thailand in connection with business associations. Compulsory membership in a business organization is not imposed on individuals, firms, or associations. Although extensive public intervention in the affairs of business associations is legally permitted, in practice there is little control of the internal operation and leadership selection processes of the associations by the government.Public measures regarding organized business during the past decade have been overwhelmingly promotive rather than restrictive. Business associations can lobby the government at various levels and through numerous channels. Moreover, in contrast with the period Montri described as authoritarian corporatism, over the past decade several business associations have displayed their effectiveness in initiating, transforming, or blocking important official policies.

TABLE 7.2 Ratings of Selected Countries in Terms of Their Observation of Civil Liberties

Country	1978	1979	1980	1981	1982	1983	1984	1985
Thailand	5	4	3	4	4	4	4	4
S.Korea	5	5	5	6	6	6	5	5
Taiwan	4	4	5	6	5	5	5	5
Singapore	5	5	5	5	5	5	5	5
Malaysia	4	3	4	4	4	4	5	5
Philippines	5	5	5	5	5	5	4	3
Indonesia	5	5	5	5	5	5	6	6
India	2	2	2	3	3	3	3	3
US	1	1	1	1	1	1	1	1

Source: Gastil, *Freedom in the World*, pp. 59-71. Reprinted by permission.

The recent role of business in creating corporatist arrangements and peak associations is also prominent. To restate the points made earlier, although the government had an important role in the development of the JPPCC system, it is the three flagship associations that have continually lobbied for and experimented with this kind of government-business consultative arrangement since 1978. While the formation of peak organizations in the heyday of the bureaucratic polity, such as the Board of Trade and the TCC, was initiated or sponsored by the government, recent peak organizations have risen to their present status by their own efforts. The ATI and the TBA started as ordinary trade associations but were eventually accepted as their principal representatives by the industrial and banking communities, and the government had to accept their new status. The Mining Industry Council and the FTI were legally recognized as peak business organizations as a result of the decade-long lobbying efforts of the business community. Of equal relevance, the Inter-Provincial Chamber of Thailand and other federations of associations have not even cared for a legal or juridical entity status.

All things considered, the present government-business relationship is better conceived of as liberal corporatism than as authoritarian corporatism. It is readily accepted that as compared with liberal corporatism in advanced industrial countries, the Thai liberal corporatism is incipient and more dependent on the role of the government. However, by and large it is characterized by a two-way direction of influence between the government and business. Both sides have a crucial role in the development and functioning of the corporatist system. Government leadership has coexisted with the political autonomy and effective policy role of business associations. Increasingly, an interaction—cooperative or conflictual—between two relatively equal parties, not a domination by one party over the other, is the building block of the emerging liberal corporatism.

Finding liberal corporatism arising in a democratizing regime is not peculiar to this study. A recent study of Turkey by Robert Bianchi also characterizes the relations between the government and interest groups in that country since 1960 as a liberal, multilateral corporatist system.[36] Nevertheless, so far there have been few studies of liberal corporatism in countries outside the industrial, democratic world. As does the Turkish case, the Thai case suggests a correlation between a liberal corporatism and a semi-industrial democratizing regime. For such a regime, liberal corporatism may be more effective than pluralism or authoritarian corporatism as a means to "reconcile rapid economic development with democracy and to avoid a return to overt authoritarian rule."[37] Further studies of other similar cases would be needed to deny or confirm this insight suggested by the Thai and Turkish cases.

Regarding the scholarly debate on the nature of the current political regime in Thailand, the findings of this study support Ansil Ramsay and others who have argued that Thailand is no longer a bureaucratic polity as business groups have a substantial impact on the public policy-making process. However, it also suggests that the assertion of Chai-anan Samudavanija and others that the bureaucratic elite are still formidable is also right—witness the role of Prime Minister Prem and the technocratic NESDB in the formation of the JPPCCs and the development of business associations in recent years. How can one reconcile this contradiction? One way is to deny the authenticity of business power, or to argue that business has little autonomy or effectiveness. This line of reasoning, however, is refuted by the findings of this study. More reasonable then is to reconceptualize the power equation between bureaucratic and extra-

a condition — the beats must be technocrats

bureaucratic forces as capable of taking a style other than a zero-sum game.[c]

Therefore, it may be argued that with the emergence of a form of liberal corporatism, power relations between bureaucratic and nonbureaucratic forces in the domain of economic policy-making in recent years have taken on the characteristics of a positive-sum game. The political regime at work in Thailand, at least in the realm of economic affairs, is no longer a bureaucratic polity, but not because nonbureaucratic forces have gained power at the expense of the bureaucratic forces. Instead, it is because both forces are strong and autonomous, and the decision-making of the regime has ceased to be monopolized by the military-bureaucratic elite.

This study also indicates the important role of the foreign actors in the development of the present business representative system. It thus agrees, though only in a broad sense, with Patcharee Thanamai, whose work can be seen as part of the current debate on regime change in Thailand.[38] While admitting that the concept of bureaucratic polity fits the pattern of Thai economic policy-making up to the 1950s, Patcharee contends that since the 1960s the concept of "triple alliance" has been more consistent with the new realities. In her view, the state, the local bourgeoisie and the international bourgeoisie or their "agencies" (such as organizations of the leading capitalist states or international organizations under the influence of the international bourgeoisie) share political economic power in Thailand.[39]

As shown earlier, American actors such as the AID, the National Endowment for Democracy, and the Center for International Private Enterprises, in conjunction with local business and the Thai government, have been involved in the development of the JPPCCs. However, instances in this study suggest that the role of local actors is more important than that of the external actors. The role of American actors, though important, is supplemental. We have noted that leading business associations had lobbied for a joint consultative committee since 1978, well before the advent of the Reagan administration's emphasis on the development of the private sector in aid-receiving countries. American funds poured in after the central JPPCC had been launched, and in most cases they were matched with substantial Thai funds. Furthermore, in the main it is not the American idea of pluralism that has been accepted by the local actors as their guideline in the recent building of a Thai business representative system.

---

[c] I am indebted to Alfred Stepan's discussion of the possibility of a non-zero sum logic of state-society relationship of power. See his article, "State Power and the Strength of Civil Society in the Southern Cone of Latin America," in Peter Evans et al, eds., *Bringing the State Back In* (Cambridge: Cambridge University Press, 1985), pp. 317-343.

The assertiveness of their associations, coupled with their rising political and economic power in general over the past decade, seems to extricate local businessmen as much from the status of submissive "clients" of "bureaucratic patrons" as from the status of compliant "compradores" of the international bourgeoisie.

Moreover, this study confirms the observation made by several scholars of Third World studies that the impact of external actors on local events is more complicated than is usually portrayed by writers of the "dependency" perspective. While these scholars, in their analysis of external actors or factors, often stress only the role of the international bourgeoisie or their agencies, this study suggests that international organizations based on the regional cooperation of developing countries may play a major role as well. It has been found that a primary source of inspiration and a training ground for the three flagship associations and several trade associations and federations of business organizations was the ASEAN-CCI. The association between the intent and the effect of the action of external actors cannot be easily drawn either. Evidently, while American agencies spend most resources and energy, Japanese ideas and institutions have the most important impact on Thai business associations.

Although business associations have moved Thailand considerably from the bureaucratic polity, they have not made a substantial contribution to the development of Thai democratic institutions. The major democratic impact of business associations has been confined to limiting the power and arbitrariness of the government in the handling of the economy. The government can no longer monopolize economic policy-making. However, democracy is more than the participation of interest groups in the public policy process and government responsiveness to problems and demands of the groups. It also entails the ability of citizens to compete for public office and to change the government through a fair electoral process. To evolve into a mature multi-party democracy, Thailand needs a strong and responsive political party system. By strengthening parties and electoral institutions, business associations presumably could advance the democratization process, but they have not yet done so.

Legal barriers do prevent associations from getting involved in the development of political parties or electoral activities. Actually, however, if business associations had a strong interest in political activities they could, presumably, move to amend the obstructive legislation. They have not done so. Most business associations are uninterested in improving political parties. In fact, they usually dissociate or distance themselves from political parties since the latter have been highly criticized by the military and the general public as weak, divisive, and self-serving. Thus far only a small group of provincial chamber leaders have planned to contribute to the development of political parties; and their plan is long-term oriented, exerting no immediate impact on either the parties or the electoral process.

If associations have not sought to strengthen parties, the reverse is also true. Thai political parties have been largely indifferent to the development of business associations. The parties had no role in the creation of the JPPCCs and the promotion of business associations in recent years. It was the nonelected element in the government and leading business associations who played the important roles. Political parties certainly recruit businessmen as individuals into their memberships and seek their financial support in the elections as well as in daily operations, but they have not tried to enlist the support of business associations.

A Thai Model for Third World Development

The significant role of Thai business associations in the economy and their working relations with the government suggests an alternative to what has come to be called the "East Asian statist" model for Third World development. That model, derived from the experience of Taiwan, Singapore, and South Korea up to the early 1980s, emphasizes the central role of the autonomous state in the development of export-oriented, capitalist economies.[40] The governments in these countries have interfered extensively with the operation of the economies. As do most governments in the Third World, they provide the legal and political framework for the functioning of the market system. They do medium- or long-term national economic planning and formulate macro-economic policies. On top of this, these governments have exerted direct influence on particular economic sectors, industries, or even firms. Taiwan and South Korea have substantial public industrial investment to ensure that investment in strategic areas or fields is undertaken. For example, throughout the 1970s, some 30 percent of total industrial investment in South Korea was made by public enterprises, while the share of the public sector in Taiwan manufacturing production, though declining, was still about 20 percent in the early 1980s.[41]

More importantly, the governments of these East Asian NICs have relied on economic incentives or penalties to lead private enterprises to undertake investments deemed pivotal to the progress of the overall economy in particular periods. With substantial control over the commercial banking systems, these governments can direct the allocation of low-interest loans and credits to favored sectors, industries, or firms.[42] Tax and tariff reduction or elimination can also be used to lure firms into certain trades or industries. On the other hand, tax and tariff policies are occasionally used to punish firms not proceeding along the lines set by governments.

While government intervention in developing countries in general has ended in fiasco, in the East Asian NICs it has worked effectively. There are several reasons for this success. To begin with, following the Japanese example, the intervention of these governments has been market-augmenting, rather than market-repressing.[43] Public enterprises have been kept to a minimal level and efforts have been made to privatize them in due course. In Taiwan, for example, the share of public corporations in total industrial production dropped from almost 60 percent to less than 20 percent between the early 1950s and the early 1980s.[44] Private enterprises, while receiving some official benefits, have been subjected to considerable competition at home or abroad. Secondly, contrary to the situation in many other Third World countries, the interventions of the governments of the NICs were in pursuit of an efficient export-oriented industrialization strategy. This was a strategy which took full advantage of their inexpensive labor, and evaluated imaginatively the opportunities in the expanding world market.

Finally, the most crucial factor in the success of the economies following this model has been a high degree of state autonomy and bureaucratic efficiency and integrity. By autonomy is meant here the ability of the state to devise and enforce its development strategy or policy, without having to take account of societal viewpoints, or regardless of potential or actual opposition from social classes or groups. If a comparative advantage in industrial labor costs is to be maintained, for example, workers must be persuaded or forced to refrain from making "excessive" wage demands. To this end, labor unions must be kept weak and often put under close government control. Their direct role in public policy-making must be prevented or at least constrained.[45] In addition, in both Taiwan and South Korea, the landlords have not been important public policy actors in the formation of public economic policy. Indeed, they were even victims of government land reform programs. But, most striking is the fact that even business, the mainstay of the modern economy in these countries, has been largely excluded from the making of government policy.

These "East Asian Statist" regimes have certainly paid close attention to business problems and quickly formulated policies to deal with them, but they have not tolerated the resistance of business to the leadership of the government in economic matters. Even gigantic corporations have sometimes been compelled to do what they did not want to. For example, to reduce undesired competition in the machine tool industry, in the early 1980s the Korean government ordered Daewoo, one of the world's largest industrial conglomerates, to cease its marine-engine manufacture.[46] The chairman of Daewoo complied while registering his complaints as follows: "The government tells you it's your duty and you have to do it, even if there's no profit. Maybe after the year 2000, Korean businessmen will be able to put their company's interests ahead of those of society or government."[47]

It is true that as in Japan, the government-business relationship is intimate in the East Asian NICs. Meetings between public officials and representatives of business are extensive and regularized. Associations, especially those related to export activities, are numerous and active in these countries. In Singapore, organized business is permanently represented on the Trade Development Board, which is responsible for the formation and implementation of export policies and programs.[48] In South Korea, all registered exporters are members of the Korean Traders Association, the peak business association of export businesses.[49] Together with 30 specific export associations, the Korean Traders Association has cooperated with the government to set goals and targets for various export items and to promote the marketing of South Korean products all over the world.[50] More significantly, export associations are represented in the monthly National Trade Promotion meetings. Chaired by the president, these meetings provide a forum for top leaders in the government and the private sector to monitor the progress of public policies and programs that have been designed to boost the exports of the nation.[51]

While business associations are important in the public policy process in the East Asian NICs, their part in policy-making is largely limited to giving advice or assisting in the implementation of government-initiated programs. Until recently, there were few reports of the role of organized business in initiating, transforming, or blocking policies and legislative measures of the governments in these countries.[52] Business associations in these countries have been closely controlled. In Taiwan, business associations are controlled by the ruling KMT Party through its Committee on Social Affairs and appointment of staff members in the associations.[53] In South Korea, the Korean Traders Association is financed by a government-mandated levy of 0.55 percent on all imports.[54]

As a result, associations in the East Asian NICs have functioned much more as a channel through which official policies are relayed to businessmen than as representatives of business interests to the government. In South Korea, for example:

All of the business associations . . . are extremely susceptible to government manipulation, and spend most of their energies reacting to various drafts prepared by the government rather than initiating policies. Association leaders are occasionally consulted in the decision phase of the policy process, but their effective ability to initiate rational policy is viewed somewhat contemptuously by government policy-makers.[55]

Governments of the East Asian NICs have been distinguishable from the rest of the Third World also by the high degree of efficiency and integrity of their bureaucracies. In these nations bureaucratic corruption has been held to a modest level. In Taiwan, Thomas Gold reports, "Cronyism and corruption existed, but so did genuine opportunity [for the business community in general]. This sets Taiwan off from such Asian neighbors as the Philippines, Indonesia, and, to a lesser extent, Thailand."[56]

Even in South Korea, where officials are left with sizable discretionary powers to promote or penalize particular firms, Leroy Jones and Il Sakong report that they have used these powers to good effect.[57] The economic bureaucracy in these countries is staffed with capable, highly motivated and adequately paid personnel. Compared to those in other developing countries, bureaucratic inefficiency and delays in the East Asian NICs are much less frequently reported.

Since the early 1980s the Thai development strategy has come to resemble that of the East Asian NICs in some crucial respects. In the first place, Thailand has recently relied more on labor-intensive, export-oriented industrialization. Though still important, agricultural exports now rank second after manufactured exports as the major foreign exchange earner. Moreover, the government has tried to increase its intervention in the economy. Since 1982, the first year under the Fifth National Economic and Social Development Plan, the government has embarked on industrial sectoral restructuring, beginning with the electrical/electronic and the automobile industries. In the mid-1980s the government moved to restructure the capital market and devalue the currency to step up investment and enhance the competitiveness of Thai exports. Last but not least, the government has tried to increase bureaucratic efficiency to improve its economic leadership. A major means to achieve this has been relying on business pressure and inputs in the JPPCCs to push implementing agencies to tackle bureaucratic red tape.

Like the East Asian NICs, Thai public intervention is market-conforming. According to the World Bank, Thailand has a very low "price distortion index."[58] This index is concerned with the deviation of prices from their opportunity costs, caused by monopolistic tendencies in the private sector or by public intervention, in the pricing of foreign exchange, factor inputs, and products. In 1983 Thailand ranked second among 31 developing nations as having the least price distortion. Its performance was better than all other countries in ASEAN (Singapore was not included in the study), and even better than that of South Korea. (See Table 7.3.)

More directly relevant to the concern of this study, a system of regular consultation between high officials and business representatives has been vigorously developed. Approaching the pattern of the East Asian NICs, government-business interaction in Thailand is becoming more intimate, and public officials are now paying close attention to business problems and demands.

TABLE 7.3 Price Distortion Index of 31 Countries

Country	Index	Ranking as Country with Least Price Distortion among 31 Selected Countries
Malawi	1.14	1
Thailand	1.43	2
Cameroon	1.57	3
South Korea	1.57	3
Malaysia	1.57	3
Philippines	1.57	3
Tunisia	1.57	3
Kenya	1.71	8
Yugoslavia	1.71	8
Colombia	1.71	8
Ethiopia	1.71	11
Indonesia	1.86	11
India	1.86	11
Sri Lanka	1.86	11
Brazil	1.86	11
Mexico	1.86	11
Ivory Coast	2.14	17
Turkey	2.14	17
Egypt	2.14	17
Senegal	2.29	20
Pakistan	2.29	20
Jamaica	2.29	20
Uruguay	2.29	20
Bolivia	2.29	20
Peru	2.29	20
Argentina	2.43	26
Chile	2.43	26
Tanzania	2.57	28
Bangladesh	2.57	28
Nigeria	2.71	30
Ghana	2.86	31

Source: World Bank, *World Development Report 1983* (New York: Oxford University Press, 1983), Table 6.1, pp. 60-61. Reprinted by permission.

See p 179: the flagships?

A marked departure from the situation in the East Asian NICs, however, is that business associations in Thailand have played a substantial role in initiating or resisting public policies and legislative measures. As shown earlier, the shift to an export-oriented industrialization strategy at the end of the 1970s was facilitated to a great extent by the advocacy of the TBA, the ATI and the TCC. Following the adoption of the new development strategy by the government, several industry associations pushed for the elimination of specific laws or rules to clear the way for the export of products of their concerns. Just as important, the JPPCC system came into being in large part as a result of the persistent lobbying efforts of business since the time of Premier Kriangsak. Provincial chambers of commerce are also becoming crucial nonbureaucratic policy actors in their provinces or regions. Acting collectively, these provincial chambers have begun to exert policy influence even in the national policy arena.

At the heart of the matter, the East Asian statist model presupposes that the government is both enlightened in setting economic policies and efficient in their implementation. On the other hand, it views societal actors as short-sighted, self-serving, and obstructive to the making of good policies. Their exclusion from public policy-making is therefore said to be justifiable. Extensive public intervention in the private business sector is not counter-productive, not only because it is market-conforming, but also because the bureaucracy is efficient and honest. While the main task of public policy formation is to insulate the decision-making process from the pressure of societal actors, the major concern of policy implementation is to induce or coerce business to follow the directions set by the government. Bureaucratic inefficiencies and rigidities are rarely viewed as burning issues in the analysis of the East Asian statist model.

The emerging Thai liberal corporatism, by contrast, neither idolizes the government nor belittles business in terms of policy-making. Strategy or policy formulation is not a monopoly of the "smart" government. Indeed the model implies that the government can be as "smart" or "stupid" as business. Useful ideas can come from business and useless ideas from the government. In addition, policy implementation in the Thai liberal corporatism is less a question of how to manipulate resistant and ignorant entrepreneurs than of how to improve the performance of the bureaucracy. Throughout the last decade both top public officials and the business community realized that the bureaucracy was ridden with red tape, delays and corruption. The airing of problems and demands by business was thus valued by the government as a means to prod the bureaucracy to work more effectively and efficiently.

Evidently, the Thai liberal corporatism is less statist than the East Asian NICs model, since the role of business in the formation of public policy is

169

substantial.[d] Just as important, the degree of public intervention in the economy is lower than that of the East Asian NICs. For example, relying on conventional means such as moral suasion or the provision of low-interest loans to commercial banks to be allocated in turn to firms in certain areas or sectors, the Thai government has a modest control on industrial sectoral development. In marked contrast, the South Korean government appoints its own men to the top management of commercial banks to ensure that those banks allocate credits and loans at favorable interest rates to private enterprises in high-priority sectors.[59] Moreover, while the application for foreign loans by private firms is relatively unencumbered in Thailand, the South Korean government insists that all foreign loans be subject to government approval and guarantee.[60] Another noteworthy point is that the Thai government usually employs only category-based incentives to persuade private firms to undertake preferred activities. The South Korean government, on the other hand, coerces individual firms to follow its instructions with measures that sometimes verge on bullying tactics. Edward Mason and others have had this to say for the situation in South Korea, "A firm that does not respond as expected to particular incentives may find that its tax returns are subject to careful examination, or that its application for bank credit is studiously ignored, or that its outstanding bank loans are not renewed."[61]

Despite the impressive growth record of the East Asian NICs, there is reason to believe that the liberal corporatism of Thailand is more feasible as a model for most Third World countries than is the East Asian statist model: it is more compatible with the capacity of their governments. Most Third World countries, democratic or authoritarian, are governed by what Gunnar Myrdal has called "soft states" in the sense that formulated public policies are rarely enforced effectively.[62] Third World bureaucracy is usually ridden with nepotism, corruption and abuses of power, especially at the local level. This is partly due to inadequate public compensation to officials and partly due to the patrimonial legacy inherited from the pre-modern societies.

Nepotism and corruption, often combined with the problems of inadequately trained staff and the lack of public funds to meet the costs of implementing projects and programs, frequently lead to a retardation, distortion, or complete failure of enacted laws, rules or policy measures. Of course, implementation is not the only policy-making problem in the developing world. Even the formulation of good public policies is

---

[d] For a related, similar view about the differences between the Thai model and the East Asian statist model, see Richard Doner, "Weak State-Strong Country: The Thai Automobile Case" *Third World Quarterly* (October, 1988).

questionable in much of the Third World. Among other things, Third World policy formation is plagued by the lack of sufficient and reliable information. This, in turn, is often caused by the poor data-gathering services of the government or the distortion of data for political purposes by responsible officers or agencies.[63]

With such incompetent governments it would be counter-productive for most Third World market economies to adopt the East Asian statist model of development. The more the Third World soft states are insulated from societal information, opinions and demands, the more their goals turn out to be unrealistic or even damaging to the economy, and so the enforcement of their policies ends in a fiasco.

As Goran Hyden has pointed out in an African case, there are two approaches to rectifying the weakness of the states in the developing world: one is state-oriented, the other society-oriented.[64] The East Asian NICs in fact have adopted a state-oriented approach which entails the installation of the right kind of political leadership and bureaucracy—those which are enlightened, capable, and relatively free of neo-patrimonial abuses. However, until Third World countries possess such strong states, their development will be better served by a society-oriented approach which encourages an active participation of societal actors in economic policy-making. As the Thai case suggests, business associations can improve the formulation of public measures by supplying statistics, operational information and advice to decision makers. Even more important is their role in initiating or opposing strategies or laws and rules regarding the overall or sectoral development of the economy. In addition, organized business can be a constant pressure for the improvement of bureaucratic efficiency and impartiality.

While the Thai model of business-government relations may be more feasible for most Third World soft states, it is dependent upon the presence of a vigorous local business class. Such a class, however, is not finding it easy to emerge in several developing countries. The role of the government in fostering local business and soliciting its contribution to economic decision-making is therefore necessary in the developing world. It is here that the evolving Thai model seems to be even more appropriate to conditions in the developing world since it does not deny the leadership of the government. By launching the JPPCC system and encouraging the formation of business associations nationwide, the government has become a leading force in the improvement of economic policy-making. However, it should be noted that in doing so the government has in the main employed a society-oriented, rather than a state-oriented, approach.

Needless to say, the relationship between the state and organized business in Thailand is not without weaknesses. A major criticism of this relationship is that, not unlike that in the East Asian model, it keeps the popular sector out of the economic policy-making process. Despite intermittent calls from the press and the academia for the inclusion of farmer and worker groups in the JPPCC system, as late as the beginning of 1991 senior officials at the NESDB still insisted that the inclusion was undesirable for it would slow down and complicate the deliberation process of the system to the point of unmanageability.[65] Another relevant criticism is that the government-business collaboration has focused almost exclusively on the reduction of government-caused costs in order that Thai businesses compete more effectively in the international market. Socially relevant issues, such as: how to cope with environmental degradation, or, how to correct the highly skewed income distribution of the nation, have been simply left out of government-business dialogues.

Even with these limitations, the participation of business in the policy-making process and its exertion of influence over the bureaucracy may be considered as a progressive stage in the political development of a country with a strong tradition of operating as a bureaucratic polity. What two prominent scholars from opposed traditions, Fred Riggs, a "modernization" scholar,[66] and Goran Hyden, a Marxist-oriented scholar,[67] hope to see in the Third World—the emergence of assertive extra-bureaucratic forces or a local bourgeoisie, respectively, that are capable of bringing the government under some control—have eventually arisen in Thailand as business associations.

Notes

1. Fred Riggs, *Thailand: The Modernization of a Bureaucratic Polity* (Honolulu: East-West Center Press, 1966), p. 396.

2. Charles Lindblom, *Politics and Markets: The World's Political Economic System* (New York: Basic Books, 1977), pp. 172-173.

3. Ibid., p. 173.

4. Ibid., pp. 172-175.

5. Fred Block, "Beyond Relative Autonomy: State Managers as Historical Subjects" *New Political Science* 2 (Fall 1981): 36-37.

6. Ibid., p. 38.

7. Kevin Hewison, "The Development of Capital: Public Policy and the Role of the State in Thailand" (Ph.D. thesis, Murdoch University, Australia, 1983).

8. Ibid., pp. 21-30.

9. The World Bank, *Thailand: Toward a Development Strategy of Full Participation* (Washington, D.C.: World Bank Publication, 1980), Table 2.2, p. 7.

10. The International Bank for Reconstruction and Development, *A Public Development Program for Thailand* (Baltimore: Johns Hopkins Press, 1959), p. 89.

11. Ibid., p. 91.

12. Ibid., p. 89.

13. Calculated from the data provided by IBRD, *A Public Development Program for Thailand*, Table 26, p. 252.

14. World Bank, *Thailand: Managing Public Resources for Structural Adjustment* (Washington, D.C.: World Bank Publication, 1984), Table 2.14, p. 30.

15. *Sathiraphab*, August 31, 1955, as quoted in G. William Skinner, *Leadership and Power in the Chinese Community of Thailand* (Ithaca: Cornell University Press, 1958), pp. 303-304.

16. Bob Jessop, "The Capitalist State and the Rule of Capital: Problems in the Analysis of Business Associations," in David Marsh, ed., *Capital and Politics in Western Europe* (London: Frank Cass, 1983), pp. 144-150.

17. Montri Chenvidyakarn, "Political Control and Economic Influence: A Study of Trade Associations in Thailand" (Ph.D. dissertation, University of Chicago, 1979), p. 135.

18. Ibid., p. 137.

19. Lae Dilokvidhyarat, "Tripartism: The Labour Control Strategy and Alternatives for Labour Movement in Thailand," paper presented at the United Nations University Conference on Southeast Asian Perspectives Project, at Hat Yai, Thailand, October, 1986, p. 7.

20. Ross Prizzia, *Thailand in Transition: The Role of Opposition Forces* (Honolulu: University of Hawaii Press, 1985), pp. 33-36.

21. Philippe Schmitter, "Still the Century of Corporatism?" in Frederick Pike and Thomas Stritch, eds., *The New Corporatism: Social-Political Structures in the Iberian World* (Notre Dame: University of Notre Dame, 1974), p. 102.

22. Ibid., p. 103.

23. Ibid., p. 105.

24. Ibid. p. 105.

25. Ibid., p. 103.

26. Ibid., p.102.

27. Ibid., p.105.

28. Montri, "Political Control," pp. 436-447.

29. Montri, "Political Control," pp. 448-449 and Schmitter, "Still the Century," p. 105.

30. Montri, "Political Control," pp. 436-437; Schmitter, "Still the Century," pp. 102-103.

31. Montri, "Political Control," p. 437.

32. Raymond Gastil, *Freedom in the World: Political Rights and Civil Liberties 1985-1986* (New York: Greenwood Press, 1986).

33. For a detailed discussion of the concepts political rights and civil liberties, their indicators and how to rate countries in terms of these two concepts, see Gastil, *Freedom in the World*, pp. 31-43.

34. The combined ratings (political rights and civil liberties) of Thailand in 1980 equal to 7 (4+3), while those of South Korea and Taiwan equal to 9 (4+5) and 10 (5+5) respectively. (See Table 7.1 and Table 7.2.)

35. The combined rating for Thailand in 1984 is 7 (3+4), while that of Malaysia, the second best in ASEAN, is 8 (3+5). (See Table 7.1 and Table 7.2.)

36. Robert Bianchi, *Interest Groups and Political Development in Turkey* (Princeton: Princeton University Press, 1984), pp. 142-146.

37. Ibid., p. 142.

38. Patcharee Thanamai, "Patterns of Industrial Policy-Making in Thailand: Japanese Multinationals and Domestic Actors in the Automobile and Electrical Appliances Industries" (Ph.D. dissertation, University of Wisconsin, 1985).

39. Ibid., pp. 245-251.

40. Leroy Jones and Il Sakong, *Government, Business, and Entrepreneurship in Economic Development: The Korean Case* (Cambridge: Harvard University Press, 1980); Stephen Haggard and Chung-in Moon, "The South Korean State in International Economy: Liberal, Dependent, or Mercantile?" in John Ruggie, ed., The *Antinomies of Interdependence* (New York: Columbia University Press, 1983); Frederic Deyo, ed., *The Political Economy of the New Asian Industrialization* (Ithaca: Cornell University Press, 1987).

41. Jones and Sakong, *Government, Business, and Entrepreneurship*, p. xxix; Alice Amsden, "The State and Taiwan's Economic Development," in Peter Evans et al, eds., *Bringing the State Back in*, p. 91.

42. Chalmers Johnson, "Political Institutions and Economic Performance: The Government-Business Relationship in Japan, South Korea, and Taiwan," in Deyo, ed., *The Political Economy*, pp. 147-149.

43. Chalmers Johnson, *MITI and the Japanese Miracle: The Growth of Industrial Policy, 1925-1975* (Stanford: Stanford University Press, 1982), pp. 317-319; and "Political Institutions and Economic Performance," in Deyo ed., *The Political Economy*, pp. 141-142.

44. Amsden, "The State and Taiwan's Economic Development," p. 91.

45. Frederic Deyo, "State and Labor: Modes of Political Exclusion in East Asian Development," in Deyo, ed., *The Political Economy*, pp. 182-202.

46. Nigel Harris, *The End of the Third World: Newly Industrializing Countries and the Decline of an Ideology* (London: I.B. Tauris & Co Ltd, 1986), p. 42.

47. *Financial Times*, October 31, 1984, p. 18, as quoted in Harris, *the End of the Third World, p. 42.*

48. Yung Whee Rhee, *Instruments for Export Policy and Administration* (Washington, D.C.: World Bank Publication, 1985), Annex III-A, pp. 236-238.

49. Yung Whee Rhee, Bruce Ross-Larson and Garry Pursell, *Korea's Competitive Edge: Managing the Entry into World Markets* (Baltimore: Johns Hopkins University Press, 1984), p. 53.

50. Ibid., pp. 23-25; p. 52.

51. Ibid., pp. 29-35.

52. Following the recent democratization efforts in South Korea and Taiwan, there are now some lobbying activities of business groups, mainly to attack what they perceive as bureaucratic delays and inefficiency. See Hagen Koo, "The Interplay of State, Social Class and World System in East Asian Development: The Cases of South Korea and Taiwan" in Deyo, ed., *The Political Economy*, p. 176.

53. Thomas Gold, *State and Society in the Taiwan Miracle* (Armonk, New York: M.E. Sharpe, Inc., 1986), footnote 21, p. 140.

54. Jones and Sakong, *Government, Business, and Entrepreneurship*, p. 70.

55. Moon Kyu Park, "Interest Representation in South Korea" *Asian Survey* 27 (August 1987): 906-907.

56. Gold, *State and Society*, p. 125.

57. Jones and Sakong, *Government, Business, and Entrepreneurship*, p. xxxi.

58. World Bank, *World Development Report 1983* (New York: Oxford University Press, 1983), pp. 57-73.

59. Jones and Sakong, *Government, Business, and Entrepreneurship*, p. 102.

60. Jones and Sakong, *Government, Business, and Entrepreneurship*, p. 102.

61. Edward Mason et al, *The Economic and Social Modernization of the Republic of Korea* (Cambridge: Harvard University Press, 1980), p. 265.

62. The concept of "soft state" was originally formulated from the experience of South and Southeast Asian countries. See Gunnar Myrdal, *Asian Drama: An Inquiry into the Poverty of Nations* (New York: Pantheon, 1968), p. 66 and pp. 895-900.

63. Gary Bertsch, Robert Clark and David Wood, eds., *Comparing Political Systems: Power and Policy in Three Worlds*, 2nd. ed. (New York: John Wiley and Sons, 1982), p. 469.

64. Goran Hyden, *No Shortcuts to Progress: African Development Management in Perspective* (Berkeley: University of California Press, 1983), Chapter 5, esp. pp. 128-132.

65. Conversation with senior officials at the NESDB Division of JPPCCs, February 1991.

66. Fred Riggs, "Bureaucrats and Political Development: A Paradoxical View," in Joseph LaPalombara, ed., *Bureaucracy and Political Development* (Princeton: Princeton University Press, 1967), pp. 120-122.

67. Hyden, *No Shortcuts to Progress*, pp. 180-182; pp. 211-213.

Epilogue

As this book was about to go to press in February 1991, the armed forces successfully seized power from the democratically elected government of Prime Minister Chatichai Choonhavan through a bloodless coup. The military junta abrogated the constitution, dissolved parliament and the government, and imposed martial law throughout the kingdom. Apparently, the political clock was turned back to the pre-1970s authoritarian era and it is appropriate to ask whether Thailand has returned to the bureaucratic polity model and whether the major conclusion of my study has been invalidated by this coup. These questions, I believe, must be dealt with both conceptually and empirically.

Conceptually, I did not claim that there would never be another successful military takeover. Rather, I was concerned to show that a major nonbureaucratic group, i.e., organized business, has become much stronger throughout the 1980s, and its strength has reached a point where the economic policy-making of the state has ceased to be the exclusive domain of public officials. Business associations have had a substantial and effective policy role during the semi-democratic years of Prem and the consolidating democratic years of Chatichai.

In other words, I have not taken the presence or absence of formal political institutions or processes, such as a constitution, elections, parties, and an elected legislature, as indicators of the absence or presence of a bureaucratic polity. Instead, I have asked who has taken a crucial role in the public policy-making process. If bureaucrats or nonelected political leaders with a bureaucratic background largely dominated the process, then we have a bureaucratic polity, and the latter may take authoritarian, semi-democratic, or less likely, democratic shells. If, on the contrary, elected officers and nonbureaucratic groups have a considerable or even leading role in the process, then we are out of the bureaucratic polity, and the new regime may take democratic, semi-democratic, or less likely, authoritarian shells.

177

178

Empirically, there have been signs in the immediate situation which suggest that the bureaucratic polity, or at least a pure form of it, has not come back. The military junta undoubtedly reigns supreme at the moment through its appointment and control of the prime minister and members of the legislature in the new regime. However, people with a nonbureaucratic, particularly business, background are substantially represented in the cabinet and the legislative assembly. Above all, the new prime minister, Anand Panyarachun, was at the time of his appointment the president of the Federation of Thai Industries (FTI). Two other important cabinet positions have also been taken by former FTI directors, Ajva Taolanon (now Deputy Minister of Agriculture) and Arsa Sarasin (now Minister of Foreign Affairs). Furthermore, several independent business and banking technocrats have been included in the cabinet.

The current post-coup regime, unlike virtually all of its predecessors, does not vest all power in the hands of the military-bureaucratic elite. Business is an indispensable partner of the military-bureaucratic leaders in administering the country for the time being. No less significant, with the departure of party politicians and the appointment of prominent technocrats (including Snoh Unakul, formerly a key figure in the NESDB and JPPCC system),[1] to almost all economic positions in the cabinet, it is very likely that the national JPPCC will regain its policy significance, which, the reader may recall, diminished somewhat in the Chatichai years.

While the coup tells us that the military-bureaucratic force is alive and well, the make-up of the post-coup regime reminds us that even an emergency rule of an authoritarian nature cannot do without extra-bureaucratic forces, particularly business. Certainly, we do not know how long this martial law regime will last, although the military has promised—as stipulated in the interim constitution—a quick return to democracy within about one year.[2] Nor can one guarantee that a more permanent, more legitimate regime yet to emerge after the passage of the martial law will be a fully fledged democracy. Yet, whatever political form it may take, I believe that this coup-prone nation can hardly embrace the essence of the bureaucratic polity, i.e., the virtual monopoly of political power by the military-bureaucratic elite. Thailand has indeed entered a phase beyond that of bureaucratic polity; yet, with the benefit of hindsight, we cannot rule that this will inevitably or at least shortly lead to a viable democratic rule.

Notes

1. Snoh now serves as a deputy premier in charge of the overall economic operation of the government.

2. Article 12 of the 1991 Interim Constitution.

List of Acronyms

AID	Agency for International Development
ASEAN	Association of Southeast Asian Nations
ASEAN-CCI	The ASEAN Chamber of Commerce and Industry
ATI	Association of Thai Industries
CIPE	Center for International Private Enterprise
FTI	Federation of Thai Industries
IMET	Institute for Management Education for Thailand
JPPCC	Joint Public and Private Sector Consultative Committee
NED	National Endowment for Democracy
NESDB	National Economic and Social Development Board
NIC	Newly Industrializing Countries
NIDA	National Institute of Development Administration
TAT	Tourism Authority of Thailand
TBA	Thai Bankers Association
TCC	Thai Chamber of Commerce
TPI	Thai Petro-Chemical Industry
TTMA	Thai Textile Manufacturing Association

References

I. Official Documents and Publications

a).Thai Government Agencies.

Chakrit Chulakasewi, ed. *Ha Pi Ko Ro Au: Hontang Haeng Kwam Samrej Kong Settakij Tai* [Five Years of the JPPCCs: Pathway to Thai Economic Success]. Bangkok: NESDB, 1986.

The Chamber of Commerce Act, B.E. 2509 (A.D.1966).

The Federation of Thai Industries Bill (1987 Draft).

Pan Pattana Settakij Lae Sangkom Haeng Chat Chabab Ti Sam, Po So 2515-2519 [The Third National Economic and Social Development Plan, 1972-1976]. Bangkok: NESDB.

Pan Pattana Settakij Lae Sangkom Haeng Chat Chabab Ti Ha, Po So 2525-2529 [The Fifth National Economic and Social Development Plan, 1982-1986]. Bangkok: NESDB.

Pan Pattana Settakij Lae Sangkom Haeng Chat Chabab Ti Hok, Po So 2530-2534 [The Sixth National Economic and Social Development Plan, 1987-1991]. Bangkok: NESDB.

Pramual Pol-Ngarn Kana Kammakarn Ruam Pak Rattaban Lae Ekachon Pua Kaekai Panha Tang Settakij (Ko Ro Au) [Collections of Achievements of the Joint Public and Private Sector Consultative Committee (JPPCC)]. Bangkok: NESDB, 1986.

Pramual Pol-Ngarn Kwam Ruammuu Pak Rattaban Lae Ekachon Pua Kaekai Panha Tang Settakij (Ko Ro Au) [Collections of Achievements in Public-Private Cooperation to Solve Economic Problems]. Bangkok: NESDB, 1987.

Rai-Ngarn Pol Karn Sammana Kana Kammakarn Ruam Pak Rattaban Lae Ekachon Pua Kaekai Panha Tang Settakij (Ko Ro Au) Nai Pumipak Krang Ti Song [A Report on the Results of the Second JPPCC Seminar on Regional Economic Problems]. Bangkok: NESDB, 1985.

Rai-Ngarn Pol Karn Sammana Kana Kammakarn Ruam Pak Rattaban Lae Ekachon Pua Kaekai Panha Tang Settakij (Ko Ro Au) Nai Pumipak Krang Ti Sam [A Report on the Results of the Third JPPCC Seminar on Regional Economic Problems]. Bangkok: NESDB, 1986.

Sawaeng Rattanamongkolmas. *Satanapab Botbat Panha Lae Naeotang Kaekai Kiaokab Kwam Ruammuu Pak Rattaban Lae Ekachon* [Status, Role, Problems and Solutions, Regarding Cooperation between the State and the Private Sector]. Report submitted to the NESDB in 1986.

Statistical Yearbook Thailand 1985-1986. Bangkok: National Statistical Office.

182

The Tourism Authority of Thailand. *Annual Report 1985.*
The Trade Association Act, B.E. 2509 (A.D.1966).

b).Business Associations and Private Agencies in Thailand.
Annual Reports (in Thai) of Selected Associations available in the files of the Central
Trade Associations and Chambers of Commerce Registrar's Office, Ministry of
Commerce:
--The Association of Finance Companies (1987).
--The Association of Members of the Securities Exchange (1987).
--ATI (1986).
--The Board of Trade (1981, 1984, 1986).
--The Chinese Construction Association (1982, 1983, 1984, 1985).
--The Condominium Trade Association (1985, 1986).
--The General Insurance Association (1983, 1984).
--The Government Lottery Dealers Association (1982, 1983, 1984, 1985).
--The Palm Oil Refiners Association (1985-86).
--TCC (1985, 1986).
--The Thai Fishery and Frozen Products Association (1985).
--The Thai Food Processing Association (1985).
The American Chamber of Commerce in Thailand. *How the Chamber Can Benefit
You.* Brochure, undated.
The Association of Financing Companies. *Turakij Ngern-Tun Nai Pratet Tai 2529*
[Financial Business in Thailand, 1986]. Bangkok: no date.
The Association of Members of the Securities Exchange. *Turakij Laksap Nai Pratet Tai*
[Securities Exchange Business in Thailand]. Bangkok: 1987.
The Board of Trade. *Annual Report 1986.*
_____.*Yisipha Pi Sapa Ho Karnka Tai* [Twenty-Fifth Anniversary Commemoration of
the Board of Trade]. Bangkok: no publication data.
The Employers' Confederation of Thailand. *Krobrob Sip Pi Sapa Ongkarn Naichang
Haeng Pratet Tai 2529* [Commemorating the Tenth Anniversary of the Employers'
Confederation of Thailand, 1986]. Bangkok: 1986.
The German-Thai Chamber of Commerce. *Handbook 1976/77.* Bangkok: no
publication data.
_____.*Handbook 1979.* Bangkok: no publication data.
"Joint Standing Committee on Commerce, Industry and Banking." Background
paper for the Third Regional Meeting of the Joint Public and Private Sector
Consultative Committee, January 26, 1986, Konkaen, Thailand.
NIDA-IMET. *Krong Karn Sammana Pattana Nak Turakij Channam Suan Pumipak* [A
Seminar Project for the Upgrading of Leading Provincial Businessmen].
Brochure, 1987.
The Project for the Development of Provincial Chamber of Commerce. *Karn
Sammana Pattana Ho Karnka Changwat Krang Ti Nung* [The First Seminar on the
Development of Provincial Chambers of Commerce]. Brochure, undated.
TBA. *Samakom Tanakarn Tai: Prawat Lae Kijjakam* [The Thai Bankers Association:
History and Activities]. Brochure, undated.

The Thai-Chinese Chamber of Commerce. *Handbook 1980.* Bangkok: no publication data.

Viraj Puengsunthorn."Prawat Samakom Poka Tai"[History of the Thai Merchants Association]. In *Nangsuu Perd Akarn Samakom Poka Tai* [Commemorative Book on the Occasion of the Opening of the New Building of the Thai Merchants Association]. Bangkok: Krung Sayam Press, 1971.

c).Foreign Government and Private Agencies, and International Agencies.

Bell, John, et al. "End of Project Evaluation of the Institute for Management Education for Thailand, Inc., (IMET) Project." Submitted to the Office of Policy and Program Review, Bureau of Private Enterprise, AID, July 19, 1985.

Bureau of Private Enterprise, AID. "Economic Growth and the Third World: A Report on the AID Private Enterprise Initiative." Washington, D.C.: April 1987.

Center for International Private Enterprise. "1986 Annual Report." Washington, D.C.

The International Bank for Reconstruction and Development. *A Public Development Program for Thailand.* Baltimore: John Hopkins University Press, 1959.

_____. *Current Economic Position and Prospects of Thailand*, Vol.I, January 11, 1972.

National Endowment for Democracy. *Statement of Principles and Objectives.* Brochure.

Rhee, Yung Whee. *Instruments for Export Policy and Administration.* Washington, D.C.: World Bank Publication, 1985.

Rhee, Yung Whee; Ross-Larson, Bruce; and Pursell, Garry. *Korea's Competitive Edge: Managing the Entry into World Markets.* Baltimore: John Hopkins University Press, 1984. Published for the World Bank.

US AID/Thailand. "Thailand: Private Sector in Development." Project No. 493-0329, July 1982.

World Bank.Thailand: *Industrial Development Strategy in Thailand.* Washington, D.C.: East Asia and Pacific Regional Office, 1980.

_____.*Thailand: Managing Public Resources for Structural Adjustment.* Washington, D.C.: World Bank Publication, 1984.

_____.*Thailand: Toward a Development Strategy of Full Participation.* Washington, D.C.: World Bank Publication, 1980.

_____.*World Development Report 1983.* New York: Oxford University Press, 1983.

_____.*World Development Report 1988.* New York: Oxford University Press, 1988.

_____.*World Development Report 1990.* Oxford: Oxford University Press, 1990.

II. Periodicals and Newspapers

Asia Yearbook (Hong Kong, in English)

Bangkok Post (Bangkok, daily, in English)

Chodmaikao (Official newsletter of the Thai Printing Association)

Dok Bia (Bangkok, monthly)

Ho Karnka Changwat (Official newsletter of the Inter-Provincial Chamber of Thailand)

Ho Karnka Changwat Lampang (Official newspaper of the Lampang Chamber of Commerce)

184

Ho Karnka Changwat Nakorn Ratchasima (Official newspaper of the Nakorn Ratchasima Chamber of Commerce)
Ho Karnka Changwat Rayong (Official newspaper of the Rayong Chamber of Commerce)
Ho Karnka Changwat Songkhla (Official newspaper of the Songkhla Chamber of Commerce)
Kemtit (Bangkok)
Ko Ro Au Sampan (Official newsletter of the central JPPCC)
Naeo-Na (Bangkok, daily)
Ruam Prachachart Turakij (Bangkok, twice weekly)
Sapa Karn Muang-Rae (Official newsletter of the Mining Industry Council)
Tarn Settakij (Bangkok, twice weekly)
Thailand Business (Bangkok, in English)
Thailand Investment News (Official newsletter of the Board of Investment, in English)
Warasarn Settakij Lae Sangkom (Official journal of the NESDB)

III. Books, Articles, Papers and Theses

(Thai authors are alphabetized by their first names.)

Almond, Gabriel, and Powell, G. Bingham. *Comparative Politics: System, Process, and Policy.* Boston: Little, Brown and Company, 1978, 2nd ed.
Alavi, Hamza."The State in Post-Colonial Societies: Pakistan and Bangladesh." *New Left Review* 74 (July-August 1972): 59-81.
Amsden, Alice."The State and Taiwan's Economic Development." In *Bringing the State Back In*, pp.78-106. Edited by Peter Evans, Dietrich Rueschemeyer and Theda Skocpol. Cambridge: Cambridge University Press, 1985.
Anek Laothamatas."Business and Politics in Thailand: New Patterns of Influence." *Asian Survey* 28 (April 1988): 451-470.
Ariff, Mohamed, and Hill, Hal. *Exported-Oriented Industrialization: The ASEAN Experience.* Sydney: Allen and Unwin, 1985.
Ayal, Eliezer. "Thailand." In *Underdevelopment and Economic Nationalism in Southeast Asia*, pp. 267-340. Edited by Frank Golay et al. Ithaca: Cornell University Press, 1969.
Baran, Paul. *The Political Economy of Growth.* New York: Monthly Review Press, 1969.
Becker, David. *The New Bourgeoisie and the Limits of Dependency: Mining, Class, and Power in "Revolutionary" Peru.* Princeton: Princeton University Press, 1983.
Bertsch, Gary; Clark, Robert; and Wood, David. *Comparing Political Systems: Power and Policy in Three Worlds.* 2nd ed. New York: John Wiley and Sons, 1982.
Bianchi, Robert. *Interest Groups and Political Development in Turkey.* Princeton: Princeton University Press, 1984.
Block, Fred. "Beyond Relative Autonomy: State Managers as Historical Subjects." *New Political Science* 2 (Fall 1981): 33-49.
Boonchu Rochanasathian. *Kwam Kid Tang Karnmuang Kong Boonchu Rochanasathian* [Poltical Ideas of Boonchu Rochanasathian]. Bangkok: Image Publication, 1982.

Cardoso, Fernando, and Faletto, Enzo. *Dependency and Development in Latin America*. Translated by Marjory Urquidi. Berkeley: University of California Press, 1979.

Cawson, Alan. *Corporatism and Political Theory*. Oxford: Basil Blackwell, 1986.

Chai-anan Samudavanija."Democracy in Thailand: A Case Study of a Stable Semi-Democratic Regime." Paper presented at the Conference on the Comparative Study of Democracy in Developing Nations, Stanford University, 1985. Later published in *Democracy in Developing Countries: Asia*, pp. 305-346, edited by Larry Diamond, Juan Linz and Seymour Martin Lipset. Boulder, Colorado: Lynne Reinner, 1989.

_____."The Military and Politics in Thailand." Paper presented at the annual meeting of the American Association for Asian Studies, Philadelphia, 1985

Chai-anan Samudavanija and Suchit Bunbongkarn. "Thailand." In *The Military-Civilian Relations in South-East Asia*, pp. 78-117. Edited by Zakaria Haji Ahmad and Harold Crouch. Singapore: Oxford University Press, 1985.

Deyo, Frederic."Coalition, Institutions, and Linkage Sequencing—Toward a Strategic Capacity Model of East Asian Development." In *The Political Economy of the New Asian Industrialism*, pp. 227-247. Edited by Frederic Deyo. Ithaca: Cornell University Press, 1987.

_____."State and Labor Modes of Political Exclusion in East Asian Development." In *The Political Economy of the New Asian Industrialism*, pp.182-202. Edited by Frederic Deyo. Ithaca: Cornell University Press, 1987.

Doner, Richard."Weak State-Strong Country: The Thai Automobile Case." *Third World Quarterly* (October 1988).

Doner, Richard, and Ramsay, Ansil. "Thailand as a Case of Flexible Strength." Paper presented at the annual meeting of the American Association for Asian Studies, Washington, D.C., March 1989.

Doner, Richard, and Wilson III, Ernest."Business Interest Associations in Developing Countries." Paper presented at the annual meeting of the International Political Science Association, September 1988.

Evans, Peter. *Dependent Development: The Alliance of Multinational, State, and Local Capital in Brazil*. Princeton: Princeton University, 1979.

_____."Reinventing the Bourgeoisie: State Entrepreneurs and Class Formation in Dependent Capitalist Development." In *Marxist Inquiries: Studies of Labor, Class, and States*, supplement to *American Journal of Sociology*, 88 (1982):S210-S247. Edited by Michael Burawoy and Theda Skocpol. Chicago: University of Chicago Press, 1982.

Frank, Andre G. *Capitalism and Underdevelopment in Latin America: Historical Studies of Chile and Brazil*. New York: Monthly Review Press, 1969.

Gastil, Raymond. *Freedom in the World: Political Rights and Civil Liberties 1985-1986*. New York: Greenwood Press, 1986.

Girling, John. *The Bureaucratic Polity in Modernizing Societies: Similarities, Differences and Prospects in the ASEAN Region*. Singapore: The Institute of Southeast Asian Studies, 1981.

_____.*Thailand: Society and Politics*. Ithaca: Cornell University Press, 1980.

Gold, Thomas. *State and Society in the Taiwan Miracle*. Armonk, New York: M.E. Sharpe, Inc., 1986.

Grit Permtanjit. "Political Economy of Dependent Development: Study of the Limits of the Capacity of the State to Rationalize in Thailand." Ph.D. dissertation, University of Pennsylvania, 1982.

Hagen, Everett. *The Economics of Development*. Homewood, Illinois: Richard D. Irwin Inc., 1975.

Haggard, Stephen, and Moon, Chung-in. "The South Korean State in International Economy: Liberal, Dependent, or Mercantile?" In *The Antinomies of Interdependence*, pp. 131-189. Edited by John Ruggie. New York: Columbia University Press, 1983.

Harris, Nigel. *The End of the Third World: Newly Industrializing Countries and the Decline of an Ideology*. London: I.B. Tauris & Co. Ltd., 1986.

Herrick, Bruce, and Kindleberger, Charles. *Economic Development*. New York: McGraw-Hill, 1983.

Hewison, Kevin."The Development of Capital, Public Policy and the Role of the State in Thailand." Ph.D.thesis, Murdoch University, Australia, 1983.

_____."The State and Capitalist Development in Thailand." In *Southeast Asia: Essays in the Political Economy of Structural Change*, pp. 266-294.Edited by Richard Higgot and Richard Robison. London: Routledge & Kegan Paul, 1985.

Hyden, Goran. *No Short Cut to Progress: African Development Management in Perspective*. Berkeley: University of California Press, 1983.

Jackson, Karl."Bureaucratic Polity: A Theoretical Framework for the Analysis of Power and Communications in Indonesia." In *Political Power and Communications in Indonesia*, pp. 3-22. Edited by Karl Jackson and Lucian Pye. Berkeley: Universityf California Press, 1978.

Jessop, Bob."The Capitalist State and the Rule of Capital: Problems in the Analysis of Business Associations." In *Capital and Politics in Western Europe*, pp. 139-162. Edited by David Marsh. London: Frank Cass, 1983.

Johnson, Chalmers. *MITI and the Japanese Miracle: The Growth of Industrial Policy, 1925-1975*. Stanford: Stanford University Press, 1982.

_____. "Political Institutions and Economic Performance: The Government-Business Relationship in Japan, South Korea, and Taiwan." In *The Political Economy of the New Asian Industrialism*, pp. 136-164. Edited by Frederic Deyo. Ithaca: Cornell University Press, 1987.

Jones, Leroy, and Sakong, Il. *Government, Business, and Entrepreneurship in Economic Development: The Korean Case*. Cambridge: Harvard University Press, 1980.

Katzenstein, Peter. *Corporatism and Change: Austria, Switzerland, and the Politics of Industry*. Ithaca: Cornell Uiversity Press, 1984.

_____. *Small States in World Markets: Industrial Policy in Europe*. Ithaca: Cornell University Press, 1985.

Kochanek, Stanley. *Business and Politics in India*. University of California Press, 1974.

_____.*Interest Groups and Development: Business and Politics in Pakistan*. Delhi: Oxford University Press, 1983.

Kraisak Choonhavan."The Growth of Domestic Capital and Thai Industrialization." *Journal of Contemporary Asia* 14 (1984): 135-146.

Krirkkiat Pipatseritham. *Wikroh Laksana Karn Pen Chaokong Turakij Kanad Yai Nai Pratet Tai* [The Distribution of Ownership in the Thai Big Business].Bangkok: Thammasat University Press, 1982.

_____.*Karn Plianplang Tang Setttakij Kab Panha Sitti Manusayachon Nai Pratet Tai* [Economic Change and Human Rights Issue in Thailand]. Bangkok: Thai Khadi Research Institute, 1985.

Lae Dilokvidhyarat. "Tripartism: The Labour Control Strategy and Alternatives for Labour Movement in Thailand." Paper presented at the United Nations University Conference on Southeast Asian Perspectives Project, Hat Yai, Thailand, October 1986.

Lande, Carl. "Introduction: The Dyadic Basis of Clientelism." In *Friends, Followers and Factions*, pp. xiii-xxxvii. Edited by Steffen Schmidt et al. Berkeley: University of California Press, 1977.

Landon, Kenneth. *Siam in Transition: A Brief Survey of Cultural Trends in the Five Years since the Revolution of 1932*. Chicago: University of Chicago Press: 1939; reprint ed., New York: Greenwood Press, 1968.

Lehmbruch, Gerhard."Liberal Corporatism and Party Government." *Comparative Political Studies* 10 (April 1977): 91-126.

Leys, Colin. "Capital Accumulation, Class Formation and Dependency: The Significance of the Kenyan Case." In *Socialist Register 1978*, pp. 241-266. Edited by Ralph Miliband and John Saville. London: Merlin Press, 1978.

Likhit Dhiravegin. *The Bureaucratic Elite of Thailand: A Study of Their Sociological Attributes, Educational Backgrounds and Career Advancement Pattern*. Bangkok: Thai Khadi Research Institute, Thammasat University, 1978.

Lindblom, Charles. *Politics and Markets: The World's Political Economic Systems*. New York: Basic Books, 1977.

MacIntyre, Andrew. *Business and Politics in Indonesia*. Sydney: Allen and Unwin, 1991.

Malloy, James, ed. *Authoritarianism and Corporatism*. Pittsburgh: University of Pittsburgh, 1977.

Mason, Edward; Kim, Mahn Je; Perkins, Dwight; Kim, Kwang Suk; and Cole, David. *The Economic and Social Modernization of the Republic of Korea*. Cambridge: Harvard University Press, 1980.

Montri Chenvidyakarn."Political Control and Economic Influence: A Study of Trade Associations in Thailand." Ph.D. dissertation, University of Chicago, 1979.

Morell, David. "Power and Parliament in Thailand: The Futile Challenge, 1968-1971." Ph.D.dissertation, Princeton University Press, 1974.

Mosel, James. "Thai Administrative Behavior." In *Toward the Comparative Study of Public Administration*, pp. 278-331. Edited by William Siffin. Indiana University's Department of Government, 1957.

Myrdal, Gunnar. *Asian Drama: An Inquiry into the Poverty of Nations*. New York: Pantheon, 1968.

Nakarin Mektrairat, "Song Krasae Pumpanya Nai Karn Patiwat Sayam Tosawat Ti 2470." In *Kwamkid Kwamru Lae Amnat Karnmuang Nai Karn Patiwat Sayam 2474* [Idea, Knowledge, and Political Power, Regarding the Siamese Revolution of 1932]. Edited by Nakarin Mektrairat. Bangkok: Sataban Sayam Suksa, 1990)

Narong Petchprasert."Samakom Karnka Lae Ho Karnka Nai Pratet Tai" [Trade Associations and Chambers of Commerce in Thailand]. M.A. thesis, Thammasat University, Bangkok, 1975.

Olson, Mancur. *The Logic of Collective Action*. Cambridge: Harvard University Press, 1965.

Panitch, Leo."The Development of Corporatism in Liberal Democracies." *Comparative Political Studies* 10 (April 1977): 61-90.

Park, Moon Kyu. "Interest Representation in South Korea." *Asian Survey* 27 (August 1987): 903-917.

Patcharee Thanamai."Patterns of Industrial Policy-Making in Thailand: Japanese Multinationals and Domestic Actors in the Automobile and Electrical Appliances Industries." Ph.D. dissertation, University of Wisconsin-Madison, 1985.

Pisan Suriyamongkol and Guyot, James. *The Bureaucratic Polity at Bay*. Bangkok: Graduate School of Public Administration, the National Institute of Development Administration, no date.

Pisan Suriyamongkol, and Douglas, Stephen."Government-Business Relations in Thailand." *Thai Journal of Development Administration* 21 (July 1981): 460-483.

Pempel, T.J., and Tsunekawa, K. "Corporatism without Labor: The Japanese Anomaly." In *Trends towards Corporatist Intermediation*, pp. 231-270. Edited by Philippe Schmitter and Gerhard Lehmbruch. Beverly Hills: Sage Publication, 1979.

Prizzia, Ross. *Thailand in Transition: The Role of Opposition Forces*. Honolulu: University of Hawaii Press, 1985.

Prudhisan Jumbala."Towards a Theory of Group Formation in Thai Society and Pressure Groups in Thailand after the October 1973 Uprising." *Asian Survey* 14 (June 1974): 530-545.

Ramsay, Ansil."Thai Domestic Politics and Foreign Policy." Paper presented at the Third US-ASEAN Conference, Chiangmai, Thailand, 1985. Later published in *ASEAN in Regional and Global Context*, pp. 30-51, edited by Karl Jackson, Sukhumbhand Paribatra and J. Soedjati Djiwandono. Berkeley: Institute of East Asian Studies, University of California, Berkeley, 1986.

_____. "Thailand: Beyond the Bureaucratic Polity." Paper presented at the annual meeting of the American Association for Asian Studies, Boston, April 10-12, 1987.

Rattakorn Asdorntirayut. *2527 Pi Haeng Prawatsart Karn-Ngern* [1984: An Historical Year in Monetary History]. Bangkok: Dok Bia Press, no date.

Riggs, Fred. *Thailand: The Modernization of A Bureaucratic Polity*. Honolulu: East-West Center Press, 1966.

_____."Bureaucrats and Political Development: A Paradoxical View." In *Bureaucracy and Political Development*, pp. 120-167. Edited by Joseph LaPalombara. Princeton: Princeton University Press, 1967.

Rudolph, Lloyd, and Rudolph, Susanne. *In Pursuit of Lakshmi: The Political Economy of the Indian State*. Chicago: University of Chicago Press, 1987.

Samrit Meewongukos. *Sayam Almanac 2528* [Siam Almanac 1985]. Bangkok: Sayamban, 1985.

Sangsit Piriyarangsan. *Tunniyom Khunnag Tai (Po So 2475-2503)* [The Thai Bureaucratic Capitalism, 1932-1960]. Bangkok: Sangsan, 1983.

Sarn Prachachon Co. *Thailand's Commercial Associations Handbook Directory (1982-1983)*. Bangkok: Sarn Prachachon Co., 1981.

Schmitter, Philippe. "Still the Century of Corporatism?" In *The New Corporatism: Social-Political Structures in the Iberian World*, pp. 85-131. Edited by Fredrick Pike and Thomas Stritch. Notre Dame: University of Notre Dame Press, 1974.

Schmitter, Philippe and Streeck, Wolfgang."The Organization of Business Interests: A Research Design to Study the Associative Action of Business in the Advanced Industrial Societies of Western Europe." (October 1981 version).

Skinner, G. William. *Chinese Society in Thailand: An Analytical History*. Ithaca: Cornell University Press, 1957.

_____."Chinese Assimilation and Thai Politics." *The Journal of Asian Studies* 16 (February 1957): 237-250.

_____. *Leadership and Power in the Chinese Community of Thailand*. Ithaca: Cornell University Press, 1958.

Sklar, Richard."Postimperialism: A Class Analysis of Multinational Corporate Expansion." *Comparative Politics* 9 (October 1976): 75-92.

Suehiro, Akira. *Capital Accumulation And Industrial Development In Thailand*. Bangkok: Chulalongkorn University Social Research Institute, 1985.

Sukhumbhand Paribatra and Suchit Bunbongkarn." Thai Politics and Foreign Policy in the 1980s." Paper presented at the Third US-ASEAN Conference, Chiangmai, Thailand, 1985. Later published in *ASEAN in Regional and Global Context*, pp. 52-76, edited by Karl Jackson, Sukhumbhand Paribatra and J. Soedjati Djiwandono. Berkeley: Institute of East Asian Studies, University of California, Berkeley, 1986.

Suthy Prasartset. *Thai Business Leaders: Men and Careers in a Developing Economy*. Tokyo: Institute of Developing Economics, 1980.

_____."Some Aspects of Government-Business Relations in Thailand and Japan." In *Papers and Proceedings of the Conference on Comparative Study of the Role of Government in Economic Development in Japan and Thailand*, pp. 4i-4.48. Bangkok: Faculty of Economics, Chulalongkorn University, December 1982.

Stepan, Alfred. *The State and Society: Peru in Comparative Perspective*. Princeton: Princeton University Press, 1978.

_____."State Power and the Strength of Civil Society in the Southern Cone of Latin America." In *Bringing the State Back In*, pp. 317-343. Edited by Peter Evans, Dietrich Rueschemeyer and Theda Skocpol. Cambridge: Cambridge University Press, 1985.

Todaro, Michael. *Economic Development in the Third World*. New York: Longman, 1985.

Vella, Walter. *Chaiyo: King Vajiravudh and the Development of Thai Nationalism*. Honolulu: University of Hawaii Press, 1978.

Visut Thamviriyawong. "Chonchan Nam Tang Turakij Kab Karnmuang Tai: Suksa Chapo Korani Karn Kao Ma Mi Botbat Tang Karnmuang Douytrong" [Business Elites and Thai Politics: A Case Study of Direct Political Participation]. In *Karnmuang Tai Yuk Mai* [Modern Thai Politics], pp. 122-166. Edited by Anothai Watanaporn. Bangkok: Praepittaya Press, 1984.

190

Wehmhorner, Arnold. "Trade Unionism in Thailand-A New Dimension in a Modernising Society." *Journal of Contemporary Asia* 13 (1983): 481-497.

Weiner, Myron. *The Politics of Scarcity: Public Pressure and Political Response in India.* Chicago: University of Chicago, 1962.

Wilson, David. *Politics in Thailand.* Ithaca: Cornell University Press, 1962.

IV. Selected Interviews

Amorn Wongsurawat, president of the Nakorn Ratchasima Chamber of Commerce, February 9, 1987; January 9, 1991.

Boonchu Rochanasathian, former deputy premier and TBA president, November 10, 1987.

Boonlert Laparojkij, president of the Songkhla Chamber of Commerce, July 25, 1987.

Boonsong Srifuangfung, president of the Chinese Chamber of Commerce, August 14, 1987.

Chakramont Pasukwanij, director of the JPPCC Division, NESDB, July 20, 1987; January 3, 1991.

Chanond Aranyakananda, executive secretary of the TCC, July 24, 1987; January 10, 1991.

Chumchun Poolswat, Naeo-Na business news section chief, June 9, 1987.

Kamol Tantivanich, manager of the Thai Textile Manufacturers Association, June 30, 1987.

Kongsak Lopongpanitch, secretary-general of the Thai Printing Association, September 29, 1987.

Nikorn Wattanapanom, June 11 and October 1, 1987; February 12, 1991.

Nipaporn Bunyanun, manager of the Thai Fishery and Frozen Products Association, July 3, 1987.

Nipon Wongtrangan, president of the Pijit Chamber of Commerce and vice-president of the Thai Rice Mills Association, June 8, August 26, 1987.

(M.L.) Prachaksilp Thongyai, August 18, 1987.

Pairoj Kesmankij, executive secretary of the FTI, January 18, 1991.

Pornsit Sriorathaikul, president of the Thai Gems and Jewelry Traders Association, October 29, 1987.

Prapat Suthaves, manager of the Association of Thai Travel Agents, November 12, 1987.

Pratuan Ngarm-Kham, senior officer of the TCC, January 7, 1991.

Prayong Wattanaprateep, manager of the TBA, July 14, 1987.

Prayoon Chivasantikarn, president of the Lampang Chamber of Commerce, June 13, 1987.

Preecha Tanprasert, vice-president of the TCC, July 6 and 16, 1987; January 29, 1991.

Santiparb Rakbumrung, manager of the Thai Tapioca Trade Association, July 1, 1987.

Sataporn Kawitanont, assistant secretary of the central JPPCC, November 17, 1987.

Savali Siripol, marketing executive of the Thai Convention Promotion Association, October 30, 1987.

Seree Wangspaichit, deputy governor of the Tourism Authority of Thailand, November 19, 1987.

Siriporn Apirakkunwong, former manager of the Thai Plastic Industry Association, June 25, 1987.

Snoh Unakul, NESDB secretary-general, August 4, 1987; January 17, 1991; February 18, 1991.

Somboon Pataichant, manager of the Rice Exporters Association, June 10, 1987.

Songkram Chivaprawatdamrong, president of the National Federation of Textile Industries, August 5, 1987.

Sunthorn Srisattana, adviser of the Inter-Provincial Chamber of Thailand, June 10, 1987.

Surin Totabtiang, president of the Trang Chamber of Commerce, February 7, 1991.

Taworn Pornprapa, former president of the ATI, August 13, 1987.

Vijit Na Ranong, president of the Federation of the Regional Tourist Business, July 19, 1987.

Winyu Kuwanan, president of the Konkaen Chamber of Commerce, February 8, 1991.

STUDIES OF THE EAST ASIAN INSTITUTE

Yenan and the Great Powers: The Origins of Chinese Communist Foreign Policy, by James Reardon-Anderson. New York: Columbia University Press, 1980.

Uncertain Years: Chinese-American Relations, 1947–1950, edited by Dorothy Borg and Waldo Heinrichs. New York: Columbia University Press, 1980.

The Fateful Choice: Japan's Advance into Southeast Asia, edited by James William Morley. New York: Columbia University Press, 1980.

Tanaka Giichi and Japan's China Policy, by William F. Morton. Folkestone, England: Dawson, 1980; New York: St. Martin's Press, 1980.

The Origins of the Korean War: Liberation and the Emergence of Separate Regimes, 1945–1947, by Bruce Cumings. Princeton: Princeton University Press, 1981.

Class Conflict in Chinese Socialism, by Richard Curt Kraus. New York: Columbia University Press, 1981.

Education Under Mao: Class and Competition in Canton Schools, by Jonathan Unger. New York: Columbia University Press, 1982.

Private Academies of Tokugawa Japan, by Richard Rubinger. Princeton: Princeton University Press, 1982.

Japan and the San Francisco Peace Settlement, by Michael M. Yoshitsu. New York: Columbia University Press, 1982.

New Frontiers in American-East Asian Relations: Essays Presented to Dorothy Borg, edited by Warren I. Cohen. New York: Columbia University Press, 1983.

The Origins of the Cultural Revolution: II, The Great Leap Forward, 1958–1960, by Roderick MacFarquhar. New York: Columbia University Press, 1983.

The China Quagmire: Japan's Expansion of the Asian Continent, 1933–1941, edited by James William Morley. New York: Columbia University Press, 1983.

Fragments of Rainbows: The Life and Poetry of Saito Mokichi,

1882–1953, by Amy Vladeck Heinrich. New York: Columbia University Press, 1983.

The U.S.–South Korean Alliance: Evolving Patterns of Security Relations, edited by Gerald L. Curtis and Sung-joo Han. Lexington, MA: Lexington Books, 1983.

Discovering History in China; American Historical Writing on the Recent Chinese Past, by Paul A. Cohen. New York: Columbia University Press, 1984.

The Foreign Policy of the Republic of Korea, edited by Youngnok Koo and Sungjoo Han. New York: Columbia University Press, 1984.

State and Diplomacy in Early Modern Japan, by Ronald Toby. Princeton: Princeton University Press, 1983 (hc); Stanford: Stanford University Press, 1991 (pb).

Japan and the Asian Development Bank, by Dennis Yasutomo. New York: Praeger Publishers, 1983.

Japan Erupts: The London Naval Conference and the Manchurian Incident, edited by James W. Morley. New York: Columbia University Press, 1984.

Japanese Culture, third edition, revised, by Paul Varley. Honolulu: University of Hawaii Press, 1984.

The Foreign Policy of the Republic of Korea, edited by Youngnok Koo and Sung-joo Han. New York: Columbia University Press, 1985.

Japan's Modern Myths: Ideology in the Late Meiji Period, by Carol Gluck. Princeton: Princeton University Press, 1985.

Shamans, Housewives, and other Restless Spirits: Women in Korean Ritual Life, by Laurel Kendell. Honolulu: University of Hawaii Press, 1985.

Human Rights in Contemporary China, by R. Randle Edwards, Louis Henkin, and Andrew J. Nathan. New York: Columbia University Press, 1986.

The Pacific Basin: New Challenges for the United States, edited by James W. Morley. New York: Academy of Political Science, 1986.

The Manner of Giving: Strategic Aid and Japanese Foreign Policy, by Dennis T. Yasutomo. Lexington, MA: Lexington Books, 1986.

Security Interdependence in the Asia Pacific Region, James W. Morley, Ed., Lexington, MA: D.C. Heath and Co., 1986.

China's Political Economy: The Quest for Development since 1949, by Carl Riskin. Oxford: Oxford University Press, 1987.

Anvil of Victory: The Communist Revolution in Manchuria, by Steven I. Levine. New York: Columbia University Press, 1987.

Urban Japanese Housewives: At Home and in the Community, by Anne E. Imamura. Honolulu: University of Hawaii Press, 1987.

China's Satellite Parties, by James D. Seymour. Armonk, NY: M.E. Sharpe, 1987.

The Japanese Way of Politics, by Gerald L. Curtis. New York: Columbia University Press, 1988.

Border Crossings: Studies in International History, by Christopher Thorne. Oxford & New York: Basil Blackwell, 1988.

The Indochina Tangle: China's Vietnam Policy, 1975–1979, by Robert S. Ross. New York: Columbia University Press, 1988.

Remaking Japan: The American Occupation as New Deal, by Theodore Cohen, edited by Herbert Passin. New York: The Free Press, 1987.

Kim Il Sung: The North Korean Leader, by Dae-Sook Suh. New York: Columbia University Press, 1988.

Japan and the World, 1853–1952: A Bibliographic Guide to Recent Scholarship in Japanese Foreign Relations, by Sadao Asada. New York: Columbia University Press, 1988.

Contending Approaches to the Political Economy of Taiwan, edited by Edwin A. Winckler and Susan Greenhalgh. Armonk, NY: M.E. Sharpe, 1988.

Aftermath of War: Americans and the Remaking of Japan, 1945–1952, by Howard B. Schonberger. Kent, OH: Kent State University Press, 1989.

Single Sparks: China's Rural Revolutions, edited by Kathleen Hartford and Steven M. Goldstein. Armonk, NY: M.E. Sharpe,

1989.

Neighborhood Tokyo, by Theodore C. Bestor. Stanford: Stanford University Press, 1989.

Missionaries of the Revolution: Soviet Advisers and Chinese Nationalism, by C. Martin Wilbur Julie Lien-ying How. Cambridge, MA: Harvard University Press, 1989.

Education in Japan, by Richard Rubinger and Edward Beauchamp. New York: Garland Publishing, Inc., 1989.

Financial Politics in Contemporary Japan, by Frances Rosenbluth. Ithaca: Cornell University Press, 1989.

Suicidal Narrative in Modern Japan: The Case of Dazai Osamu, by Alan Wolfe. Princeton: Princeton University Press, 1990.

Thailand and the United States: Development, Security and Foreign Aid, by Robert Muscat. New York: Columbia University Press, 1990.

Race to the Swift: State and Finance in Korean Industrialization, by Jung-En Woo. New York: Columbia University Press, 1990.

Anarchism and Chinese Political Culture, by Peter Zarrow. New York: Columbia University Press, 1990.

Competitive Ties: Subcontracting in the Japanese Automotive Industry, by Michael Smitka. New York: Columbia University Press, 1990.

China's Crisis: Dilemmas of Reform and Prospects for Democracy, by Andrew J. Nathan. Columbia University Press, 1990.

The Study of Change: Chemistry in China, 1840–1949, by James Reardon-Anderson. New York: Cambridge University Press, 1991.

Explaining Economic Policy Failure: Japan and the 1969–1971 International Monetary Crisis, by Robert Angel. New York: Columbia University Press, 1991.

Pacific Basin Industries in Distress: Structural Adjustment and Trade Policy in the Nine Industrialized Economies, edited by Hugh T. Patrick with Larry Meissner. New York: Columbia University Press, 1991.

Business Associations and the New Political Economy of

Thailand: From Bureaucratic Polity to Liberal Corporatism, by Anek Laothamatas. Boulder, CO: Westview Press, 1991.

Constitutional Reform and the Future of the Republic of China, edited by Harvey J. Feldman. Armonk, NY: M.E. Sharpe, 1991.

Asia for the Asians: Japanese Advisors, Chinese Students, and the Quest for Modernization, 1895–1905, by Paula S. Harrell. Stanford: Stanford University Press, forthcoming.

Driven by Growth: Political Change in the Asia-Pacific Region, edited by James W. Morley. Armonk, NY: M. E. Sharpe, forthcoming.

Locality and State: Schoolhouse Politics During the Chinese Republic, by Helen Chauncey. Honolulu: University of Hawaii Press, forthcoming.

The Lukang Rebellion: Pollution, Politics and Foreign Investment in Taiwan, by James Reardon-Anderson. Armonk, NY: M. E. Sharpe, forthcoming.

About the Book and Author

This outstanding contribution to our understanding of Thailand's political economic system is perhaps the first major English-language work that provides an up-to-date analysis of the country widely hailed as Asia's next newly industrialized country. Dr. Laothamatas argues that, at least in the realm of economic decision-making, Thailand has moved away from a pure form of bureaucratic polity to a system he refers to as liberal corporatism. He presents detailed empirical data regarding chambers of commerce, their peak organizations, and the nation's trade associations, all of which will have a profound influence on the direction Thailand's political economy takes.

The book should be of great interest to students of Thai politics, as it directly challenges Fred Riggs' "bureaucratic polity" model, which has so long dominated the thinking of both Western and Thai scholars. Policymakers and development specialists interested in the state-business relationship also will find the study useful, given the author's deft placement of the Thai case in the context of the debate on modernization theory and the recent spate of writings on the role of the state in newly industrializing countries.

Anek Laothamatas is a member of the faculty of political science at Thammasat University, Bangkok. He received his Ph.D. from Columbia University, where from 1989 to 1990 he was an adjunct assistant professor of Southeast Asian politics. Dr. Laothamatas has done extensive research on government-business relations as well as on the interaction between economic development and democratization. He is now engaged in a World Bank research project on the political economy of structural adjustment reform in new democracies.

His English-language publications include "Business and Politics in Thailand," *Asian Survey* (April 1988), and "Thailand and Indonesia: Bureaucratic Polities in Transformation" (coauthored), in Colin Mackerras (ed.), *East Asia: An Introductory History*. He also has written numerous articles for leading Thai-language scholarly journals and newspapers.

Index

political vision of, 115–116
problems and achievements of, 62–65
Prudhisan Jumbala, 103

Rama VI, 25
Ramsay, Ansil, 6–7, 160
Restricted democracy, 6
Revolution of 1932, 1, 22, 25
Riggs, Fred, 1–3, 171

Sarit Thanarat, 27–28, 150
Sawaeng Rattanamongkolmas, 12
Schmitter, Philippe, 8, 13, 157
Semi-democracy, 5
Siamese Chamber of Commerce, 22–23
Skinner, G. William, 24, 26
Sklar, Richard, 10
Snoh Unakul
 early work with organized business, 81–82
 political vision of, 81–82, 154
 in the post-coup government, 178
 on the role of tourism, 127
 on state administration as an obstacle to development, 135
 on state-business cooperation as key to economic success, 81
Soft state
 problems for the East Asian model, 169–170
State
 run by/for capitalists, 152
Streeck, Wolfgang, 8
Structural influence of business
 Hewison on, 150
 limit of, 150–152

Lindblom and Block on, 150
Suchit Bunbongkarn, 6
Sukhumbhand Paribatra, 6
Sunthorn Srisattana, 61–62
Suthy Prasartset, 12, 77

Taworn Pornprapa, 81, 83, 125
TBA, 8, 30, 32, 36, 38–39, 46–47, 49–52, 59, 71–74, 83–84, 93–94, 138, 141, 143, 154, 159, 168
TCC, 8, 27–30, 32, 36, 38–39, 45–52, 59, 64–65, 71–74, 83–84, 92–94, 99, 112, 142, 154–155, 159, 168
Thai-ification
 of association members and presidents, 30, 77
 of the operation of Chinese associations, 30
Thailand, Inc., 39, 84
Thanin Kraivixian, 35–36, 151
Thanom Kittikachorn, 3, 28, 32
Tourist-industry associations, 56–57, 127
Trade associations
 classification of, 47, 54–57
 general profile of, 53–54
Trade Association Act, 28–30, 49, 86, 92
Triple alliance approach, 7, 161

USAID
 aid to the JPPCCs, 82–83
 direction under Reagan, 82

Winyu Kuwanan, 101–102

Young Turks, 80